Information Technology

VIKRANT MALVIYA

'A' Level, PGDCM

Cyber Security Advisor and Trainer

HPH

Himalaya Publishing House

MUMBAI • NEW DELHI • NAGPUR • BENGALURU • HYDERABAD • CHENNAI • PUNE
LUCKNOW • AHMEDABAD • ERNAKULAM • BHUBANESWAR • INDORE • KOLKATA • GUWAHATI

First Edition : 2012

Published by	:	Mrs. Meena Pandey for **Himalaya Publishing House Pvt. Ltd.,** "Ramdoot", Dr. Bhalerao Marg, Girgaon, **Mumbai - 400 004.** Phone: 022-23860170/23863863, Fax: 022-23877178 **E-mail: himpub@vsnl.com; Website: www.himpub.com**
Branch Offices	:	
New Delhi	:	"Pooja Apartments", 4-B, Murari Lal Street, Ansari Road, Darya Ganj, New Delhi - 110 002. Phone: 011-23270392, 23278631; Fax: 011-23256286
Nagpur	:	Kundanlal Chandak Industrial Estate, Ghat Road, Nagpur - 440 018. Phone: 0712-2738731, 3296733; Telefax: 0712-2721215
Bengaluru	:	No. 16/1 (Old 12/1), 1st Floor, Next to Hotel Highlands, Madhava Nagar, Race Course Road, Bengaluru - 560 001. Phone: 080-32919385; Telefax: 080-22286611
Hyderabad	:	No. 3-4-184, Lingampally, Besides Raghavendra Swamy Matham, Kachiguda, Hyderabad - 500 027. Phone: 040-27560041, 27550139; Mobile: 09390905282
Chennai	:	No. 8/2, Madley 2nd Street, Ground Floor, T. Nagar, Chennai - 600 017. Phone: 044-28144004/28144005; Mobile: 09345345051
Pune	:	First Floor, "Laksha" Apartment, No. 527, Mehunpura, Shaniwarpeth (Near Prabhat Theatre), Pune - 411 030. Phone: 020-24496323/24496333; Mobile: 09370579333
Lucknow	:	Jai Baba Bhavan, Church Road, Near Manas Complex and Dr. Awasthi Clinic, Aliganj, Lucknow - 226 024 (U.P.). Phone: 0522-2339329, 4068914; Mobile: 09307501550
Ahmedabad	:	114, "SHAIL", 1st Floor, Opp. Madhu Sudan House, C.G. Road, Navrang Pura, Ahmedabad - 380 009. Phone: 079-26560126; Mobile: 09377088847
Ernakulam	:	39/176 (New No: 60/251) 1st Floor, Karikkamuri Road, Ernakulam, Kochi - 682011, Phone: 0484-2378012, 2378016; Mobile: 09344199799
Bhubaneswar	:	5 Station Square, Bhubaneswar - 751 001 (Odisha). Phone: 0674-2532129, Mobile: 09338746007
Indore	:	Kesardeep Avenue Extension, 73, Narayan Bagh, Flat No. 302, IIIrd Floor, Near Humpty Dumpty School, Indore - 452 007 (M.P.). Mobile: 09301386468
Kolkata	:	108/4, Beliaghata Main Road, Near ID Hospital, Opp. SBI Bank, Kolkata - 700 010, Phone: 033-32449649, Mobile: 09883055590, 07439040301
Guwahati	:	House No. 15, Behind Pragjyotish College, Near Sharma Printing Press, P.O. Bharalumukh, Guwahati - 781009, (Assam). Mobile: 09883055590, 09883055536
Typeset by	:	Elite-Art, New Delhi
Printed at	:	M/s Sri Sai Art Printers, Hyderabad. On behalf of HPH.

PREFACE

This book is intended to make learning computers easy. The content of this book is especially helpful for students who are good but could not perform well in the examinations. The format of this book not only helps in getting insight into the topics but also prepares one for the examination. The questions given are exam oriented.

This book is meant for

1. Students preparing the paper "IT Tools and Applications" paper for DOEACC 'O' and 'A' level examinations.

2. Students who are doing computer courses of duration up to 1 year from various computer institutes.

3. Candidates who will appear in competitive examinations for Government jobs in which computer knowledge is essential or desirable. The book covers questions both for the written tests and interview.

4. People in Government services and who are new to computers.

5. Anyone who wants to learn and acquire sharp knowledge in computers.

This book is not for people who just want to pass an examination by learning without understanding.

I hope that this book would do wonders to the reader's performance in the examination. People buying this book would get free consultation with me and all their queries would be answered by me personally through email. Also they would get free updates to the book. On request, they can get more questions absolutely free about any topic they specially require. Suggestions about the book are welcome. Coming up shortly is the book titled **"Internet and Network"** for DOEACC paper "Internet Technologies and Tools".

Thanks a lot and all the best.

Vikrant Malviya

PGDCM, 'A' Level

Cyber Security Advisor and Trainer

Word of thanks

I thank all my family members and people close to me. I also thank the authors I have read in gaining knowledge about Computers since I started. Last but not the least, I thank you for reading this book.

How to use this book?

The book in your hand is designed to provide more knowledge in less amount of time. All the topics in the book are divided into 3 levels, Level-1, Level-2 and Level-3. Note that these levels are according to the level of depth in respect of that particular topic. Now, for each level, types of questions fall in three categories. A "D" denotes that what follows is a short description about the topic. An "S" denotes that there is one option which is correct among the given options. An "M" denotes that the question have many options as correct. Lastly, an "FIB" indicates that in the examinations, this question could be asked as a filler in the blank question. So while reading a chapter, you get the description about the topics and answer of fill in the blanks type of questions (for which no options are given) and your knowledge so far is also tested by Single answer and Multiple answer questions. What you should do is use a pencil to tick mark the questions which you wrongly answer. Just before the examination, besides reading the descriptions, you could go through those questions which you have marked previously. This would be enough for performing well. Don't try to memorize the questions and answers because it is not like that you would get exactly the same question in the examination. So, try to get good knowlege about every topic. This will help you in long term and make you successful. Thanks and all the very best.

Vikrant Malviya
Author

1

INTRODUCTION TO COMPUTERS

Communication

L-1 D 1. This type of dialing uses multiple tone signaling. Push button phones usually use it. It is required for dial up connections used to connect to the internet.

Ans Touch-tone dialing

Data

L-1 D 2. Data processing is the restructuring or reordering of data by humans or by machines, to increase their usefulness and value for some particular purpose.

L-1 D 3. Data mining tools search databases for hidden patterns to find information that is predictive in nature. This information is difficult to be produced manually even by the experts.

L-1 D 4. Data mining tools predict future trends based on available data and try to find behaviours, allowing businesses to make proactive, knowledge driven decisions.

L-1 F 5. Data is the plural of the word ————.

Ans Datum

Data Processing

L-1 D 6. Characteristics of useful information are relevancy, timeliness, accuracy, conciseness and completeness.

E-commerce

L-1 S 7. Three kinds of e-commerce are ————————, ———————— and ————————.

A. B2C B. C2B C. A2B D. B2B

Email

L-1 D 8. Sending an email in all capital letters is considered to be the equivalent of shouting and comes under bad manners.

File Access

L-2 S 9. Combining two or more records into a single physical block to reduce read or write time.

A. Union B. Adding C. Concatenation D. Blocking

File Handling

L-1 M 10. Among the following, which are wild card characters?

A. & B. * C. " D. ?

L-1 T/F 11. Wild card characters are used in searching files.

A. TRUE B. FALSE

File Organization

L-2 S 12. In ——————————, a process could read the bytes or records of a file out of order, or to access records by key, rather than by position.

A. Inverted access B. Random access

C. Sequential access D. Direct sequential

L-2 S 13. A process could read a file only in order, starting from the beginning.

A. Sequential access B. Random access

C. Indexed sequential D. Direct sequential

L-2 S 14. A process could not skip around and read the file out of order.

A. Random access B. Inverted access

C. Sequential access D. Direct sequential

File System

L-1 D 15. In a single-level directory system, all the files are placed in one directory. Such a directory system has significant limitations if the number of files increases or when there is more than one user. Since all files are in the same directory, they must have unique names.

L-2 S 16. A file organization technique in which address of records is calculated rather than then searched.

A. Encrypting B. Hashing

C. Indexing D. None of the above

Fonts

L-2 D 17. Fonts that are scalable and sometimes generated as bitmaps or soft fonts, depending on the type and capability of the printer.

Ans TrueType fonts

L-2 T/F 18. True type fonts are device independent fonts.

A. TRUE B. FALSE

General

L-1 D 19. The three-character that identifies the type of file.

Ans Extension

L-1 D 20. Email button is located in ———————— toolbar in MsWord.

Ans Formatting

L-1 D 21. On the keyboard, a ———————————— is a horizontal bar in the lowermost row, which is significantly wider than most of the other keys.

Ans Shift bar

L-2 D 22. Self-extracting zip file also need a zip unzip software.

L-2 D 23. Use a ———————————— to join, or concatenate, one or more text strings to produce a single piece of text. This is known as a text concatenation operator.

Ans Semicolon

L-1 D 24. In many window-based softwares, Zoom range is 10 per cent to 400 per cent.

L-1 D 25. The singular for the word 'data' is datum.

L-1 D 26. A Decimal number could be converted into an equivalent binary number and *vice versa.*

L-2 D 27. With the use of an internal computer memory chip, a ———————— can be used to store a large amount of information securely.

Ans Data card

L-1 D 28. In the context of computer hardware, full form of CAM.

Ans Content Addressable Memory

L-1 D 29. The bak extension is used to denote a

Ans Backup file

L-1 D 30. The .gif extension is used to denote a

Ans Graphical interchange format file

L-1 D 31. Alias is a term which means

Ans Another name for an object, entity

L-1 D 32. A file is a

Ans Collection of related data.

L-1 D 33. Backup means ———————— for the purpose of using it if the main data is lost due to hardware or software malfunction or user's mistake.

Ans Archived data

L-1 D 34. An Offline system is the one.

Ans Which is not connected to the network

L-1 D 35. Path name.

Ans Location of the file in the directory structure of the computer

L-1 D 36. GIGO means

Ans Garbage In Garbage Out. It means that the quality of the output or the results given by the computer/program depends on the quality of the input.

L-1 D 37. A Picosecond is equal to

Ans One trillionth of a second

L-1 D 38. Cut vs. copy

Ans Cut copies the selected text in the clipboard and removes the selected text.

L-1 D 39. A Millisecond is equal to

Ans One thousandth of a second

L-1 D 40. Transaction

Ans In computer programming, a transaction usually means a sequence of related operations that is treated as a unit for the purposes of satisfying a request and for ensuring database integrity. For a transaction to be completed and database changes to make permanent, a transaction has to be completed in its entirety.

L-1 D 41. Public folder is another term for a ——————————.

Ans Shared folder

L-1 D 42. Some attributes of a file are (known as file attributes)

Ans Read only, hidden, archive etc.

L-1 D 43. Output devices

Ans A device, such as a printer, video display, or speaker, that presents data from a computer to a user.

L-1 D 44. Root Directory

Ans The topmost directory in the hierarchy of directories containing files and other directories

L-1 D 45. Save vs.-Save as

Ans Use "Save" to save changes made to an already saved and named file. "Save as" is used to save a new file which is not saved yet.

L-1 D 46. Analog computers

Ans An analog computer uses continuous physical phenomena such as electrical, mechanical or hydraulic quantities to model the problem being solved.

L-1 D 47. The following are File Descriptors which represents various information about a file.

Ans Name, title, author, version etc.,

L-1 D 48. Multi-programming

Ans Parallel processing in which several programs are run at the same time on a single processor. There is no true simultaneous execution of different programs. Instead, the operating system executes part of one program, then part of another, and so on. To the user, it appears that all programs are executing at the same time.

L-1 D 49. Dedicated devices.

Ans Devices that have to be dedicated to the single user until the work of that user is finished

L-1 D 50. Logical Functions.

Ans Logical functions provide basic comparison and return TRUE or FALSE values based on the evaluation of the formula.

L-1 D 51. Multi-threading is

Ans The ability of an operating system to execute different parts of a program, called threads, simultaneously. The programmer must carefully design the program in such a way that all the threads can run at the same time without interfering with each other.

L-1 D 52. What is an email?

Ans A message from a user to recepients sent usually using a computer

L-1 D 53. In a image processing/displaying software, enlarging a picture is known as

Ans Zooming

L-1 D 54. In computers, Line feed character is

Ans Chr(13)

L-1 D 55. Web-enabled software are

Ans Those software that can be accessed using an internet connection and a browser and used to do work such as order billing, accounting, sales etc.

L-1 D 56. What is a resource?

Ans Data, program or hardware e.g., printer etc. which is used by a computer or human for carrying out some task.

L-1 D 57. ENIAC was created for the US Army.

L-1 D 58. What is file processing?

Ans Accessing a file and reading the data available in it and deriving some conclusions from it through a set procedure and storing the results somewhere in the same file or the other.

L-1 D 59. What is an output device?

Ans The computer system transfers results of processing to these objects.

L-1 D 60. Information is refined data.

L-1 D 61. What are natural languages?

Ans A human written or spoken language as opposed to a computer language.

L-1 D 62. Decimal no. 9912 in binary is.

Ans 10011010111000

L-1 D 63. What is an operating system?

Ans A software which makes the hardware of the computer usable by human. The interface provided by the operating system is used by humans to interact with the computer.

L-1 D 64. Decimal number 34 in binary is
Ans 00100010

L-1 D 65. The term 'Embedded' means contains within. For e.g., Software that are present in smart cards are said to be embedded in it.

L-1 D 66. Latest version of MS-Office is
Ans Office 2007

L-1 D 67. Full form of CAI is Computer Aided Instruction.

L-1 D 68. The program group 'Entertainment' is located in 'Accessories'.

L-1 D 69. This key is used to delete the character to the right of the insertion point.
Ans DELETE

L-1 D 70. In the context of software, CAM is Computer Aided Manufacturing.

L-1 D 71. A word can contain one or more bytes

L-1 D 72. In the context of software and engineering, CAE stands for ———————.
Ans Computer Aided Engineering

L-1 D 73. Left Alt + Left Shift + Print Screen
Ans Switch High Contrast on and off

L-1 D 74. Who is known to be the world's first programmer?
Ans Ada Lovelace

L-1 D 75. To display the bottom of the active window, ———— key is used.
Ans End

L-1 D 76. Latest Operating System by Microsoft is
Ans Windows 7

L-1 D 77. A nanosecond is one billionth of a second.

L-1 D 78. Intel, Cyrix & Amd manufacture CPU.

L-1 D 79. PDA stands for Portable Digital Assistant.

L-1 D 80. Digital computers from smallest to largest.
Ans Microcomputers, Minicomputers, Mainframes, Supercomputers

L-1 D 81. Difference between laptop and a subnotebook.
Ans Laptop usually have cd/dvd drive/writer. Subnotebook does'nt. Laptops are bigger than notebook. Subnotebooks are usually for small tasks such as web browsing.

L-1 D 82. Information is organized or classified data.

L-1 D 83. A Nanosecond is equal to one billionth (10^{-9}) of a second. Repeated at D 77.

L-1 D 84. What are the characterstics of the internet?
Ans Internet is scaleable, open, easy to use, centralized resource etc.

L-1 D 85. IPOS cycle — Input, Processing, Output and Storage.

L-1 D 86. Timeliness means that information is free from bias.

L-1 D 87. ——————— is computer instruction or data.
Ans Software

L-1 D 88. What is the difference between data and information?

Ans Information is processed data.

L-1 D 89. The data entered into a data processing system is known as Input.

L-1 D 90. Information is nothing but refined ____________.

Ans Data

L-1 D 91. ALT+4 "Delete the selected folder or file (Delete button)?

L-1 D 92. What is the difference between batch and online processing?

Ans A user get updated data if it query an online processing system. In batch processing, a group of jobs is performed in a single lot. The time of this processing is mostly lesser than the time of actual happening of the transaction.

L-1 D 93. A rectangular group of cells is called a ____________.

Ans Grid

L-1 D 94. To connect a laptop or notebook computer to a docking station.

Ans Dock

L-1 D 95. The four steps of IPOS (Input, Processing, Output and Storage) do not have to occur in a rigid sequence.

L-1 D 96. Email is an electronic message sent from one computer to another.

L-1 D 97. A person who uses a computer that is not connected to a network.

Ans Local User

L-1 D 98. Leading or trailing spaces in a cell affect sorting and searching.

L-1 D 99. People who use office automation could be termed as

Ans Knowledge workers

L-1 D 100. Why does today's software applications need more powerful hardware?

Ans Computers are being used in numerous areas and since many calculations and processing is involved, powerful hardware is required.

L-1 D 101. The ease with which a software or a service could be accessed by a user is known as

Ans Usability

L-1 D 102. Advantages of computers — Speed, Accuracy, Reliability, Memory Capability—

L-1 D 103. Open the folder up one level from the open folder (Up One Level button).

Ans ALT + 2

L-1 D 104. Memory beyond one megabyte in 80286, 80386, 80486, and Pentium computers is known as.

Ans Extended memory

L-1 D 105. A Printer that is directly connected to one of the ports on your computer.

Ans Local Printer

L-1 D 106. In the task pane, press CTRL + SPACE to display a menu of additional commands.

L-1 D 107. A set of unique names for entities used in a shared computing environment.

Ans Namespace

L-1 D 108. Hardware is the mechanical and electronic devices, which we can see and touch.

L-1 D 109. A program which defragments volumes on a computer so that the computer runs faster and more efficiently.

Ans Disk defragmenter

L-1 D 110. Every general purpose computer must have an operating system to run other program.

L-1 D 111. Special keys — Function keys, Control keys, Arrow keys, Caps Lock key, etc.

L-1 D 112. Five elements of computing process — Hardware, Software, Data, Human and Procedure..

L-1 D 113. Summarized data is classified into two: ——————— and ————.

Ans Lightly and highly

L-1 D 114. If not specified otherwise, a print from a computer always go to the ————.

Ans Default printer

L-1 D 115. In Ms-Word or Ms-Excel, a hyperlink is automatically created when an internet address or email address is typed.

L-1 D 116. A microcomputer is a ful-fledged computer system that uses a microprocessor as its CPU.

L-1 D 117. A data processing system accepts data as input and processes it into information as output.

L-1 D 118. In formatting, # displays only significant digits and does not display insignificant zeros.

L-1 D 119. Computer data is processed in two fundamental ways ——————— and ———————.

Ans Batch and online

L-1 D 120. A system can be defined as a group of interrelated components working to achieve a common goal.

L-1 D 121. Use 'Print screen' button to capture the entire screen to the clipboard or to print the entire screen.

L-1 D 122. A text management system is a computer system designed to work with the written or typewritten word.

L-1 D 123. Steps in data processing are — Recording, Classifying, Sorting, Calculating, Summarizing and Reporting.

L-1 D 124. A system which permits direct communication between system users and the operating program in the CPU.

Ans Interactive system

L-1 D 125. Transaction files created from source documents are used for logging or recording transactions.

L-1 D 126. When the recipients can get the information when they need it, then the information is known to be ——————.

Ans Timely

L-1 D 127. A Briefcase command that separates the copy of the file inside Briefcase from the copy outside Briefcase.

Ans Splitting

L-1 D 128. Canned programs — Programs prepared by a third party vendor and provided to the used in a machine-readable form.

L-1 D 129. Data can be defined as any fact, observation, assumption or occurrence. These when processed becomes information.

L-1 D 130. ________________ is a set of rules that provides a way of instructing the computer to perform certain operations.

Ans Programming languages

L-1 D 131. A technique for generating new ideas. People sit together and find ideas and solutions and the best one is selected.

Ans Brainstorming

L-1 D 132. ________________ is a subset of an enterprise-wide data warehouse, which typically supports an enterprise element.

Ans Data mart

L-1 D 133. A GIS stores information about the world as a collection of thematic layers that can be linked together by geography.

L-1 D 134. A computer is programmable that is, what the computer does depends totally on the program, which the computer is using.

L-1 D 135. Information stored on a local disk drive. It is a list of files and folders that have been backed up in a backup set.

Ans On-disk catalog

L-1 D 136. A fixed number of adjacent bits that represent a particular character or symbol. Normally, it consists of eight bits.

Ans Byte

L-1 D 137. If an input to a program is able to distinguish between upper case characters and lower case characters, it is said to be

Ans Case-sensitive

L-1 D 138. ________________ is defined as using computer and communication technology to help people better use and manage information.

Ans Office automation

L-1 D 139. Intelligent terminals do some of the processing tasks and they relieve the central computer from doing all of the processing.

L-1 D 140. A stand alone computer system is one that is not connected to or does not communicate with another computer system or network.

L-1 D 141. A person who uses a computer that is not connected to a network. A local user is most likely someone using a computer at home.

Ans Local User

L-1 D 142. The Microsoft Software Library (MSL) is a collection of free, binary (non-text) files located on the Web for all Microsoft products.

L-1 D 143. A set of characters that includes the 10 decimal digits, the 26 letters of the alphabet and a number of special characters is called.

Ans Alphanumeric character set

L-1 D 144. A thin device made of silicon on which integrated electronic components are arranged to form a circuit which does a specific thing.

Ans Chip

L-1 D 145. The number of characters or words that the device can transfer per second, after it has been positioned at the beginning of the record is called bit rate.

L-1 D 146. One can develop professional looking multimedia presentations using tools like Microsoft PowerPoint, Lotus Freelance Graphics and so on.

L-1 D 147. The ability to store and execute instructions, the stored program concept, is the most important property of a general purpose computer.

L-1 D 148. ——————————— lets networked PCs and workstations share information and electronic documents from both corporate and on-line sources.

Ans Groupware

L-1 D 149. Microsoft Press offers the training and support materials a user need about Microsoft Office, Microsoft Windows 98, and Microsoft Windows 2000.

L-1 D 150. The primary source of product information for Microsoft support engineers and customers. This comprehensive collection of articles are updated daily.

Ans Microsoft Knowledge Base (KB)

L-1 D 151. A computer is an electronic data processing device capable of receiving input, storing sets of instructions to process the data and generating accurate output.

L-1 D 152. Information about a file such as its identification details, descriptive title, the author name, the subject, or a keyword related to the contents of the file.

Ans File property

L-1 D 153. A data storage and retreival system. Usually removable storage is used. A library consists of removable media and a hardware device that can read from or write to the media.

Ans Library

L-1 D 154. A folder name or file name longer than the 8.3 file name standard (up to eight characters followed by a period and an extension of up to three characters) of the FAT file system.

Ans Long name

L-1 D 155. The terminal of bank's computer network which is operated by the customer through a visual display unit and a numeric keyboard. To input a touchscreen, or buttons on the side of the display unit are used.

Ans Automated Teller Machine (ATM)

L-1 D 156. The comprehensive source of programming information and toolkits for those who write programs for Microsoft Windows 98 and Microsoft Windows 2000 operating systems, and for those who use Microsoft product.

Ans Microsoft Developer Network (MSDN) CD-ROM Library

L-1 D 157. Information technology (IT) encompasses any combination of equipment (hardware) that facilitates the acquisition, creation, modification, retrieval, storage and transmission of information using electronic media.

L-1 D 158. Microsoft End-User License Agreement ("EULA") is a legal agreement between you (either an individual person or a single legal entity, who will be referred to in this EULA as "You") and Microsoft Corporation for the Microsoft.

L-1 D 159. A credit card-sized device that is used with an access code to enable certificate-based authentication and single sign-on to the enterprise. Smart cards securely store certificates, public and private keys, passwords, and other types of personal information.

Ans Smart card

L-2 D 160. File system.

Ans In computing, a file system (often also written as filesystem) is a method for storing and organizing computer files and the data they contain to make it easy to find and access them. File systems may use a data storage device such as a hard disk or CD-ROM and involve maintaining the physical location of the files, they might provide access to data on a file server by acting as clients for a network protocol (e.g., NFS, SMB, or 9P clients), or they may be virtual and exist only as an access method for virtual data (e.g., procfs). It is distinguished from a directory service and registry.

L-2 D 161. Portability.

Ans Portability is a characteristic of a computer program and it denotes the ease with which it can be used in an operating systems other than the one in which it was created without requiring major rework.

L-2 D 162. Defragmentation.

Ans Puts the scattered parts of files in continuous locations so that data is stored in the media in one heap.

L-3 D 163. Directed Acyclic Graph

Ans In mathematics, a directed acyclic graph, also called a DAG, (also acyclic directed graph), is a directed graph with no directed cycles; that is, for any vertex v, there is no non-empty directed path that starts and ends on v.

L-2 D 164. What is CAD/CAM system?

Ans Computer Aided Design, Computer Aided Manufacturing

L-2 D 165. What is virtual reality?

Ans Virtual reality (VR) is a technology which allows a user to interact with a computer-simulated environment. This environment is a simulation of the real world or an imaginary world.

L-2 D 166. Ctrl + shift while dragging an item.

Ans Create shortcut to selected item

L-2 D 167. A drive attached to an empty folder on an NTFS volume.

Ans Mounted Drive

L-2 D 168. Any node within a tree, along with connected dependants.

Ans Subtree

L-2 D 169. Mainframes have large on line secondary storage capacity.

L-2 D 170. Scalable fonts designed to work with PostScript devices.

Ans Type 1 fonts

L-2 D 171. A search method that can be used to direct the search using conversational language.

Ans Natural language searching

L-2 D 172. A set of unique names for resources or items used in a shared computing environment.

Ans Namespace

L-2 D 173. Multi-dimensional views are inherently representative of an actual ————.

Ans Business Model

L-2 D 174. Mainframes have high speed cache memory, capacity of multi programming and time sharing.

L-2 D 175. The source code that contains the data to be printed as well as the commands for print.

Ans Print job

L-2 D 176. FAQ — A frequently asked question. A file or a document containing frequently asked questions and their answers.

L-2 D 177. The on-disk catalog contains a list of files "and folders that have been backed up in a backup set.

Ans On-disk catalog

L-2 D 178. ———— is a computer based tool for mapping and analyzing things that exist and events that happen on earth.

Ans Geographic Information System

L-2 D 179. An automated process called ———— is used to create explicit geographic references from implicit references.

Ans Geocoding

L-2 D 180. The process of distributing a computer system's facilities to different components of a job in order to perform the job.

Ans Resource allocation

L-2 D 181. ———— is a collection of computer-based information that is critical to successful execution of enterprise initiatives.

Ans Management Information System

L-2 D 182. In personal computers, the Front Side Bus (FSB) is the bus that carries data between the CPU and the memory controller hub (MCH).

L-2 D 183. ____________, ____________ and ____________ are three technologies that supports data mining.

Ans Neural network, Case based reasoning, Decision tree

L-2 D 184. An entity, such as a file, folder, shared folder, printer, or Active Directory object, "described by a distinct, named set of attributes.

Ans Object

L-2 D 185. The process of trying out a new product at a location other than where it was manufactured and people who test are not from the manufacturing party.

Ans Beta testing

L-2 D 186. The scattering of parts of the same disk file over different areas of the disk. Fragmentation occurs as files on a disk are deleted and new files are added.

Ans Fragmentation

L-2 D 187. A working GIS integrated five key components ____________, ____________, ____________, ____________ and ____________.

Ans Hardware, Software, Data, People and Method

L-2 D 188. A logical dump starts at one or more specified directories and recursively dumps all the files and directories found there that have changed since some give base date.

L-2 D 189. A font created by a series of dots. These dots are connected by lines. The resultant font can be scaled to any size. Some dot-matrix printers also support plotter fonts.

Ans Plotter font

L-2 D 190. A code page is a table that relates the binary character codes used by a program to keys on the keyboard or to characters on the display. Useful for working on computers in languages other than English.

L-3 D 191. Cold boot means

Ans The start-up of a computer from a powered-down, or off state. Also called hard boot.

L-3 D 192. What are the uses of virtual reality?

Ans Flight simulation, games, medicine, architect, weather, chemistry

L-3 D 193. Creating a physical or theoretical model on a computer and trying various things that would otherwise be difficult to in an actual system and then analyzing the experience and result so that they would help if the same things are done on the actual system. This technique is known as simulation.

L-1 D 194. Multi processing

Ans Multi processing is the use of two or more central processing units (CPUs) in a single computer system. It is the ability of a system to support more than one processor and/or the ability to allocate tasks between them.

L-2 D 195. A mounted drive's name is resolved to a fill full system path.

L-3 D 196. Warm boot means

Ans Refers to restarting a computer that is already turned on via the operating system. Restarting it returns the computer to its initial state. A warm boot is sometimes necessary when a program encounters an error from which it cannot recover. On PCs, a user can perform a warm boot by pressing the Control, Alt, and Delete keys simultaneously. On Macs, you can perform a warm boot by pressing the Restart button. Also called a soft boot.

L-1 F 197. Full form of GUI is

Ans Graphical User Interface

L-1 F 198. Full form of CBIS is

Ans Computer Based Information System

L-1 F 199. Full form of EULA

Ans End User License Agreement

L-1 F 200. ________________ means reading each word (and punctuation mark) in a document slowly and carefully while looking for errors.

Ans Proofing or proof reading

L-1 F 201. One billionth of a second

Ans A nanosecond

L-1 F 202. Bit is a ____________.

Ans Binary digit

L-1 F 203. "#" is known as ____________.

Ans Hash

L-1 F 204. "Con' means ____________.

Ans Console

L-1 F 205. @ is known as ____________

Ans at the rate of

L-1 F 206. In the context of software, EIS is ________________.

Ans Executive Information System

L-1 F 207. ____________ describes the type of file.

Ans File extension

L-1 F 208. VRML stands for ________________.

Ans Virtual Reality Modeling Language

L-1 F 209. Enter key is also known as ____________.

Ans Return key

L-1 F 210. A group of related records maintained in a specific order is called a ________ ________.

Ans Data file

L-1 F 211. An action that cannot be broken down further to a group of actions is known as a ______.

Ans Atomic action

L-1 F 212. The time between issuing a command and getting the result is called ______.

Ans Response time

L-1 F 213. ______ is the study of how to create safety, comfort and ease of use for people who use machines.

Ans Ergonomics

L-1 F 214. Each location of a computer system can store a fixed number of characters or bits called its ______.

Ans Word Length

L-2 F 215. MIPS is ______.

Ans Million Instructions Per Second

L-2 F 216. OLAP is the abbreviation of ______.

Ans Online Analytical Processing

L-2 F 217. 32 bit computer has a word length of ______.

Ans 32

L-2 F 218. With Microsoft ______, a person can have virtual meetings with anyone in the world.

Ans Netmeeting

L-3 F 219. Computer software are designed to perform adequately with other products that would come up in the near future. Same applies to hardware.

Ans Upward compatibility

L-1 F 220. ______ education allows one to proceed at one's own pace.

Ans Online

L-3 F 221. Programs developed on a more advanced system which can also be executed on a less advanced (earlier) version. This is known as ______.

Ans Downward compatibility

L-1 M 222. Text editors

A. MS-Word B. Wordstar C. Lotus D. Edit

L-1 M 223. Memory Stores

A. Data B. Instructions

L-1 M 224. Relational Operators.

A. = B. > C. Add D.2's complement

L-1 M 225. Main characteristics of computers.

A. Word Length B. Speed and Stor C. Accuracy and D. Forgething
E. Automation

L-1 M 226. These portals provide free email accounts.
A. Hotmail B. Yahoo mail C. Rocketmail D. Snail mail
E. Acb Cement

L-2 M 227. Speed of computers can be measured in
A. Nanoseconds B. Picoseconds

L-3 M 228. Biometric identification
A. Fingerprint B. Hand geometry C. Voice D. Iris
E. Face recongition

L-1 M 229. Carriage return
A. Escape key B. Return key C. Enter key D. All of the above

L-1 M 230. Limitations of computers
A. Productivity B. Reasoning C. Accuracy D. Volume

L-1 M 231. ———— is a page orientation
A. Landslide B. Landscape C. Photoframe D. Vertical
E. Portrait

L-2 M 232. Text file are of two types
A. Decimal B. ASCII C. Binary D. EBCDIC

L-1 M 233. Basic file operations
A. Create B. Send C. Delete D. Open
E. Encrypt

L-1 M 234. These are known as wildcard characters.
A. * B.+ C. & D. ?

L-1 M 235. The main functions of the computer are
A. Receive input and produce output B. Information processing
C. Information storage D. All of the above

L-1 M 236. The major components of a computer are
A. Memory B. CPU C. I/O Devices D. All of the above

L-1 S 237. Which of the following is an operating system?
A. DOS B. OS/2 C. UNIX D. All of the above

L-2 S 238. Types of Operating Systems
A. Mainframe OS B. Server OS C. Multiprocess OS D. PC OS
E. All of the above

L-2 S 239. Types of Operating Systems
A. Embedded OS B. Smart Card OS
C. Real-time OS D. All of the above

L-1 S 240. ATM is
A. Automated Transaction Machine B. Automated Teller Machine
C. American Teller Machine D. Automated Transaction Module

L-1 S 241. A4 page size

A. 10 × 12 inch | B. 8.27 × 11.69 inch
C. 8.50 × 11.70inch | D. None of the above

L-1 S 242. EDP stands for

A. Electronic Data Program | B. Electronic Data Processing
C. E-commerce Data Processing | D. None of these

L-1 S 243. Open search window

A. Alt + S | B. F3 | C. ALT + 2 | D. Ctrl + S

L-1 S 244. In many softwares, ———————— is used to cancel the current task.

A. Alt | B. Esc | C. F1 | D. Home

L-1 S 245. A microsecond is equal to

A. Thousandth of a second | B. Millionth of a sec
C. Billionth of a second | D. Trillionth of a second

L-1 S 246. Temporary files are stored in

A. C: Temp | B. C:\Windows\Temp | C. C:\Program | D. All of the above

L-1 S 247. Typically, the capacity of CD-ROM is

A. 1 GB | B. 640-700 MB | C. 300-400 MB | D. 800 MB

L-1 S 248. Font size is commonly measured in ————.

A. Inches | B. Points | C. Cms | D. All of the above

L-1 S 249. The process of arranging data into a desired sequence.

A. Arranging | B. Sorting | C. Sequencing | D. Setting

L-1 S 250. Windows supports long file names upto ———————— characters.

A. 30 | B. 255 | C. 128 | D. 8

L-1 S 251. Units in which information is stored on disk and other external media and it is in this unit that a user sees his/her data in windows explorer.

A. Field | B. Files | C. Blocks | D. Characters

L-1 S 252. Anything that is useful and is allotted to a process, program or a user.

A. Device | B. Resources | C. Authorization | D. None of these

L-1 S 253. ———————— is the means using which an object communicates/interacts with another.

A. Interactor | B. Interface | C. Messenger | D. Spooler

L-1 S 254. In a ————————————, devices can be added or removed while the computer is running.

A. Cold system | B. Hot pluggable system
C. Both of the above | D. None of the above

L-1 S 255. The running of several computer programs one after the another without the need of a human operator.

A. Online program | B. Batch program
C. Automatic program | D. None of the above

L-1 S 256. In a dialog box, the command button that is selected or highlighted when the dialog box is displayed. It has a bold border, indicating that it will be chosen automatically if the ENTER key is pressed.

A. Main button B. Default button C. Enter button D. Only button

L-2 S 257. PDF stands for

A. Presentable Document For B. Portable Document
C. Portable Document D. Presentable Document File

L-2 S 258. Measure of the efficiency of a computer system.

A. Speed B. Throughput C. Volume D. Clock speed

L-2 S 259. Number of bits a computer can process at a time in parallel is called

A. Binary system B. Word Length C. Processing power D. Word gauge

L-2 S 260. Which is the technology that is used as a direct-entry method in banks?

A. OCR B. MICR C. OMR D. None of the above

L-2 S 261. The ability to input data directly into a computer system by speaking to it.

A. Direct input B. Speech recognition C. Manual input D. None of the above

L-2 S 262. The total amount of processing carried out by a computer system within a given time period.

A. Speed B. Throughput C. Volume D. Clock speed

L-2 S 263. ________ rely on servers for services such as printing, database and even processing power.

A. Nodes B. Clients C. Host D. None of the above

L-2 S 264. The ability of computer hardware or software to ensure data integrity when a hardware failures occur

A. Data protection B. Fault tolerance C. Data Integrity D. None of the above

L-2 S 265. With the ________________ type e-commerce, the company first established a website on the internet.

A. B2B B. B2C C. C2B D. All of the above

L-2 S 266. A backup that copies only files that are created or changed since the last normal or incremental backup.

A. Selective backup B. Full backup
C. Additional backup D. Incremental backup

L-1 S 267. Letter page size

A. 8.5 × 11inches B. 9 × 11inches C. 8.5 × 14inches D. None of the above

L-1 S 268. Giga is ________________.

A. 1073741824 B. 100000000 C. 99999 D. None of the above

L-1 S 269. EDI stands for ________________.

A. Electronic Data Interchange B. Electronic Data Interaction
C. E-commerce Data D. Electronic Data Independence

L-1 S 270. Usually, the number of "Enter" keys in the keyboard is
A. 2 B. 1 C. 3 D. None of the above

L-1 S 271. ———————— can be used to create web pages.
A. Frontpage B. HtmlPager
C. Internet information server D. None of the above

L-1 S 272. Which among the following entries of year is better?
A. 1901 B. 59
C. Both of the above D. None of the above

L-1 S 273. Verifying that an entity is who or what it claims to be.
A. Authentication B. Authorization
C. Auditing D. Rights evaluation

L-1 S 274. The following software creates and edits text files using basic text formatting
A. Notepad B. Wordpad C. MS-Word D. MS-Outlook

L-1 S 275. If "Caps" light is on, it means the characters would be typed in
A. Capital Letters B. Lowercase C. Propercase D. None of the above

L-1 S 276. The highest level in a hierarchically organized set of information.
A. Root B. Top C. Node D. None of the above

L-1 S 277. To detach a laptop or other portable computer from a docking station.
A. Undock B. Disconnect C. Remove D. None of the above

L-1 S 278. The technology that is used in evaluation of aptitude tests is called.
A. OCR B. OMR C. MICR D. MCR

L-1 S 279. ———————— is the most important program that runs on a computer.
A. Operating System B. Compiler
C. Word D. Excel

L-1 S 280. A computer that works with discrete quantities. It uses numbers to simulate real time processes.
A. Digital Computer B. Analog Computer
C. Dedicated Computer D. Workstation

L-1 S 281. ———————— is an umbrella term describing the electronic technologies that support person to person collaboration.
A. Groupware B. Software C. Hardware D. Firmware

L-1 S 282. A backup that copies all selected files and marks each file as having been backed up (in other words, the archive attribute is cleared).
A. Normal backup B. Differential backup
C. Incremental backup D. Decremental backup

L-2 S 283. The period during which due to a hardware or software failure, the computer is unavailable for use.
A. Downtime B. Turnaround time
C. Lapse time D. None of the above

L-2 S 284. The spoken words are interpreted by the computer and converted into computer readable form. This is

A. Speech recognition B. Voice input

C. Both of the above D. Verbal interaction

L-2 S 285. Which of the following is used to send and receive files stored on other computer on the Internet?

A. FTP B. Telnet C. FAQ D. SLIP

L-1 S 286. Zip is related to

A. Transmission B. Copy C. Compression D. None of the above

L-1 S 287. Full form of FIFO

A. First In Function Output B. Function Input First Output

C. First In First Out D. None of these

L-1 S 288. Microsecond

A. One thousandth of a second B. One hundredth of a second

C. One millionth of a second D. Million of a second

L-1 S 289. Legal page size

A. 8.5 × 11 inches B. 9 × 11inches

C. 8.5 × 14inches D. None of the above

L-1 S 290. Full form of CAD is

A. Computer Automated Design B. Compiled Aided Design

C. Computer Aided Design D. None of the above

L-1 S 291. In most window-based softwares, the shortcut for help is

A. F10 B. F8 C. F1 D. None of the above

L-1 S 292. Keyboard shortcut to print a file is ——————

A. Alt + P B. Ctrl + P C. ALT + 2 D. ALT + 1

L-1 S 293. Example of system software.

A. Word processors B. Games

C. Spreadsheets D. None of the above

L-1 S 294. A Megabyte is ——————

A. 1024 bytes B. 100024 bytes C. 100000 bytes D. 1048576 bytes

L-1 S 295. Collection of facts in raw form.

A. Information B. Field C. File D. Data

L-1 S 296. This key deletes character to the left of the insertion point.

A. Del B. Enter C. Backspace D. None of the above

L-1 S 297. Comma, period, semicolon, and so on.

A. Control keys B. Grammatical keys C. Punctuation keys D. English keys

L-1 S 298. Prevent the CD from automatically playing on inserting into the drive.

A. Press Pause break B. Press escape

C. Press Shift D. Press Ctrl when you insert a CD

L-1 S 299. GIS stands for ——————————.

A. Geographical instruction system B. Geographical information software

C. Geographical information system D. Generator information system

L-1 S 300. Which of the following is an output device?

A. Printer B. Monitor C. Plotter D. All of the above

L-1 S 301. The finished result of processing by a system is called a ——————————.

A. Print B. Hard copy C. Input D. Output

L-1 S 302. Microcomputers are also called ——————————.

A. Minicomputer B. Supercomputer

C. Mainframe D. . Personal computers

L-1 S 303. Norton, Mcafee and AVG are names of some common

A. File compression utilities B. Excel programs

C. Antivirus D. Word processors

L-1 S 304. A combination of letters, digits and special characters

A. Beta numeric B. Non-numeric C. Word D. Alphanumeric

L-1 S 305. Typing, layout settings, printing, designing of images etc.

A. Printing B. Software development

C. Desktop publishing D. Data entry

L-1 S 306. If on the edit menu "Paste" option is disabled, it means that

A. The option cannot be used B. Software is corrupt

C. No text have been copied to the clipboard. D. None of the above

L-1 S 307. Node or software program that requests services from a server.

A. Server agent B. Computer C. Host D. Client

L-1 S 308. The result of data processing which is useful in making decisions.

A. Processed data B. Results C. Information D. File

L-1 S 309. Which of the following is the most important program in a computer?

A. Word processors B. Spreadsheets

C. Presentation graphics D. None of the above

L-1 S 310. The abnormal end of a program because of a system fault error or operator intervention.

A. Run time error B.Program fault C. Program failure D. Abort

L-1 S 311. Computer output which is displayed on the screen of a terminal without a printed copy.

A. Hard copy B. Display copy C. Visible copy D. Soft copy

L-1 S 312. A small button which on clicking performs a specific tasks. One of the components of GUI.

A. Button B. Link C. Icon D. Menu

L-1 S 313. To type numbers using numeric keys on right side of the keyboard, ———— indicative light should be on.

A. Caps lock B. Scroll lock C. Num lock D. All of the above

L-1 S 314. Files created on previous versions of a software can be opened in the latest version of the same software. This feature is called ————.

A. Compatibility B. Portability

C. Backward compatibility D. None of the above

L-1 S 315. The science that studies and discover ways in which machines should be designed so that they become comfortable and efficient to be used.

A. Ergodesign B. Architecture C. Ergonomics D. Ergocom

L-1 S 316. Latest processor from Intel is

A. Core2Duo B. Dual core C. i-series D. Cyrix

L-2 S 317. Among the following, ———— is a file compression utility.

A. Internet explorer B. FTP

C. Winrar D. Disk defragmenter

L-2 S 318. MIS is

A. Magnetic instruction system B. Management instruction system

C. Magnetic input system D. Management information system

L-2 S 319. MIDI stands for

A. Magnetic Instruments Digital Interface

B. Magnetic Ink Digital Interface

C. Musical Instruments Interpace

D. Musical Information Digital Interaction

L-2 S 320. JVM is ————.

A. Java very important machine B. Java virtual machine

C. Jittery virtual machine D. None of the above

L-2 S 321. Java control panel is usually available in

A. My documents B. My computer C. Control panel

D. All programs E. Desktop

L-2 S 322. BPR is the abbreviation of ————.

A. Business process restruct B. Big process reengineering

C. Business procedure reinstallation D. Business process reengineering

L-2 S 323. Mainframe Operating Systems provide the following services.

A. Batch B. Transaction Processing

C. Timesharing D. All of the above

L-2 S 324. Which of the following is generally used for backups?

A. CD-ROM B. Hard disk

C. 8-mm Helical Scan D. Magnetic tape

L-2 S 325. A technique used to reduce the number of characters transmitted without losing data.

A. Transmission B. Zip

C. Modem compression D. None of the above

L-2 S 326. If used, this method ensures continued system operation even if a component of the system fails.

A. Replication B. Quick correction C. Fault tolerance D. None of these

L-2 S 327. A measure of how well a computer, service, or application can be expanded to meet increasing demands.

A. Growth potential B. Increasability

C. Expandibility D. Scalability

L-2 S 328. The total time elapsed between submission of command and data to a computer and availability of results.

A. Throughput B. Access time C. Turnaround time D. Response time

L-2 S 329. ______________ looks like a standard credit card, but instead of a magnetic strip it contains embedded microprocessors and memory.

A. Debit Card B. Credit Card C. Smart Card D. Identity card

L-2 S 330. With most terminals, nothing is automatically displayed when a key is pressed. It is entirely up to the software to display the character, if desired. This process is known as

A. Displaying B. Printing C. Echoing D. Copying

L-1 S 331. Large databases are analyzed to get some useful information

A. Data analysis B. System analysis C. Data audit D. Data mining

L-1 D 332. Prerecorded list of instructions is called a

Ans Program

L-1 D 333. Cashless payment of amounts using the internet.

Ans Electronic Funds Transfer

L-1 S 334. A service that manages an Uninterruptible Power Supply (UPS) connected to a computer.

Ans UPS service

L-1 S 335. Windows Media Server can be used to broadcasting to more than 10 people at the same time.

L-1 S 336. CAD systems allow the designers to view a product from different perspectives including three-dimensional rotations and various cross sections.

L-1 S 337. Electronic Data Interchange EDI is the exchange of electronic messages from one organization to another using a network. These data pertains mainly to business.

Ans TRUE

L-1 T/F 338.OS/2 is a programming language.

A. TRUE B. FALSE

L-1 T/F 339. Today, all computers are analog.

A. TRUE B. FALSE

L-1 T/F 340. Wordprocessors has not replaced typewriters.

A. TRUE B. FALSE

L-1 T/F 341. My Documents folder cannot be accessed via desktop.

A. TRUE B. FALSE

L-1 T/F 342. Data stored in smart cards cannot be password protected.

A. TRUE B. FALSE

L-1 T/F 343. Programs written in high level language are executed by the computer in the form in which it is written.

A. TRUE B. FALSE

L-1 T/F 344. If you have saved a file and given a name to it, then afterwards if you press "Save" icon on the toolbar, a dialog box will appear.

A. TRUE B. FALSE

L-2 T/F 345. Winzip utility is used to transfer files from one computer to another.

A. TRUE B. FALSE

L-1 T/F 346. A gigabyte is 1073741824 bytes.

A. TRUE B. FALSE

L-1 T/F 347. Data after processing becomes information.

A.TRUE B. FALSE

L-1 T/F 348. The question mark character "?" represents any single character.

A. TRUE B. FALSE

L-1 T/F 349. The asterisk character represents any group of one or more characters.

A. TRUE B. FALSE

L-1 T/F 350. A computer needs both hardware and software for its proper functioning.

A. TRUE B. FALSE

L-1 T/F 351. If the file is not saved and you close the file, you are asked to save the file.

A. TRUE B. FALSE

Generation of Languages

L-1 D 352. The third generation languages, or 3GL are high-level languages such as C.

L-1 D 353. The first generation languages, or 1GL are low-level languages that are machine language.

L-1 D 354. The second generation languages, or 2GL are also low-level languages that generally consist of assembly languages.

L-1 D 355. The fifth generation languages, or 5GL are programming languages that contain visual tools to help develop a program. A good example of a fifth generation language is Visual Basic.

L-1 D 356. The fourth generation languages, or 4GL are languages that consist of statements similar to statements in a human language. Fourth generation languages are commonly used in database programming and scripts.

Hard disk

L-2 S 357. The time required to position a movable read-write head over the recording track to be used is called.

A. Rotational delay
B. Data transfer time
C. Seek time
D. Stoppage time

Hardware

L-1 D 358. Even if the power is switched off, non-volatile devices does not loses its content

L-1 D 359. EPROM

Ans. EPROM The information stored in an EPROM chip can be erased by exposing the chip to strong UV light. EPROM chips are easily recognized by the small quartz window used for erasing. Once erased, the chip can be re-programmed. EPROM is more expensive to buy per unit cost, but can prove cheaper in the long run for some applications.

L-1 D 360. "Tab" key is used to

Ans. Move the cursor directly to next tab stop.

L-1 D 361. What is the difference between RAM and ROM?

Ans. Both are random access but RAM is volatile.

L-1 D 362. An intelligent terminal has an inbuilt processing capability.

L-1 D 363. A group of consecutive sectors written at once in CD-ROM XA are called

Ans CD-ROM Track

L-1 D 364. With portable computers, ______________________ are more popular than the mouse.

Ans Touchpad

L-1 D 365. The primary task of a CPU is to execute a sequence of stored instructions called a program.

L-1 D 366. CD-Rs look like regular CD-ROMs, except that they are gold colored on top instead of silver colored.

L-1 D 367. If you connect two MIDI keyboards with a cable, the note you play on one keyboard (the master) is mimicked on the other (the slave).

L-2 D 368. Seek operation is

Ans Set the current position to a place from/to which/where data transfer is required.

L-2 D 369. Full form of SCSI is

Ans Small Computer System Interface

L-2 D 370. The concept in which the name of the file or a device should be string or an integer and not depend on the device in any-way

Ans Uniform naming

L-2 D 371. Available disk space that is not allocated to any volume. The type of disk determines the type of volume that can be created on the unallocated space.

Ans Unallocated space

L-1 D 372. EEPROM

Ans This has the added advantage that the information stored can be rewritten in blocks and hence can be used to store system settings that the user may want to change periodically. Commonly used to store system settings such as BIOS settings.

L-1 D 373. This interface is used for connecting microcomputers to peripheral devices such as hard disks and printers, and to other computers and local area networks.

Ans SCSI

L-1 F 374. GDI is ______________.

Ans Graphics Device Interface

L-1 F 375. MULTICS is ______________.

Ans Multiplexed Information and Computing Service

L-2 F 376. A feature that automatically compresses the data that is being stored on the device. This feature is available on some tape drives.

Ans Hardware compression

L-1 F 377. UPS is ______________.

Ans Uninterruptible Power Supply (UPS)

L-1 M 378. Examples of mass storage devices are

A. Disk Drives B. Tapes C. CD-ROM D. All of the above

L-1 S 379. CMOS is used to hold

A. Operating system B. Date and Time Information
C. Application process D. System startup parameters

L-1 S 380 Full form of WORM is

A. Write-on-resuable media B. Write-once-read many
C. Write-on-random media D. None of the above

L-1 S 381. Data can be erased and rewritten on

A. CD-R B. CD-RW C. Both of the above D. None of the above

L-1 S 382. The physical components of a computer system and its peripherals.

A. Software B. Hardware C. System D. All of the above

L-1 S 383. ______________ are software that has been permanently written onto read only memory.

A. Software B. Firmware C. Fixware D. Hardware

L-1 S 384. Caches in which all modified blocks are written back to the disk immediately are called ______________caches.

A. Immediate write B. Write-through
C. Immediate writable D. None of the above

L-1 S 385. It is connected between a computer and a power source to ensure that electrical flow is not interrupted in case of a power failure.

A. Universal power supply B. Uninterruptible power supply
C. Uninterrupted power supply D. Universal power saver

L-2 S 386. CMOS is

A. Complementary Metal Oxide
B. Complementary Metal Oxide Semiconductor
C. Common Metal Oxide Semiconductor
D. Common Manipulative Optional Semiconductor

L-2 S 387. The bus used for attaching peripheral devices such as disks and CD-ROMs to the system.

A. PCI B. IDE C. RAM D. None of the above

L-2 S 388. A type of digital video disc (DVD) decoder that allows a DVD drive to display movies on computer.

A. Coder B. Software decoder
C. Encoder D. Decrypter

L-2 S 389. ——————interface allows asynchronous transmission of data characters one bit at a time.

A. Parallel port B. Serial port C. USB port D. Printer port

L-1 S 390. Cordless devices uses

A. Infrared light B. Ultraviolet light C. Both of the above D. Radiowaves

L-1 S 391. The actual machinery in a computer is called the

A. Hardware B. Software C. Motherboard D. All of the above

L-1 S 392. —————— can be considered to be the "Heart" of the computer.

A. Central Processing Unit B. Motherboard C. IC D. RAM

L-3 S 393. A calculated value which is used to reconstruct data after a failure in a Raid-5 volume.

A. Parity B. Checksum C. Log D. None of the above

L-1 S 394. Which has maximum capacity?

A. Floppy disk B. Zip disk C. Jaz cartridge D. Superdisk

L-1 S 395. The "Wheel" on the mouse is called

A. Mouse roll B. Roller C. Scroll key D. Wheel

L-1 S 396. The Physical components of a computer system are called

A. Software B. Mother board C. Hardware D. None of the above

L-1 S 397. Usually for "Clicking", there are ——— mouse buttons

A. 5 B. 1 C. 2 D. None of the above

L-1 S 398. A type of storage devices which does not uses optical disk storage technology.

A. CD B. CD-R C. Tapes D. VCD

L-1 S 399. Following transmits data from one part of the computer to other.

A. Wires B. PCI cards C. RAM D. Bus

L-1 S 400. Which is a device that draws pictures on paper based on commands from a computer?

A. Synthesizer B. Monitor C. Plotter D. None of the above

L-1 S 401. ―――――――― is used to permanently retain large amounts of data for future use.

A. CPU B. Cache

C. Mass storage device D. None of the above

L-1 S 402. UPS devices use ―――――――― to keep the computer running for a period of time after a power failure has occurred.

A. Electrical connection B. Inverter

C. Batteries D. None of the above

L-2 S 403. 1,024 megabytes or approximately one billion bytes.

A. Byte B. Megabyte C. Gigabyte (GB) D. Terabyte

L-3 S 404. When power is turned on, the hardware of the computer sets the program counter to the first address of the ――――――――

A. System.ini B. Active partition C. Bootstrap loader D. Boot.ini

L-1 S 405. Which component of the computer executes the instructions?

Ans Central Processing Unit

L-2 S 406. An interface on the computer that allows asynchronous transmission of data characters one bit at a time.

Ans Communication port

L-1 T/F 407. A CD stores greater amount of data than a DVD.

A. TRUE B. FALSE

L-1 T/F 408. Data once written on CD ROMs could be replaced.

A. TRUE B. FALSE

L-2 T/F 409. SCSI is high speed serial interface.

A. TRUE B. FALSE

L-1 T/F 410. Full form of DVD is Digital Versatile Disk.

A. TRUE B. FALSE

Hardware and software

L-2 S 411. A measure of the fault tolerance of a computer and its programe.

Ans Tolerance B. Availability C. Portablility D. Contactability

L-2 S 412. The statistically average time from the moment that a batch job is submitted until the moment it is completed is called

Ans Response time. B. Performance C. Throughput D. Turnaround time.

History

L-1 D 413. ―――――――― was the first all-electronic computer.

Ans ENIAC

L-1 D 414. UNIVAC stands for

Ans Universal Automatic Computer

L-1 D 415. Fourth Generation Computers

Ans 1980+ (Personal Computers)

L-1 D 416. Fourth Generation Computer uses

Ans LSI (Large Scale Integrated circuits)

L-1 D 417. First Generation Operating systems

Ans 1944-55 (Vacuum tubes and plugboards)

L-1 D 418. First significant Timesharing system

Ans CTSS (Compatible Time Sharing System)

L-1 D 419. The first true digital computer was designed by

Ans Charles Babage (an English Mathematician)

L-1 D 420. The first supercomputer was ILLIAC IV made by Burroughs.

L-1 D 421. In the late 1950s transistors 1/200th the size of a vacuum tube came into use.

L-1 D 422. UNIVAC was the first computer to handle both numerical and alphabetic information with equal ease.

L-1 D 423 **Mark I** was programmed by punch cards, weighed 5 tons and could do multiplication operation in about 6 seconds.

L-1 D 424. The UNIVAC was a vacuum tube computer, and its input was through magnetic tape, storage was magnetic tapes or a magnetic drum.

L-1 D 425 The first computer to have the Von Neumann Architecture was the Electronic Discrete Variable Automatic Computer, or EDSAC which became operational in 1952.

L-1 D 426. In a typical Von Neumann system, instructions and data are loaded together in the same memory. The instruction is placed first with data immediately following it.

L-1 F 427. Personal computers are also known as ——————————.

Ans Microcomputers

L-1 F 428. ENIAC stands for ——————————.

Ans Electronic Numerical Integrator And Computer

L-1 S 429. A high level programming language named after Ada Augusta.

A. Augusta B. Ada C. Charles D. Darwin

L-1 S 430. First computer was

A. UNIVAC B. ABACUS C. ENIAC D. None of the above

L-1 S 431. Which is the operating system for IBM PS/2 computer?

A. CICS/2 B. DB/2 C. OS/2 D. None of the above

L-1 S 432. The first major computer line to use Small Scale Integrated Circuits (SSIC).

Ans 360 from IBM

Input/Output

L-1 S 433. In ————————, synchronization of hardware and software is achieved to produce electronic tones.

A. Synthesizer B. Plain Talk C. VoiceType D. MIDI

L-2 T/F434. Same superdisk drive cannot be used to read and write to 1.44 MB diskettes as well as 120MB super disk.

A. TRUE B. FALSE

Internet

L-1 D 435. The address of a website is written on ———————— of the internet explorer.

Ans Address bar

L-1 D 436. AltaVista is a meta -search engine.

L-1 D 437. ———————————— are mailing list management system.

Ans Listserv, Majordomo

L-1 D 438. Companies like Amazon bookstore are examples of virtual shops.

L-1 D 439. There are two main types of search tools ———————— and ————————

Ans Web index and search engine

L-1 D 440. ———————————— is a place where contact information about the people is stored

Ans Address book

L-1 D 441. A ———————— is a single unit of information, often called a document that is available via the World Wide Web (WWW).

Ans A webpage

L-1 D 442. Dynamic content, such as a stock ticker, a weather map, or news, that is usually updated from the World Wide Web or a channel.

Ans Active content

L-1 D 443. ———————————— provides a single interface that enables users to search many different search engines, indexes and databases simultaneously.

Ans Meta search engine

L-2 D 444. ———————————————— is a protocol designed to search, retrieve and display documents from remote sites on the internet.

Ans Gopher

L-2 D 445. ———————————— is a protocol, or set of rules, that enables one computer to connect to another computer and this process is referred to as ————————————.

Ans Telnet, Remote login

L-2 F 446. Any site or remote computer which is not harmful to this computer in any way and there exist some preset mechanism to determine this.

Ans Trusted site

L-1 M 447. List some activities that can be done on the internet.

Ans Email B. Web surfing C. Scanning D. File transfer

L-2 M 448. The major categories for top-level domains are

Ans A. com B. net and gov C. edu and org D. All of the above

L-1 S 449. The WWW is a brainchild of

A. Tim Berners Lee B. EF Codd

C. JCR Licklider D. None of the above

L-1 S 450. Which of the following is a search engine?

A. Altavista B. Excite C. Lycos D. All of the above

L-1 S 451. Which of the following is a characterbased browser?

A. Mosaic B. Netscape C. Internet Explorer D. Lynx

Internet

L-1 T/F 452. It is not possible to send formatted documents, photos, sound files, and video files as attachments through email.

A. TRUE B. FALSE

Internet Explorer

L-1 S 453. To refresh a window/desktop following key is used

A. F1 B. F2 C. F3 D. F4

E. F5

Keyboard

L-1 D 454. Windows key is used to get start menu.

L-1 D 455. "*" is known as

Ans Asterisk

L-1 D 456. Scroll Lock button on the keyboard is used to

Ans To prevent the cursor to change the position if the scroll bars are used to view different pages of a document.

L-2 D 457. A feature that sets your keyboard to beep when one of the locking keys (CAPS LOCK, NUM LOCK, or SCROLL LOCK) is turned on or off.

Ans Toggle Keys

L-2 M 458. These are called modifier keys.

A. Ctrl B. Escape C. Shift D. Alt

L-1 S 459. "\" is

A. Backward slash B. Forward slash

C. Junk character D. Relational operator

L-1 S 460. "/" is

A. Backward slash B. Forward slash

C. Junk character D. Relational operator

L-2 S 461. ———— enables a user to press a modifier key or windows key and have it remain active until a non-modifier key is pressed.

A. Important keys B. StickyKeys C. Toggle keys D. None of the above

L-1 S 462. Usually the key located at top left corner is

A. Esc key. B. Enter key C. Pause key D. F1 key

L-1 T/F 463. Normally, there are two window keys on a keyboard

A. TRUE B. FALSE

L-1 T/F 464. The lock keys include Scroll lock, Num lock (which allows the use of the numeric keypad), and Caps lock.

A. TRUE B. FALSE

L-2 T/F 465. Modifier keys are useful for people who have difficulty in pressing two keys simultaneously.

A. TRUE B. FALSE

Mainframe

L-2 D 466. An example of mainframe operating system.

Ans OS/390

Memory

L-2 D 467. Buffering enables the processor to execute another instruction while input or output is taking place rather than being idle while transfer is completed.

L-2 S 468. An area in memory used to hold input and output records.

A. Cache B. Register C. Buffer D. Stack

Monitor

L-1 D 469. Clear Type fonts are intended for display on flat screen monitors.

MS-DOS

L-1 D 470. CLS command in Dos.

Ans Clear the screen

L-1 D 471. Break command in Dos

Ans Sets or clears extended Ctrl + C checking.

L-1 D 472. Displays the name of or changes the current directory.

Ans CHDIR

L-2 D 473. In Dos directory structure, Dot refers to the current directory. Dotdot refers to its parent.

MS-Office

L-1 S 474. —————————— can be used for moving text from one place to another.

A. Cut and paste B. Formatting C. F10 D. Dragging

Multimedia

L-1 D 475. An image file which contains many images and when viewed, all images run one by one to present an animated effect.

Ans GIF

L-1 D 476. Draw programs are also called ——————.

Ans Vector graphics programs

L-1 D 477. There are two basic forms of computer graphics —————— and ——.

Ans Bitmap and Vector graphics

L-1 D 478. Bitmap images are formed from a matrix of pixels with different colors

L-1 D 479. What is a Bitmap image?

Ans A bitmap is one of many types of file formats for images stored in a computerized form. It carries the extension. BMP. Computers use bits of 1 and 0 to store data. A bitmap is literally a map of bits that form a particular picture when rendered to a display like a computer monitor.

L-1 D 480. What is a Vector image?

Ans Vector graphics is the use of geometrical primitives such as points, lines, curves, and shapes or polygon(s), which are all based on mathematical equations, to represent images in computer graphics.

L-1 D 481. Vector graphics are a set of objects such as lines, rectangles, ellipses, arcs, or curves called primitives that the program stores as numerical coordinates and mathematical formulas specifying their shape and position in the image.

L-1 D 482. Multimedia is also used for special effects in movies.

L-1 D 483. —————— blends two images to create a third.

Ans Morphing

L-1 D 484. A Hypermedia is a network containing several inter-linked information units.

L-1 D 485. In color management, the purity of a color's hue, moving from gray to the pure color.

Ans Saturation

L-1 D 486. There are two basic types of multimedia presentations —————— and —.

Ans Interactive and non-interactive

L-1 D 487. In a hypermedia system the mouse cursor is sensitive to link spots, changing its shape when on a link spot.

L-1 D 488. Multimedia is becoming popular because it is attractive and audio, video, text and graphic are all included.

L-1 D 489. The offset distance from the start of the previous track so that the head has time to switch from top of platter to bottom of platter and be at the start of the new track.

L-1 D 490. —————— smooths the edges of the image by altering the contrast and color of its edge pixels, making the contours of the image appear truer and easier to see.

Ans Anti-aliasing

L-1 D 491. Using animation software, one creates beginning and ending frames for an action and after specifying these as key features, the computer uses a process called —— —————— to create the intermediate frames.

Ans Overweening or twining

L-1 D 492. After 2D or 3D vector graphics are created in a wire frame view the next step is to add a surface to the wire frame to give the image body and solidity and the programs used to do this are called ______________.

Ans Shades

L-1 D 493. What is a Digital Sound?

Ans Reproduction and transmission of sound stored in a digital format. This includes CD as well as any sound files stored on a computer.

L-1 D 494. The effect of action and motion in the animated movies or cartoons is created by projecting still pictures, called cells, one after another at a rate of 30 per second or higher.

L-2 D 495. Bitmap pictures are made from a series of small dots, much like a piece of graph paper with specific squares filled in to form an image. Bitmaps are created with and edited in Image editors such as MS Paint, Adobe Photoshop etc.

L-2 D 496. What are Multimedia Authoring Tools?

Ans Also known as author ware, a program that helps to write hypertext or multimedia applications. They also support a scripting language for more sophisticated applications.

L-1 D 497. WMF is

Ans Windows Meta File

L-1 D 498. Bitmap pictures are also called paint type or raster images.

L-1 D 499. Two types of graphics.

Ans Vector and raster

L-1 S 500. EMF file is

A. Expert Meta File
B. Enhanced Meta File
C. Enriched Meta File
D. Enhanced Image Meta File

L-1 S 501. PNG is

A. Portable Network Graphics
B. Presentable Network Graphics
C. Portable Network GIF
D. Portable New Graphics

L-1 S 502. Full form of GIF is

A. Graphics Interchange Format
B. Graphics Interoperable Format
C. General Interchange Format
D. None of the above

L-1 S 503. Bitmap pictures are often saved with a ______________ extension.

A. BMP
B. PNG
C. JPG
D. GIF
E. All of the above

L-1 S 504. TIFF file is

A. Transferred Image File Format
B. Tagged Interchangeable Format
C. Tagged Image File Format
D. Tagged Image File Function

L-1 S 505. JPG is short form for

A. Joint Presentable Experts
B. Joint Photo Exchange Group
C. Joint Photographic Expert Group
D. Joint Photographic Exchange Group

L-1 S 506. File name extension of a bitmap file is

A.Map B. Bitmap C. Bit D. BMP

L-1 S 507. ———— contains multiple images which stream to create an animation effect.

A.JPG B. JPEG C. GIF D. BMP

L-1 S 508. ———— technology helps games and other programs in using advanced multimedia capabilities of the hardware.

A.DOT pitch B. Resolution C. Flash D. DirectX

L-1 S 509. A set of images, pictures or drawing displayed in sequence to give an effect of movement.

A.Film B. Projection C. Animation D. Play

L-1 T/F 510. A GIF file may include animation.

A.TRUE B. FALSE

Networking

L-2 S 511. A unit for measuring data transmission speed. It is used to describe the capacity of a carrier.

A. Bit rate B. Band C. Bandwidth D. None of the above

Number System

L-1 D 512. Adding 1 to the 9's complement produces 10's complement.

L-2 D 513. If the two carries (carry in and carry out) of the sign bit position are not equal, it means that an ———— has occurred.

Ans Transmission error

L-1 D 514. 4 in EBCDIC is

Ans 11110100

L-1 D 515. Octal or hexadecimal code.

Ans This is equivalent translation of the binary code to octal or hexadecimal representations.

L-1 D 516. What is octal number system?

Ans Octal number system uses digits 0. 1, 2, 3, 4, 5, 6, 7 as part of the number system

L-1 D 517. The binary equivalent of 15 is 1111

L-1 D 518. ABCD stands for Add Decimal with Extend

L-1 D 519. Mantissa is the signed fixed point number

L-1 D 520. Binary number system is a positional number system

L-1 D 521. Exponent is the position of the binary or decimal point

L-1 D 522. The 8 symbols of octal number system are 0, 1, 2, 3, 4, 5, 6, 7

L-1 D 523. In the decimal number system, there are ten digits 0 to 9.

L-1 D 524. The binary equivalent of 45 is 101101 and its BCD code is 01000101.

L-1 D 525. The R's complement is obtained by adding 1 to the (r-1)'s complement.

L-1 D 526. EBCDIC code uses eight bits for each character and a ninth bit for parity.

L-1 D 527. A standard single byte character encoding scheme used for text-based data.

Ans American Standard Code for Information Interchange (ASCII)

L-1 D 528. The 16 symbols of hexadecimal number system are 0, 1, 2, 3, 4, 5, 6, 7, 8, 9, A, B, C, D, E, F.

L-1 D 529. A number system of base or radix r is the system that uses distinct symbols for r digits.

L-1 D 530. To perform basic mathematical operations such as addition, subtraction and multiplication.

Ans Arithmetic operators

L-1 D 531. When converted to binary number, the decimal no. 99 is 1100011, and in BCD it is 1001 1001.

L-1 D 532. Excess-3 code is formed by adding 4 to the decimal number and then forming the binary coded number.

L-1 D 533. In the fixed point number representation system, all number are represented as integers or fraction.

L-1 D 534. The BCD code can be assigned the weights 8421 and for this reason it is sometimes called the 8421 code.

L-1 D 535. Each octal digit corresponds to three binary digits and each hexadecimal digit corresponds to four binary digits.

L-1 D 536. A number which has both an integer part and a fractional part, is called a real number or a floating point number.

L-1 D 537. ASCII-8 code is the new version of ASCII. It is a 8 bit code. With 8 bits, the code capacity is extended to 256 characters.

L-1 D 538. The BCD is the simplest binary code that is used to represent a decimal number. In the BCD code, 4 bits represent a decimal number.

L-1 D 539. The number system in which the weight of each digit depends on its relative position within the numbers is called the ——————————.

Ans Positional number system

L-1 D 540. The number of bits needed to store a decimal number in a binary code is greater than the number of bits needed for its equivalent binary representation.

L-1 D 541. Computer circuitry and media possess binary characteristics. So, this is the reason behind the use of binary number system for data representations in computers.

L-1 D 542. To determine the quantity that the number represents, it is necessary to multiply each digit by an integer power of r and then form the sum of all weighted digits

L-2 D 543. What is the significance of 2' complement in binary arithmetic?

Ans Subtraction can be performed using addition.

L-2 D 544. A gigaflop is one billion floating point arithmetic operations per second.

L-2 D 545. In ASCII, the first 3 bits are zone bits and the remaining 4 bits represent digit values.

L-2 D 546. The 1's complement of a binary number is formed by changing 1's into 0's and 0's into 1's.

L-2 D 547. The decimal digits in ASCII can be converted to BCD by removing the three high order bits 011.

L-2 D 548. A floating point number is said to be normalized if the most significant digit of the mantissa is non-zero.

L-2 D 549. In ASCII-8 and EBCDIC, the first 4 bits are known as zone bits and the remaining 4 bits represent digit values.

L-2 D 550. The number n can be expressed as $n = mr^e$ where m is the mantissa, r is the radix of the number system and e is the exponent.

L-2 D 551. To obtain the 10's complement of a BCD number, we first take the 9's complement and then add one to the least significant digit.

L-2 D 552. When subtracting with complements, the negative answer is recognized by the absence of the end carry and the complemented result.

L-2 D 553. The r-1's complement of a octal or hexadecimal number is obtained by subtracting each digit from 7 or F (decimal 15) respectively.

L-2 D 554. In computers, data is represented by either the presence or absence of electronic or magnetic signals in its circuitry or the media it uses.

L-2 D 555. A boolean function whose terms contain all variables or their complements. This is unreduced form of the boolean function in minterm or maxterm form.

Ans Canonical form

L-2 D 556. The binary numbers in the signed-2's complement system are added and subtracted by the same basic addition and subtraction rules as unsigned numbers.

L-2 D 557. The 10's complement of 246700 is 753300 and is obtained by leaving the two zeros unchanged, subtracting 7 from 10 and subtracting the other three digits from 9.

L-2 D 558. To convert a binary number to its decimal equivalent, the following expression is used — the weight of nth bit of a number from the right hand side = n^{th} bit × 2^{n-1}

L-2 D 559. When all the bits of the computer word are used to represent the number and no bit is used for sign representations, it is called unsigned representation of numbers.

L-2 D 560. The 2's complement can be formed by leaving all least significant 0's and first 1 unchanged and then replacing 1's by 0's and 0's by 1's in all other. Higher significant bits.

L-2 D 561. Unicode: A character encoding standard developed by the Unicode Consortium. By using more than one byte to represent each character, Unicode enables almost all of the written languages in the world to be represented by using a single character set.

Ans Unicode

L-2 D 562. In the fixed point number representation system, all numbers are represented as integers or fractions. Signed integer or BCD numbers are referred to as fixed point numbers because they contain no information regarding the location of the decimal point.

L-2 D 563. The conversion of a decimal integer into a base r representation is done by successive divisions by r and accumulation of the remainders. The conversion of a decimal fraction to radix r representation is accomplished by successive multiplications by r and accumulation of remainders.

L-3 D 564. Comparing the binary coded octal and hexadecimal numbers with their binary number equivalent, it can easily be seen that the bit combination in all the three representations is exactly the same.

L-1 D 565. The binary symbol 0 or 1 is known as a

Ans Bit

L-2 D 566. A system for representing numerical values. The radix point can be placed anywhere relative to the significant digits of the number. This position is indicated separately in the internal representation. Floating point representation can represent higher range of values.

L-1 D 567. In binary numbers, the leftmost bit in a number represents the sign.

L-1 F 568. EBCDIC stands for

Ans Extended BCD Interchange Code

L-1 F 569. A character encoding standard that represents almost all the written languages of the world.

Ans Unicode

L-2 F 570. A block code in which a weight has been assigned to each of the symbol positions in a codeword.

Ans Weighted code

L-3 F 571. Changes by only one bit as it sequences from one number to the next. In other words, the change from any number to the next in the sequence is recognized by a change of only one bit from 0 to 1 or from 1 to 0. This type of code is called —.

Ans Gray code

L-1 M 572. The binary system has only these symbols.

A. 1 B. 3 C. 0 D. 2

L-1 M 573. There are two types of complements for each base r system.

A. r's complement B. (r-2)'s complement

C. (r-1)'s complement D. (r+2)'s complement

L-1 M 574. Binary number system uses only two digits ———— and ————.

A. 1 B. 10 C. 2 D. 0

L-1 M 575. ASCII uses ———— or ———— number combinations to represent characters. So, 128 or 256 possible characters can be represented.

A. 7 B. 5 C. 9 D. 8

L-1 M 576. The number of digits a number system uses to represent the numbers in the system is called the ________ or ________.

A. Base B. Basis C. Radix D. All of the above

L-1 S 577. ASCII

A. Australion Standard Code for Information Interchange

B. American Standard Code for Information Interchange

C. All India Standard Code for Information Interchange

D. None of the above

L-1 S 578. D in ASCII is

A. 01100100 B. 01000100 C. 10100100 D. 010100100

L-1 S 579. K in EBCDIC is

A. 110110010 B. 11010010 C. 1010010 D. 010100110

L-1 S 580. The binary equivalent of 20 is

A. 11111 B. 10100 C. 10101 D. 10011

L-1 S 581. Binary equivalent of octal 6 is

A. 011 B. 110 C. 101 D. 111

L-1 S 582. The addition of binary 0 and 1 is

A. 0 B. 1 C. 10 D. 01

L-1 S 583. The addition of binary 1 and 1 is

A. 1 B. 10 C. 01 D. 0

L-1 S 584. Kilo byte in binary number system is

A. 1000 bits B. 1024 bits C. 1001 bits D. None of the above

L-1 S 585. The base of the binary number system is

A. 1 B. 2 C. 8 D. None of the above

L-1 S 586. The radix of the binary number system is

A. 0 B. 2 2 C. 8 D. 10

L-1 S 587. The base of the decimal number system is

A. 2 B. 10 C. 1 D. 100

L-1 S 588. The radix of the decimal number system is

A. 2 B. 10 C. 16 D. 8

L-1 S 589. The absolute value of a number is the number

A. With its sign B. Without its sign

C. Value of the number D. None of the above

L-1 S 590. The base of the octal number system is ________

A. 1 B. 2 C. 8 D. 9

L-1 S 591. In machine language, information is represented as ________ and ________

A. 0's and 2's B. 0's and 1's C. 1's and 2's D. 2's and 10's

L-1 S 592. With EBCDIC, each eight bit byte is divided into 2 portions - zone portions, and the ————.

A. Host portion B. Digit portion C. Sub-zone portion D. None of the above

L-1 S 593. The ———— of a number system is defined as the number of digits it uses to represent the numbers in the system.

A. Radix B. Base C. Mantissa D. Floating point

L-2 S 594. Tera

A. 100000000000 B. 1000000000000 C. 1000000000 D. None of the above

L-2 S 595. The 10's complement of the decimal 2389 is

A. 7610 B. 7611 C. 7612 D. 7610

L-1 S 596. K in ASCII is

A. 1001011 B. 11010010 C. 1010010 D. 010100110

L-1 S 597. A byte consists of ————.

A. 8 Bits B. 7 Bits C. 5 Bits D. 10 Bits

L-1 S 598. The addition of binary 1 and 0 is

A. 1 B.10 C. 01 D. 0

L-1 S 599. Decimal equivalent of hexadecimal A is

A. 10 B. 11 C. 9 D. 16

L-1 S 600. Conversion of decimal 41.6875 into binary.

A. 101001.1011 B. 101101.1011 C. 110101.1001 D. 101001.1101

L-1 S 601. A single character is represented in binary form as a

A. Byte B. Bit C. Octal D. Decimal

L-1 S 602. The ———— of a number system is defined as the number of digits it uses to represent the numbers in the system.

A. Radix B. Members C. Mantissa D. Significance

L-1 S 603. Full form of BCD is

A. Bit and Coded Decimal B. Bit and Corrected Decimal
C. Binary Coded Decimal D. Best Coded Decimal

L-1 S 604. 4 in ASCII is

A. 101010100 B. 100010100 C. 0101100 D. 00110100

L-1 S 605. D in EBCDIC is

A. 01100100 B. 01000100 C. 11000100 D. 010100100

L-1 S 606. Binary number system

A. Comprises of any two digit B. Comprises of 9 and 1
C. Comprises of 1 and 2 D. Comprises of 1 and 0

L-1 S 607. 9's complement of 546700 is

A. 453200 B. 453290 C. 453299 D. None of the above

L-1 S 608. BCD stands for ——————

A. Binary Calculated Decimal B. Bit Coded Decimal

C. Binary Coded Decimal D. None of the above

L-1 S 609. Kilo in binary number system is

A. 1000 B. 1525 C. 1625 D. 1024

L-1 S 610. Binary no. 1010011 in decimal is

A. 80 B. 81 C. 83 D. 91

L-1 S 611. The hexadecimal equivalent of 15 is

A. F B. D C. E D. G

L-1 S 612. The radix of the octal number system is

A. 16 B. 2 C. 8 D. 10

L-1 S 613. The binary number system uses the radix

A. 0 B. 1 C. 2 D. None of the above

L-1 S 614. The decimal number system is also known as

A. Real number system B. Floating point number system

C. Base-10 number system D. None of the above

L-1 S 615. In BCD, ——— bits represents a decimal number

A. 2 B. 3 C. 4 D. 6

L-1 S 616. Hexadecimal number system uses —————— as the base or radix.

A. 10 B. 5 C. 8 D. 16

L-1 S 617. The decimal equivalent of binary number 111111 is ——————

A. 25 B. 40 C. 63 D. None of the above

L-1 S 618. We use —————— number system for our day-to-day activities.

A. Binary B. Hexo-decimal C. Decimal D. Octal

L-1 S 619. It refers to the base-8 number system which uses just eight unique symbols.

A. Hexadecimal number system B. Binary number system

C. Octal number system D. Decimal number system

L-1 S 620. The total no. of digits symbols available to represent numbers in a positional number system.

A. Exponent B. Significant digit C. Mantissa D. Base

L-1 S 621. The 9's complement of a decimal number is obtained by subtracting each digit from ——————.

A. 1 B. 10 C. 9 D. None of the above

L-1 S 622. Complements are used for simplifying the —————— operation and for logical manipulation.

A. Multiplication B. Addition C. Subtraction D. Division

L-2 S 623. The 2's complement of binary 101100 is 010100.

A. 010100 B. N C. Y D. None of the above

L-1 S 624. A Binary Digit is called a

Ans Bit

L-1 S 625. To show the equality between decimal and binary forty-five, we will write $(101101)_2=(45)_{10}$.

Ans TRUE

L-2 S 626. 14 is represented in signed magnitude representation as

Ans 00001110

L-2 S 627 -14 is represented in signed-1's complement representation as

Ans 11110001

L-2 S 628 -14 is represented in signed-2's complement representation as

Ans 11110010

L-1 T/F 629. The radix of the hexadecimal number system is 8.

A. TRUE B. FALSE

L-1 T/F 630. Leftmost bit equal to 0 represent a negative number and 1 represents a positive number.

A. TRUE B. FALSE

L-2 T/F 631. The 1's complement of a binary number is obtained by subtracting each digit from 2.

A. TRUE B. FALSE

Number System

L-1 T/F 632. With 7 bits, upto 128 characters can be coded.

A. TRUE B. FALSE

L-1 T/F 633. Binary no. 1 in decimal is 1.

A. TRUE B. FALSE

L-1 T/F 634. A basic grouping of bits that the computer operates on as a single unit is byte.

A. TRUE B. FALSE

L-1 T/F 635. A characteristic or property involving a selection in which there are two possibilities.

A. TRUE B. FALSE

L-1 T/F 636. Adding a number to the 2's complement of another number is equivalent to subtracting the second number from the first.

A. TRUE B. FALSE

L-2 T/F 637. In binary subtraction, if a larger number is subtracted from a smaller number, the result obtained will be the 2's complement.

A. TRUE B. FALSE

L-1 T/F 638. The complement of a complement could not produce the original number.

A. TRUE B. FALSE

L-1 T/F 639. The decimal equivalent of binary number 10100 is ____________.

Ans 20

L-2 T/F 640. The 2's complement of a binary number is obtained by adding 1 to the 1's complement.

Printers

L-1 D 641. A ribbon is used to print characters on a page.

Ans Inkjet printer

Security

L-3 D 642. In Windows, Ctrl+Alt+Del is used to

A. Logon on to a system, this specific key combination is used to ensure that any trojan could not be executed. This key combination is already assigned to the appearance of task manager. If some trojan program is presenting the logon screen, task manager would open.

L-1 F 643. The issues of protecting data from unauthorized use, tampering or destruction is called ________.

Ans Security

L-2 F 644. A ________ is a person who is an expert in computers and test any software, protocol etc. to its limit to find out any weakness in them to be exploited.

Ans Hacker

L-2 S 645. If there are failed logon attempts within a specified amount of time, windows security does the following.

A. Delete thc account B. Account lockout
C. Restart the system D. None of the above

L-1 S 646 If a user forget his/her password, ________ help to regain access to his/her account.

A. Password resetting B. Password recovery
C. Forgot Password D. All of the above

L-1 S 647 One should regularly ________ the antivirus to keep the system ready against infections.

A. Reinstall B. Change C. Remove D. Update

L-1 S 648 Copying files and placing it at some other location so that in case of system failure, copy of important files is available for use.

A. Xcopy B. File copy C. Backup D. Format

L-2 S 649. Dr. Watson (Drwtsn32.exe) is installed in ________ folder when you set up windows.

A. Temp B. Program files C. System folder D. None of the above

L-3 S 650. A Certification issuing authority

A. Microsoft B. Mastercard C. Verisign D. Digisign

Software

L-1 S 651. Program and data is called

A. Hardware B. Database C. Software D. Computer

L-3 S 652. ______________ is a speech recognition system.

A. IBM VoiceType B. Apple PlainTalk
C. Dragon Dictate D. All of the above

Spreadsheet

L-1 S 653. Which of the following is a spreadsheet package?

A. MS-Excel B. MS-Word C. MS-Powerpoint D. None of the above

Types

L-1 D 654. In the context of networking, RJE is

Ans Remote Job Entry

L-1 D 655. Subnotebooks

Ans A portable computer that is slightly lighter and smaller than a full-sized notebook computer. Typically, subnotebook computers have a smaller keyboard and screen, but are otherwise equivalent to notebook computers.

L-1 D 656. Palmtop computers

Ans A small computer that literally fits in the user's palm. Palmtops have limited functionality, but they are suited for certain functions such as phone books and calendars. Palmtops that use a pen rather than a keyboard for input are often called handheld computers or PDAs.

L-1 D 657. Embedded computers

Ans Such as smart card which have a computer chip installed in it.

L-1 D 658. In the context of networking, RJT is

Ans RJT

L-1 D 659. What is the specialty of ENIAC?

Ans The ENIAC was a modular computer, composed of individual panels to perform different functions. Twenty of these modules were accumulators, which could not only add and subtract but hold a ten-digit decimal number in memory. Besides its speed, the most remarkable thing about ENIAC was its size and complexity. ENIAC contained 17,468 vacuum tubes, 7,200 crystal diodes, 1,500 relays, 70,000 resistors, 10,000 capacitors and around 5 million hand-soldered joints. It weighed 30 short tons (27 t). ENIAC used ten-position ring counters to store digits; each digit used 36 vacuum tubes, 10 of which were the dual triodes making up the flip-flops of the ring counter.

L-2 D 660. Power supercomputers use ______________ technology?

Ans Nano

L-2 D 661. Difference between a minicomputer and a microcomputer?

Ans Microcomputers are personal or desktop computer designed for general use by a single person. Minicomputer are mid-range servers supporting smaller number of simultaneous users, typically 50 to 100.

L-2 D 662. A point-of-sale (POS) terminal is a computerized replacement for a cash register. The POS system can include the ability to record and track customer orders, process credit and debit cards, connect to other systems in a network, and manage inventory. A POS terminal has as its core a personal computer, which is provided with application-specific programs and I/O devices for the particular environment in which it will serve.

L-1 S 663. ____________ is smallest among digital computers.

A. Microcomputer B. Minicomputer

C. Supercomputer D. Mainframe

Types of Computers

L-1 D 664. ____________ can be considered to be scale down version of mainframe computers.

Ans Minicomputers

L-1 D 665. A Mainframe is

Ans Mainframes (often colloquially referred to as Big Iron[1]) are computers used mainly by large organizations for critical applications, typically bulk data processing such as census, industry and consumer statistics, ERP, and financial transaction processing.

L-1 D 666. A Minicomputer is

Ans A minicomputer is a class of multi-user computers that lies in the middle range of the computing spectrum, in between the largest multi-user systems (mainframe computers) and the smallest single-user systems (microcomputers or personal computers).

L-1 D 667. What is a mainframe?

Ans Large computers for processing bulky data requiring enormous storage and fast processing.

L-1 D 668. A Personal Computer is

Ans A microcomputer

L-1 D 669. IBM Thinkpad is a supercomputer.

L-1 D 670. The more powerful workstations are called supermicros.

L-1 D 671. The most popular microcomputer operating system is MVS.

L-1 D 672. A mainframe can supportmore than 1000 remote terminals.

L-1 D 673. A workstation falls between minicomputers and microcomputers in terms of processing power.

L-1 D 674. Supercomputers can operate at speeds one thousand to one million times as fast as microcomputers.

L-1 D 675. A relatively fast but small and inexpensive computer with somewhat limited input/output capabilities.

Ans Minicomputer

L-1 D 676. A supercomputer is a computer which performs at a rate of speed which is far above that of other computers.

L-1 D 677. Supercomputers can perform at upto 128 gigaflops. They use bus width of 32 or 64 bits. Even faster are being developed.

L-1 D 678. A typical microcomputer consists of a processor on a single silicon chip mounted on a circuit board together with memory chips, ROM and RAM chips etc.

L-1 D 679. In large scale computing, the processing task of multiple users is performed on a single computer which is centralised and is a mainframe or a minicomputer.

L-1 D 680. What distinguishes supercomputers from ordinary computers is their high degree of parallelism means the ability to perform a large number of operations simultaneously.

L-1 D 681. Supercomputers can process 64 bits or more at a time. Their processing speed ranges from 10000 million instructions per second to 1.2 billion instructions per second. They can support up to 10000 terminals at a time

L-2 D 682. The main distinguishing factor between Mainframes and Personal Computers.

Ans High I/O Capacity of Mainframes

L-2 D 683. Microcomputers using 8 bit word length use 7 bits to represent the basic code. The 8th bit is used for parity or it may be permanently 1 or 0

L-1 D 684. A minicomputer system consists of a CPU several disk drives, a high speed printer perhaps a few magnetic tape units and a number of terminals.

L-1 F 685. Systems connected to large computers. These systems do not have their own processing power.

Ans Dumb terminals

L-1 S 686. Which of these is more powerful?

A. Personal Computer B. Workstation

L-1 S 687. A terminal that has no local processing capability.

A. Dedicated machine B. Dumb terminal
C. Client D. None of the above

L-1 S 688. A small comparatively inexpensive computer used by individuals for applications such as accounting, entertainment, education and hobbies.

A. Minicomputer B. Personal computer
C. Both of the above D. None of the above

L-2 S 689. RISC is

A. Reduced Interval Set Computing B. Reduced Instruction Set Computing
C. Rerun Instruction Set Compiler D. None of the above

L-1 S 690. Which type of computer could support more users?

A. Mainframe B. Minicomputer

L-1 S 691. A computer that operates on data which is in the form of continuously variable physical quantities such as electrical current.

A. Analog computer B. Dedicated computer
C. Digital computer D. Microcomputer

L-2 S 692. The Operating System for mainframes have to deal mainly with

A. Processing many jobs at once B. Processing realtime jobs
C. Processing printing D. All of the above

L-1 S 693. IBM S/390 is a

A. Microcomputer B. Laptop
C. Mainframe D. Supercomputer

L-1 S 694. Which among these is the fastest computer?

A. Personal Computer B. Workstation
C. Minicomputer D. Mainframe E. Supercomputer

L-1 S 695. The first large-scale computer ever developed is

A. IBM 701 B. Mark II C. EDIVAC D. ENIAC

L-1 S 696. Workstations generally run on ——————operating system.

A. Dos B. Windows C. Both of the above D. Unix

L-1 S 697. The smallest category of computer fabricated using a microprocessor, and other integrated circuits, namely a ROM, RAM, and I/O interface chips.

A. Minicomputer B. Workstations C. Microcomputer D. Dumb terminal

L-2 S 698. MVS stands for

A. Many Very-Large System B. Multi-value System
C. Multiple Virtual Storage D. None of the above

L-2 S 699. CISC stands for ——————.

A. Common Instruction Set Computer
B. Complex Instruction Solving Computer
C. Complete Instruction Set Computer
D. Complex Instruction Set Computer

L-1 S 700. A Workstation is

Ans A workstation is a high-end microcomputer designed for technical or scientific applications. Intended primarily to be used by one person at a time, they are commonly connected to a local area network and run multi-user operating systems. The term workstation has also been used to refer to a mainframe computer terminal or a PC connected to a network.

L-1 S 701. Workstations have RISC architecture (Reduced Instruction Set Computing) which results in faster processing of instructions.

L-1 T/F 702. A laptop CPU can be put to sleep in software, reducing power usage to almost zero.

A. TRUE B. FALSE

Unix

L-1 D 703. In the X Window System, middle-clicking by default pastes the contents of the primary buffer at the pointer's position.

Windows

L-1 D 704. The use of "Pause Break" key is

Ans To pause a slide show

L-1 D 705. In Windows, directory system is

Ans Hierarchical

L-1 D 706. An option you can turn on or off by selecting or clearing it. You can have more than one check box checked on a sheet at a time.

Ans Check box

L-1 D 707. Keyboard shortcut to open My Computer.

Ans Win key + E

L-1 D 708. Keyboard shortcut to minimize all windows.

Ans Win key + M

L-1 D 709. Open the run dialog box.

Ans Win key + R

L-1 D 710. Display the System properties dialog box

Ans Win key + BREAK

L-1 D 711. Two keys on which windows mono is printed are called

Ans Win key

L-1 D 712. The question mark (?) represents a single character and astersik (*) represents one or more characters.

Ans Wildcard character

L-1 D 713. Keyboard shortcut for bold text is

Ans Ctrl + B

L-1 D 714. Alt + F4 is used to

Ans Close an active item, or quit the active program.

L-1 D 715. Alt + Enter is used to

Ans Displays properties of the selected item.

L-1 D 716. Alt + Tab is used to

Ans Switch to the next window.

L-1 D 717. Esc key is.

Ans Escape key

L-1 D 718. Keyboard shortcut to print a file.

Ans Ctrl + P

L-1 D 719. Undo an action.

Ans Ctrl + Z

L-1 D 720. Alt + Shifit + Tab is used to

Ans Switch to the previous window

L-1 D 721. There are also keys on the keyboard which could be used to play songs directly.

L-1 D 722. Use up and down arrow keys to increase or decrease volume in Windows media player.

L-1 D 723. Keyboard shortcut to switch between open items.

Ans Alt + Tab

L-1 D 724. In Windows Me, Me stands for

Ans Millennium

L-1 D 725. Keyboard shortcut to move backward through options.

Ans Shift + Tab

L-1 D 726. Command prompt is available in

Ans Accessories

L-1 D 727. Alt + Underlined letter in a menu name.

Ans Displays the corresponding menu

L-1 D 728. By hitting the "Print Screen" button

Ans Screen is captured

L-1 D 729. Display the top of the active window.

Ans Home

L-1 D 730. In MS-Word, increase the font size Ctrl + Shift + < is used.

L-1 D 731. Hold down thc Ctrl key while dragging the selected item to

Ans Copy selected item

L-1 D 732. The default place where date appears is

Ans Right side of the Taskbar

L-1 D 733. The most common use of "Ctrl" key is in

Ans Shortcut commands

L-1 D 734. Some Font types are TrueType, Screen or Printer.

L-1 D 735. Recently accessed document are listed in

Ans Documents menu

L-1 D 736. Checks a disk and displays a status report.

Ans CHKDSK

L-1 D 737. Display the contents of the selected folder.

Ans Num lock + Plus sign on numeric keypad.

L-1 D 738. To get help and other information about windows.

Ans Help and Support

L-1 D 739 Display all subfolders under the selected folder.

Ans Num Lock + Asterisk on numeric keypad

L-1 D 740. Underlined letter in a command name on an open menu.

Ans Carry out the corresponding command

L-1 D 741. What is the advantage of graphical user interface?

Ans Easy to use, quick to understand. Categorized tasks.

L-1 D 742. On resume password protect in Screensaver tab is for

Ans If a user go away from her system and later after the screensaver is initialized, someone else come to use it, he/she cannot use the system if not authorized.

L-1 D 743. Migrates files and settings from one computer to another.

Ans Files and settings transfer wizard

L-1 D 744. Starts a separate window to run specified program or command.

Ans Start menu

L-1 D 745. View the folder one level up in My Computer or windows explorer.

Ans BACKSPACE

L-1 D 746. Document properties are details about a file that help identify it.

L-1 D 747. To configure older programs to run on XP we could take the help of

Ans Program Compatibility Wizard

L-1 D 748. Associated with a performance parameter, available in system monitor.

Ans Performance counter

L-1 D 749. The programs mentioned in ———————— are executed as per the settings and time and date specified.

Ans Scheduled Tasks

L-1 D 750. Group box — Groups related controls, such as option buttons or check boxes.

L-1 D 751. Plays digital media including music, videos, CDs, DVDs and internet radio.

Ans Windows Media Player

L-1 D 752. To work in another user account, we have to first ———————— from the current user.

Ans Log-off

L-1 D 753. The act of minimizing a window and placing it in the lower right corner of the screen.

Ans DOCK

L-1 D 754. Properties of any document can be viewed by selecting the document in Windows Explorer.

L-1 D 755. A portion of the screen where programs are run. Several windows can be opened at the same time.

Ans Window

L-1 D 756. To move an item on the screen, select the item and then press and hold down the mouse button and move the mouse.

Ans Dragging

L-1 D 757. The comprehensive information resource for evaluating, implementing, and supporting Microsoft business products.

Ans Microsoft Tech Net

L-1 D 758 Choosing ClearType for your screen fonts makes the words on your computer screen look as smooth as the words on a page.

L-1 D 759. A tooltip is a small, boxed text message that pops up when a mouse cursor hovers over a toolbar icon in a software program.

L-1 D 760. A secondary window that contains buttons and various kinds of options through which you can carry out a particular command or task.

Ans Dialog box

L-1 D 761. A gradual progression of colors and shades, usually from one color to another color, or from one shade to another shade of the same color.

Ans Gradient

L-1 D 762. If you use the same name as the original file, the original is overwritten. When you see a message asking whether you want to replace the existing file if you click Ok, the original file is replaced by the current file.

L-1 D 763. A menu displays a list of commands. Some of these menu options have images with them so that mostly used commands and there options could be easily remembered.

Ans About menus and toolbars

L-1 D 764. A file that is stored inside My Briefcase and not linked to any file outside My Briefcase. When you update files, the orphan file is not synchronized with any other file.

Ans Orphan file

L-1 D 765. A TV could be used as a monitor of a computer system.

L-1 D 766. Controls are graphic objects that appear on a form to display or enter data or, perform an action. For e.g., text boxes, list boxes, option buttons, command "buttons, and others.

L-1 D 767. Scroll bar — A control that scrolls through a range of values when a user clicks the scroll arrows or drag the scroll box. A user can move through a page of values by clicking between the scroll box and a scroll arrow.

L-2 D 768. Character map

Ans Selects special characters and copies them to your document.

L-2 D 769. Press Shift 5 times to

Ans Switch sticky keys on and off

L-2 D 770. Computers in "Stand by" mode means

Ans A sleep mode in a portable computer that provides an almost immediate resumption of operation when turned back on. In standby mode, the hard disk and display are turned off, and the CPU is throttled down to its lowest-power state. However, memory is kept active, which requires battery power, but at a very slow rate. The system will typically switch to hibernation mode when it senses insufficient battery capacity to continue in standby mode.

L-2 D 771. Compressing and password protecting the compressed file.

Ans Use winzip software

L-2 D 772. Shortcut to Cycle through items in a window or on the desktop.

Ans F6

L-2 D 773. Vector fonts are rendered from a mathematical model.

L-2 D 774. Updates installed on the internet explorer can be seen in

Ans About Internet explorer message box

L-2 D 775. Shared folders on the local network can be accessed through.

Ans Network place

L-2 D 776. To change users without logging off in a workgroup environment.

Ans Click Start, click Log off and then click Switch User.

L-2 D 777. Screen review utilities — Accessibility aids for people who are blind or have learning disabilities.

L-2 D 778. TrueType and OpenType fonts are outline fonts. These type of fonts are rendered from line and curve commands.

L-2 D 779. This dialog box requires no response from the user. It is between the client computer and an intermediary device.

Ans Static dialog box

L-2 D 780. Open Type and True Type fonts can both be scaled and rotated. Both look good in all sizes and on all output devices supported by windows.

L-2 D 781. A Windows feature that produces a visual cue, such as a screen flash or a blinking title bar, whenever the computer plays a system sound.

Ans Sound Sentry

L-2 D 782. The frequency in which the Resource Monitor checks that the resource is available and operating. There are two levels of polling: Looks Alive and Is Alive.

Ans Polling intervals

L-2 D 783. Before a program can draw in a window, it needs to acquire a ———— which is an internal data structure containing the properties of the window.

Ans Device context

L-2 D 784. In the state of hibernation, computer shuts down after saving everything that is present in the memory at that time to the hard disk. When the computer is brought out of hibernation, all the programs and documents that where open are restored to the desktop.

Ans Hibernation

L-3 D 785. Fast searching runs in the background and extracts information from files. This information is organized so that subsequent searching is quick.

L-1 F 786. Reverses the latest changes done on a document.

Ans Undo

L-1 F 787. Using Windows, Xp ———— searches on all types of objects can be done.
Ans Search Companion

L-1 F 788. A file that is stored inside My Briefcase and not linked to any file outside.
Ans Orphan file

L-1 F 789. The height of the page is greater than the width. In Landscape orientation, the width of the page is greater than the height.
Ans Portrait orientation

L-2 F 790. The program which runs in the active window is called a ————.
Ans Foreground program

L-1 M 791. Personal computers Operating Systems
A. Windows 98 B. Windows 2000 C. Macintosh OS D. All of the above

L-1 M 792. In Windows XP, 3 positions of a desktop wallpaper are
A. Stretch B. Tile C. Rotate D. Center

L-2 M 793. File compression utilities.
A. Winzip B. WinRar C. Pkunzip D. comMaster

L-2 M 794. A ———— typically states who sent the document to the printer and gives the state and time of printing.
A. Separator page B. Banner page C. Status page D. Descriptor

L-1 M 795. Open the selected menu, or perform the action assigned to the selected button.
A. Spacebar B. Ctrl C. Enter D. Backspace

L-1 M 796. Display or hide the start menu.
A. Ctrl + Esc B. Win key C. Both of the above D. None of the above

L-1 S 797. Show the desktop.
A. Winkey + S B. Winkey + D C. Alt + D D. Ctrl + Esc

L-1 S 798. Paper size legal is.
A. 8.5 × 11inches B. 8.5 × 14inches C. 9 × 14inches D. 8.5 × 13.5inches

L-1 S 799. Games are located in ———— group.
A. Accessories B. Programs C. Startup D. Entertainment

L-1 S 800. Keyboard shortcut to display the Start menu.
A. Ctrl + F10 B. Ctrl + Esc C. F10 D. F1

L-1 S 801. Repeat your last action
A. Ctrl + Z B. Ctrl + Y C. Ctrl + A D. Ctrl + Home

L-1 S 802. Search for a file or folder.
A. F5 B. F3 C. F2 D. Ctrl + S

L-1 S 803. Checks or clears a check box.
A. Ctrl B. Spaccbar C. Backspace D. Win key

L-1 S 804. In Windows, shortcut for search.
A. F1 B. F3 C. Search D. Win key

L-1 S 805. Cancel a menu or dialog box action.

A. Ctrl B. ESC C. Alt D. None of the above

L-1 S 806. A box that contains a list of items.

A. Item box B. List box C. Combo box D. Serial box

L-1 S 807. Cancel a command and close a dialog box.

A. Ctrl B. Esc C. Alt D. Shift

L-1 S 808. A control that embeds a picture into a form.

A. Embedder B. Image control C. View control D. Photo bucket

L-1 S 809. Press ———— to make the menu bar active.

A. F1 B. F10 C. F5 D. Ctrl + O

L-1 S 810. ———— is a box in which text could be typed.

A. Label B. Text Box C. Check Box D. Type Box

L-1 S 811. A button that initiates an action when it is clicked.

A. Button B. Command button C. Label D. Hyperlink

L-1 S 812. Path of a file from the root of directory to the file.

A. Relative path name B. Absolute path name

C. Real path name D. None of the above

L-1 S 813. In graphical user interface, a group of buttons or icons.

A. Icon group B. Toolbar C. Menubar D. System Tray

L-1 S 814. To view files and folders on a computer ———— is used.

A. Internet explorer B. Windows explorer

C. Control panel D. Search option

L-1 S 815. Text that provides information about a control or the worksheet or form.

A. Text box B. Label C. Combo box D. List box

L-1 S 816. ———— files are the most common file format for Windows sounds.

A. mpeg B. wmv C. .sou D. .mp4

L-1 S 817. A control in which item that is selected in the list box appears in the text box.

A. Toggle box B. Check box C. Option box D. Combo box

L-1 S 818. System Information could be obtained from ———— tab of the System properties.

A. Computer name B. General C. Hardware D. L-3

L-1 S 819. A file that provides information to Windows about how best to run MS-DOS-based programs.

A. Shortcut B. Program infor mation

C. Both of the above D. None of the above

L-1 S 820. If the "Print" icon on the standard toolbar is pressed ————.

A. The "Print" dialog box appe B. The whole document

C. Only the current page gets printed. D. All of the above

L-1 S 821. Files deleted from the system moves to ———————— from where it can be restored.

A. Trash B. Recycle bin C. Deleted folder D. Temp

L-1 S 822. Provides options to customize the appearance and functionality of the computer and other settings.

A. Tool box B. Control Panel C. Windows manager D. System tools

L-1 S 823. Close the active document in programs that allow to have multiple documents open simultaneously.

A. Alt + F4 B. Ctrl + F4 C. Alt + F10 D. F10

L-1 S 824. Turns an option on or off. You can check more than one check box at a time on a sheet or in a group.

A. Toggle box B. Check box C. Option box D. Filter box

L-1 S 825. If somebody have to type a character in small letters, she/he should press that key with holding ——— key.

A. Caps key B. Shift key C. Ctrl key D. Alt key

L-1 S 826. Rewriting parts of a file to contiguous sectors on a hard disk to increase the speed of access and retrieval.

A. Fragmentation B. Defragmentation C. Ordering D. Sorting

L-1 S 827. It accepts a document sent to a printer and then stores it on disk or in memory until the printer is available for it.

A. Buffer B. Print spooler C. Print manager D. None of the above

L-1 S 828. The area of desktop which displays time and quick access to some programs, volume control etc. It is situated to the right of taskbar

A. Status bar B. Notification area C. Information bar D. None of the above

L-1 S 829. This view of windows explorer lets the user see images in the folder in small size with their names so that multiple images can be viewed simultaneously.

A. Image view B. Thumbnail C. Picture view D. None of the above

L-2 S 830. In the start-run box, %temp% is used to

A. Create a temp folder B. Open the default
C. Open history folder D. None of the above

L-2 S 831. Cycle through items in the order they were opened.

A. F6 B. Alt + Esc C. Alt + Right arrow D. Alt + Left arrow

L-2 S 832. ———————————— helps to organize, edit and share windows media.

A. Windows Media Player B. Windows Movie Maker
C. Volume Control D. Media Center

L-2 S 833. When a process wants to print a file, it enters the file name in a special.

A. Print file B. Spooler director C. Cache D. Printer port

L-2 S 834. A procedure or an expression associated with a specific menu pad, menu or menu option.

A. Script B. Code snippets C. Code D. Routine

L-2 S 835. To change the name of a computer, —————— icon in the control panel is used.

A. Computer properties B. System properties
C. Folder properties D. Peripheral properties

L-2 S 836. To delete temporary files, recycle bin files, temporary installation files, Internet history and other useless files, —————— is used.

A. Tempcleaner B. Disk cleanup C. Registry cleaner D. All of the above

L-2 S 837. A bar on the left side of open/save dialog boxes which contains icons to show 7history folder, My Documents folder, Desktop, Favorites, and Web folders.

A. My Computer B. Spacebar C. Location D. Fast access

L-3 S 838. —————— is a protocol used for exchanging data between various Microsoft Windows based programs.

A. Data query B. Dynamic Data Exchange
C. Data dictionary D. SQL

L-1 S 839. Security center is located in

A. System tools B. Accessories C. Startup D. Desktop

L-1 S 840. Accessiblity program group appears in

A. Accessories B. Program C. Both of the above D. None of the above

L-1 S 841. Open the shortcut menu for the active window.

A. Alt + SpacebarB. Alt + Shift C. Ctrl + Spacebar D. None of the above

L-1 S 842. Quits the CMD.EXE program (command interpreter).

A. Exit B. Quit C. Finish D. Stop

L-1 S 843. A hierarchical representation of folders and files.

A. Tree view B. Folder view C. File view D. None of the above

L-1 S 844. Sound recorder is located in ——— program group.

A. Entertainment B. Programs C. Setting D. Startup

L-1 S 845. Submenu of all the programs installed on the computer.

A. Program B. Setting C. Help D. Run

L-1 S 846. The menu option —————— locates specific text in a document.

A. Find B. Search C. Look D. See

L-1 S 847. The ——— menu option in start menu is used to directly execute a program.

A. Run B. Program C. Control panel D. Search

L-1 S 848. The on-screen work area on which windows, icons, menus, and dialog boxes appear.

A. Desktop B. Windows C. Screen D. Monitor

L-1 S 849. Open a folder one level up if a folder is selected in the Save as or Open dialog box.

A. Backspace B. Del C. Right arrow key D. None of the above

L-1 S 850. When a software is installed on a windows computer, its files are usually stored in —————— folder.

A. Program files B. Windows C. Temp D. My Softwares

L-1 S 851. —————————— allows you to change the way windows handles the media files it detects on a device with removable storage.

A. Autoplay B. Media detect C. Autorecover D. Autorun

L-2 S 852. ———— button can be attached to a text box and is used to increase or decrease a value.

A. Spin B. Slider C. Combo box D. Control box

L-1 S 853. Display properties can be accessed from

A. From control panel B. Right click on desktop
C. Both of the above D. None of the above

L-1 S 854. Copy

A. CTrl + X B. Ctrl + V C. Ctrl + C D. Alt + C

L-1 S 855. Ctrl + Z

A. Zip B. Control C. Undo D. Redo

L-1 S 856. Copy con

A. Copies from a file called con B. Copies to a connected device
C. Copies to another computer D. Copies from console

L-1 S 857. Paper size A4 is

A. 8.60 × 11.30 inches B. 8.69 × 11.27 inches
C. 8.27 × 11.69 inch D. 8 × 12 inches

L-1 S 858. This is in italics.

A. Hello B. Hello C. *Hello* D. ~~Hello~~

L-1 S 859. Context key works as

A. Normal Click B. Double Click C. Right Click D. Scroll

L-1 S 860. Close the active window

A. Alt + F1 B. Ctrl + F4 C. Alt + F4 D. Alt + F11

L-1 S 861. Restore minimized windows

A. Ctrl + R B. Ctrl + Esc + R
C. Win key + Shift D. Win key + Shift + M

L-1 S 862. To repeat your last action

A. F1 B. Ctrl + R
C. F4 D. Alt + R

L-1 S 863. Communication program group appears in

A. Control panel B. Administrative tools
C. Program D. Accessories

L-1 S 864. Entertainment program group appears in

A. Startup B. Control panel C. Accessories D. Search

L-1 S 865. To get help on Windows, press on desktop.

A. Help key B. Escape C. F10 D. F1

L-1 S 866. The most common use of function key F1 is
A. Shutdown B. Search C. Help D. Run a program

L-1 S 867. Activate the menu bar in the active program.
A. Alt B. F10 C. Both of the above D. None of the above

L-1 S 868. Page orientation are of ———— types.
A. Four B. Three C. One D. Two

L-1 S 869. Controls such as command buttons, scroll bars are
A. Windows controls B. GUI
C. Operating system D. ActiveX controls

L-1 S 870. One point in font size is equal to 1/——— of an inch
A. 36 B. 52 C. 72 D. 99

L-1 S 871. A bar with buttons and options to carry out specific tasks.
A. Menu bar B. Status bar C. Formula bar D. Toolbar

L-1 S 872. A button used to select one option from a group of options.
A. Check button B. List box C. Choice button D. Option button

L-1 S 873. A shortcut menu is invoked by pressing ————.
A. Ctrl B. Alt
C. Esc D. The right mouse button

L-1 S 874. Landscape and ———— are two types of page orientation.
A. Vertical B. Horizontal C. Portrait D. None of the above

L-1 S 875. A file that is created when you drag part of a document to the desktop.
A. Copy B. Drag C. Scrap D. Document

L-1 S 876. Area of memory where the system keeps the contents which is copied or cut.
A. Copy memory B. Copy board C. Clip memory D. Clipboard

L-1 S 877. To delete a file permanently, the following key combination is used on file.
A. Shift + Backspace B. Ctrl + Del
C. Shift + Del D. Alt + Del

L-1 S 878. An area of memory that holds text, graphics, or other information cut or copied from an application.
A. RAM B. Buffer C. Clipboard D. Storyboard

L-1 S 879. A button that becomes pressed in when clicked, and it remains pressed in till it is pressed again.
A. Check button B. Spinner C. Toggle button D. On-off button

L-1 S 880. ———— are used when there are many possibilities and only one among them have to be selected.
A. Combo box B. Record selector C. Check box D. Option box

L-1 S 881. Arrows key can be used to view parts of the documents that extend past the bottom, top, or sides of the screen.

A. Function keys
B. Numeric keys
C. Escape key
D. Control keys
E. Arrow keys

L-1 S 882. A portion of the document window surrounded by and separated from other portions by vertical or horizontal bars.

A. Window B. Box C. Frame D. Pane

L-1 S 883. A horizontal area at the bottom of a window which displays values of some key parameters related to that window.

A. Parament window
B. Parameter bar
C. Info bar
D. Status bar

L-1 S 884. A text box with a drop-down list box. You can either select a choice from the list or type your own entry in the box.

A. List box B. Selection box C. Spinner D. Combo box

L-1 S 885. A set of visual elements such as desktop wallpaper, button color, font etc. that provide a unified look for the computer.

A. Desktop B. Screensaver C. Theme D. None of the above

L-1 S 886. A small image displayed usually on the top of the screen below the menu. It can be clicked to perform a specific function.

A. Menu B. Scroll C. Combo box D. Icon

L-1 S 887. Microsoft Windows includes a folder named ______________ that can serve as a place to store the documents you use frequently.

A. Windows B. Temp C. My Documents D. Program files

L-1 S 887. A moving picture or pattern that appears on your screen when you have not used the mouse or keyboard for a specified period of time.

A. Desktop B. Webpage C. Movie D. Screensaver

L-1 S 889. When what's this button is clicked, the cursor changes to a question mark and then if another menu option or button is clicked it shows ______________.

A. Notes on the topic
B. Comments about the topic
C. Help about how
D. Screentip with short Description about the topic

L-2 S 890. To schedule computer tasks to run automatically

A. Startup programs
B. Batch command
C. Scheduled task
D. Autoprogramming

L-2 S 891. Enables you to clear your drive of unnecessary files

A. Registry cleaner B. Disk management

C. Disk partitioning D. Disk cleanup

L-2 S 892. Delete the selected item permanently without placing the item in the Recycle Bin

A. Backspace + Del B. Alt + Del

C. Ctrl + Del D. Shift + Del

L-2 S 893. A control which is used where increase or decrease of value is required to be input

A. List box B. Combo box

C. Spinner D. Value control

L-2 S 894. The part of the windows desktop which displays time and also contains shortcuts to certain programs

A. Informational area B. Quick launch

C. Notification area D. Message area

L-2 S 895. This technology includes accessibility aids, such as readers or screen magnifier so that people with disabilities can use computers easily.

A. Readability B. Resolution

C. Accessibility D. None of the above

L-1 S 896. Collapses the selected folder.

Ans Minus sign on numeric keypad

L-1 S 897. Synchronize option is available in

Ans Accessories

L-2 S 898. Press Shift + Del key to permanently erase a file.

Ans TRUE

L-2 S 899. In Task Manager, the current working set of a process, in kilobytes.

Ans Memory Usage

L-2 S 900. The current working set is the number of pages currently resident in memory.

Ans Current working set

L-1 T/F 901 In the context of a page, Portrait is a drawing.

A.TRUE B. FALSE

L-1 T/F 902. "My Music" folder is located on the desktop.

A.TRUE B. FALSE

L-1 T/F 903. Printers can be connected to the computer USB using ports only.

A.TRUE B. FALSE

L-2 T/F 904. By default, Windows File Protection is disabled.

A.TRUE B. FALSE

L-1 T/F 905. The title bar displays the name of the document.

A. TRUE B. FALSE

L-1 T/F 906. "My Pictures" folder is located in "My Documents" folder.

A. TRUE B. FALSE

L-1 T/F 907. If selected text is bold, Pressing Ctrl+B makes it normal.

A. TRUE B. FALSE

L-1 T/F 908. Rich Text Format (RTF) is compatible with several word processors.

A. TRUE B. FALSE

L-2 T/F 909. OpenType is an extension of TrueType.

A. TRUE B. FALSE

Windows

L-1 S 910. All opened windows appear on the

A. Quick launch tool bar B. Taskbar

C. System tray D. Start—> Run

L-1 S 911. Quick launch menu appears on the

A. Taskbar B. System tray C. Start menu D. Desktop

Windows XP

L-1 D 912. The bar that contains the Start button. It appears at the bottom of the desktop by default. A user can also hide the task bar and move it to the sides or top of the desktop.

Ans. Taskbar button

L-1 S 913. ———— button appears on the taskbar and corresponds to a running application.

A. System tray B. Desktop

C. Taskbar button D. Control Panel

Answers

Q. No.	Answer	Q. No.	Answer
7	A B D	259	B
9	D	260	B
10	B D	261	B
11	A	262	B
12	B	263	B
13	A	264	B
14	C	265	B
16	B	266	B D
18	A	267	A
222	A B D	268	A
223	A B	269	A
224	A B E	270	A
225	A B C E	271	A
226	A B C	272	A
227	A B	273	A
228	A B C D E	274	A
229	B C	275	A
230	B	276	A
231	B E	277	A
232	B D	278	B
233	A C D	279	A
234	A D	280	A
235	D	281	A
236	D	282	A
237	A B C	283	A
238	E	284	A
239	A C	285	A
240	B	286	C
241	B	287	C
242	B	288	C
243	B	289	C
244	B	290	C
245	B	291	C
246	B	292	B
247	B	293	D
248	B	294	D
249	B	295	D
250	B	296	C
251	B	297	C
252	B	298	C
253	B	299	C
254	B	300	D
255	B	301	D
256	B	302	D
257	B	303	C
258	B	304	D

Q. No.	Answer	Q. No.	Answer
305	C	357	C
306	C	378	A B
307	D	379	B D
308	C	380	B
309	D	381	B
310	D	382	B
311	D	383	B
312	C	384	B
313	C	385	B
314	C	386	B
315	C	387	B
316	C	388	B
317	C	389	B
318	D	390	A D
319	C	391	A
320	B	392	A
321	C	393	A
322	D	394	C
323	D	395	C
324	D	396	C
325	C	397	C
326	C	398	C
327	D	399	D
328	D	400	C
329	C	401	C
330	C	402	C
331	D	403	C
332	A	404	C
333	A	405	A
334	A	406	A
335	A	407	B
336	A	408	B
337	A	409	B
338	B	410	A
339	B	411	B
340	B	412	D
341	B	429	B
342	B	430	C
343	B	431	C
344	B	432	A
345	B	433	D
346	A	434	B
347	A	447	A B D
348	A	448	D
349	A	449	A
350	A	450	A
351	A	451	D

Q. No.	Answer	Q. No.	Answer
452	B	595	B
453	E	596	A
458	A B C	597	A
459	A B	598	A
460	B	599	A
461	B	600	A
462	A	601	A
463	A	602	A
464	A	603	C
465	A	604	D
468	C	605	C
474	D	606	
500	B	607	C
501	A	608	C
502	A	609	D
503		610	C
504	C	611	C
505	C D	612	C
506	D	613	C
507	C	614	C
508	D	615	C
509	C	616	D
510	A	617	C
511	B	618	C
572	A C	619	C
573	A C	620	D
574	A D	621	C
575	A D	622	C
576	A C	623	A
577	B	624	A
578	B	625	A
579	B	626	A
580	B	627	A
581	B	628	A
582	B	629	B
583	B	630	B
584	B	631	B
585	B	632	A
586	B	633	A
587	B	634	A
588	B	635	A
589	B	636	A
590	B	637	A
591	B	638	
592	B	639	A
593	B	640	A
594	B	645	B

Q. No.	Answer	Q. No.	Answer
646	C	812	B
647	D	813	B
648	C	814	B
649	C	815	B
650	C	816	B
651	C	817	D
652	D	818	B
653	A	819	B
663	A	820	B
686	B	821	B
687	B	822	B
688	B	823	B
689	B	824	B
690	A	825	B
691	A	826	B
692	A	827	B
693	C	828	B
694	E	829	B
695	D	830	B
696	D	831	B
697	C	832	B
698	C	833	B
699	D	834	B
700	A	835	B
701	A	836	B
702	A	837	B
791	D	838	B
792	A B D	839	A
793	A B C	840	A
794	A B	841	A
795	A C	842	A
796	C	843	A
797	B	844	A
798	B	845	A
799	B	846	A
800	B	847	A
801	B	848	A
802	B	849	A
803	B	850	A
804	B	851	A
805	B	852	A
806	B	853	C
807	B	854	C
808	B	855	C
809	B	856	D
810	B	857	C
811	B	858	C

Q. No.	Answer	Q. No.	Answer
859	C	886	D
860	C	887	C
861	D	888	D
862	C	889	D
863	D	890	C
864	C	891	D
865	D	892	D
866	C	893	C
867	C	894	C
868	D	895	C
869	D	896	A
870	C	897	A
871	D	898	A
872	D	899	A
873	D	900	A
874	C	901	B
875	C	902	B
876	D	903	B
877	C	904	B
878	C	905	A
879	C	906	A
880	D	907	A
881	E	908	A
882	D	909	A
883	D	910	B
884	D	911	A
885	C	913	C

2

COMPUTER AND PERIPHERALS

L-1 D 1. Full form of BCR.

Ans Bar Code Reader

L-1 D 2. A bar code reader (or bar code scanner) is an electronic device for reading printed barcodes.

L-1 D 3. Pen type bar code readers requires the operator to swipe the pen over the code.

L-1 D 4. A bar code is a series of alternating dark and light stripes that are read by an optical scanner.

L-1 D 5. In semi-automatic handheld readers, the operator need not swipe, but he must position the reader near the label.

L-1 D 6. There are also fix mount readers for automatic reading. The bar code reader reads when the label is passed over it.

L-1 D 7. The Universal Product Code (UPC) is a 12 digit numeric code. It identifies a company and product name. This information is scanned and used in invoicing.

L-2 D 8. WinWedge captures serial data, and transfers the data to the application.

L-2 D 9. Camera-based bar code readers use a small video camera to capture an image of a bar code.

L-2 D 10. CCD (Charge Coupled Device) readers use an array of hundreds of tiny light sensors lined up in a row in the head of the reader.

L-2 D 11. Working of a Laser scanners is similar to pen type readers. But they use a laser beam as the light source and employ either a reciprocating mirror or a rotating prism to scan the laser beam back and forth across the bar code.

L-1 D 12. Full form of UPC is Universal Product Code. It is used to uniquely identify a particular product. Invoicing becomes easy and fast if UPC is used.

L-1 D 13. A bar-code reader is also called a price scanner or point of sale (POS) scanner.

L-1 F 14. Bar code scanners can be connected to a computer through a serial port, keyboard port or by using a device called ——————.

Ans Wedge

Cache

L-1 S 15. A special very-high-speed memory called a —————— is used to increase the speed of processing by holding current programs and data that is likely to be accessed again.

A. Cache B. RAM C. ROM D. Auxillary

CD

L-1 D 16. —————————— are a storage medium from which data is read and to which it is written by lasers.

Ans CD

L-1 D 17. CD-RW is

Ans Rewritable compact discs can also be erased.

L-1 D 18. CD-R is

Ans Recordable compact disc.

L-2 T/F 19. Recording density in CD-ROM is lower as compared with magnetic disk.

A. TRUE B. FALSE

Data transfer

L-2 D 20. A port on a computer that allows asynchronous communication of one byte at a time.

Ans Communication port

L-2 T/F 21. Communication port is also called a serial port.

A. TRUE B. FALSE

Digitizer

L-1 D 22. A Digitizer is a tablet or board-like device which converts analog electric signals of an absolute or relative position on the tablet surface to digital x,y coordinates.

L-2 D 23. The cursor is displayed on the screen and the location is only relative to the location on the screen and is effected by the size and configuration of the monitor. A digitizer is mostly used in absolute coordinates.

File Access

L-2 D 24. A file that includes an index directory to facilitate random access.

Ans Indexed file

File Organization

L-1 D 25. Sequential access is also called

Ans Serial access

L-1 S 26. A file organization in which records are organized in order of the value of some FIELD

A. Random B. Sequential C. Both of the above

D. None of the above

L-1 S 27. Storage devices in which the access time is effectively independent of the location of the data

A. Sequential access B. Direct-access C. Both of the above

D. None of the above

L-1 T/F 28. A magnetic disk is a sequential access device.

A. TRUE B. FALSE

L-1 T/F 29. Sequential file processing is faster than direct access file processing for getting random information

A. TRUE B. FALSE

General

L-1 D 30. A set of specifications developed by Intel that allows a computer to automatically detect and configure a device and install the appropriate device drivers.

Ans Plug and play

L-1 D 31. What are peripheral devices?

Ans Peripheral devices are devices connected to the computer but external in relation to the processing unit. If a peripheral device is disconnected, the computer will still be able to work; only functions performed by this peripheral device will not be available.

L-1 D 32. A word is a smallest unit of data that can be handled by CPU.

L-2 D 33. An optical port on a computer that uses infrared light.

Ans Infrared port

L-2 D 34. A computer, or a computer peripheral such as a printer, that can communicate using infrared light.

Ans Infrared device

L-2 D 35. A set of three values that defines how a color can be represented on computer devices such as monitors, scanners, and printers.

Ans Color space

L-3 D 36. The particular range of colors that a device is able to produce

Ans Color gamut

L-1 M 37. Which among the following is a peripheral device?

A. Printer B. CPU C. Scanner D. RAM

L-2 S 38. Light that is beyond red in the color spectrum.

Ans A. Ultra red B.. Red C. Infrared (IR)

D. None of the above

L-1 S 39. ISA stands for

Ans Instruction Set Architecture

L-2 T/F 40. Infrared light is visible to the human eye.

A. TRUE B. FALSE

Hard disk

L-2 D 41. Disk arm scheduling algorithms works on the policy of

Ans First come first serve

L-2 D 42. Dynamic disks does not support volumes that span multiple disks.

L-1 D 43. Sectors

Ans A subdivision of a track on a disk (magnetic or optical). Each sector stores a fixed amount of data. 512 bytes per sector for disks and 2048 bytes per sector for optical discs.

L-1 D 44. Most disks use 512-byte sectors.

L-1 D 45. A storage medium that holds information until it is deleted or overwritten.

Ans Secondary Storage

L-1 D 46. The labelling of tracks and sectors is called performing a logical or soft format.

L-1 D 47. Auxiliary storage devices are also used to transfer data from one computer to another.

L-2 D 48. Partitions

Ans A partition can be thought of as a division or "part" of a real hard disk drive. Multiple partitions on a single hard drive appear as separate drives to the operating system.

L-2 D 49. Superblock

Ans A superblock is a record of the characteristics of a file system, including its size, the block size, the empty and the filled blocks and their respective counts, the size and location of the inode tables, the disk block map and usage information, and the size of the block groups.

L-2 D 50. Contiguous allocation of files.

Ans A file on disk that is not broken apart. All sectors are adjacent to each other. A contiguous file is faster to read and write than one that is fragmented across the disk.

L-2 D 51. Dynamic disks can be accessed only by Windows 2000 and Windows XP.

L-2 D 52. Before a hard disk could be used, each platter must receive a low level format.

L-2 D 53. In a read operation from disk, many disk controllers always read and cache multiple sectors even when only one is requested.

L-2 D 54. The seek time or access time measures the time it takes on an average to access a particular piece of information.

L-2 D 55. Addressing scheme in which disk sectors are numbered consecutively starting at 0, without regard to the disk geometric.

Ans Logical block addressing

L-2 D 56. While the controller and software are waiting for a seek to complete on one drive, the controller can initiate a seek on another.

L-2 D 57. Stored bits are detected by a change in magnetic field produced by a recorded spot on the surface as it passes through a read head.

L-2 D 58. In hard disk, concepts of magnetism are used for storing and reading the bits.

L-2 D 59. The position of sector 0 on each track of a hard disk is offset from the previous track when the low level format is done, this offset is called

Ans Cylinder skew

L-2 D 60. The recording density refers to the number of bits that can be recorded on a diskette in one inch circumference of the innermost track on diskette.

Ans TRUE

L-2 D 61. A dynamic volume made up of disk space from a single dynamic disk. A simple volume can consist of a single region on a disk or multiple regions of the same disk that are linked together.

Ans Simple volume

L-3 D 62. Reducing Disk Arm Motion when reading from the hard disk.

Ans Reduce the amount of disk arm motion by putting blocks that are likely to be accessed in sequence close to each other, preferably in the same cylinder.

L-3 D 63. When a write is issued to a ————————, the disk either correctly writes the data or it does nothing, leaving the existing data intact.

Ans Stable storage

L-2 F 64. ———————— checks disks for errors.

Ans Scandisk

L-2 F 65. A portion of a hard disk that functions as if it is a separate physical disk is known as a ————————.

Ans Partition

L-2 M 66. A disk consists of one or more metal platters that rotate at —— rpm.

A. 5400 B. 7200
C. 10800 D. None of the above

L-2 S 67. All the tracks for a given arm position form a

A. Path B. Cylinder C. Track D. Sector

L-2 S 68. In a hard disk, each track is divided into number of

A. Tracks B. Sectors C. Cylinders D. Cones

L-2 S 69. A partition on the hard disk using which the computer starts.

A. OS partition B. Active partition
C. NTFS partition D. None of the above

L-2 S 70. ———————— sectors that do not correctly read back the value just written to them.

A. Read only sectors B. Bad sectors
C. Both of the above D. None of the above

L-2 S 71. A log, a table which records the location of each file on disk and the status of each sector.

A. Partition table B. File Allocation Table

C. Event Log D. Log table

L-2 S 72. The formatted capacity of a hard disk is usually ———— per cent low than the unformatted capacity.

A. 10 B. 20 C. 5 D. 15

L-1 S 73. The most common auxiliary memory devices used in computer systems are

A. Magnetic disks B. Magnetic tapes

C. Both of the above D. None of the above

L-1 S 74. In a hard disk, at any given arm position, each of the heads can read an annular region known as

A. Track B. Sector

C. Cylinders D. None of the above

L-2 S 75. ———————— is used to deal with checkboarding.

A. Compaction B. Check box C. Fragmentation D. Cleanup

L-2 S 76. The hard disk drive that contains the system and boot partitions used to start Windows.

A. Primary disk B. Main disk

C. First disk D. None of the above

L-1 S 77. The most common method of carrying data from one place to another is by using

A. Pen drive B. CD-ROM

C. Both of the above D. None of the above

L-2 S 78. Bits are stored in the magnetized surface in spots along concentric circles called

A. Clusters B. Cylinders C. Tracks D. Sectors

L-2 S 79. Sector 0 contains the ————————————, which contains some boot code plus the partition table at the end.

A. System record B. Bootstrap loader C. Master Boot Record D. Boot.ini

L-2 S 80. A portion of the hard disk partition that contains information about the disk's file system and a small program that loads the windows operating system.

A. Primary partition B. FAT

C. Active OS D. Partition boot sector

L-1 T/F 81. A track in a given sector near the circumference is shorter than a track near the centre of the disk.

A. TRUE B. FALSE

L-2 T/F 82. The active partition may not be the primary partition of the hard disk.

A. TRUE B. FALSE

L-2 T/F 83. High level formatting of disk is done by the manufacturer of the hard disk.

A. TRUE B. FALSE

L-3 T/F 84. Stable storage is implemented in hardware.

A. TRUE B. FALSE

L-2 T/F 85. Hard disks hold more data and are faster than floppy disks.

A. TRUE B. FALSE

L-2 T/F 86. Read and write operations on a magnetic disks take equal time.

A. TRUE B. FALSE

L-2 T/F 87. A track in a given sector near the circumference is longer than a track near the centre of the disk.

A. TRUE B. FALSE

L-2 T/F 88. A type of partition that can be created on basic hard disks. A primary partition is a portion of a physical disk that functions as if it were a physically separate disk.

Ans Primary partition

Hardware

L-3 D 89. An Intel microprocessor that uses explicitly parallel instruction set computing and 64-bit memory addressing.

Ans Itanium

L-2 D 90. A program that is substituted for hardware and stored in read only memory (ROM).

Ans Firmware

L-2 D 91. What is so special about ergonomic keyboards?

Ans Easy to use, does'nt have bad effects on one's wrists, arm, body.

L-2 D 92. ROM is used in ——— to handle low level device control.

Ans I/O Cards.

L-1 D 93. ISA

Ans Industry Standard Architecture

L-1 D 94. Cluster

Ans A cluster is the minimum unit of file space on a hard disk or disk partition; also known as an 'allocation unit'. If the cluster size is 16 KB, then a 1 KB file and a 7 KB file will each take 16 KB of actual disk space; a 17 KB file will take 32 KB. Clearly smaller clusters make more efficient use of hard drive space, however there can be a small trade off in performance terms due to increased fragmentation.

L-1 D 95. AV disks

Ans Audio Visual disks

L-1 D 96. DMP means

Ans Dot Matrix Printer

L-1 D 97. EEPROM is

Ans Electrically Erasable ROM

L-1 D 98. Serial port

Ans A serial port is a serial communication physical interface through which information transfers in or out one bit at a time.

L-1 D 99. Block devices

Ans A peripheral device that transfers a group of bytes (block, sector, etc.) of data at a time such as a disk.

L-1 D 100. Bubble memory

Ans Bubble memory is a type of non-volatile computer memory that uses a thin film of a magnetic material to hold small magnetized areas, known as bubbles or domains, each of which stores one bit of data.

L-1 D 101. CPU stands for

Ans Central Processing Unit

L-1 D 102. Clock software

Ans It is a software in computers for Accounting CPU Usage.

L-1 D 103. What is a bus?

Ans Through which data transfers between various internal components of the computer.

L-1 D 104. Implications of better Bus speed in a computer system.

Ans More the bus speed in a system, more efficient would be the use of processor and storage devices because the speed with which data and instructions travel among various devices in CPU increases.

L-1 D 105. Processor slots

Ans BIOS, CMOS, Power supply connector

L-1 D 106. Eisa is of 8/16 bits

L-1 D 107. What is a block?

Ans In computing (specifically data transmission and data storage), a block is a sequence of bytes or bits, having a nominal length (a block size).

L-1 D 108. ISA are 8/16 bits

L-1 D 109. Full form of PCI is

Ans Peripheral Component Interconnect

L-1 D 110. What is a monitor?

Ans Is the main output device which helps a user to interact with the computer.

L-1 D 111. RAM is also known as

Ans Core Memory

L-1 D 112. Examples of ports and connectors in a computer

Ans Parallel ports, com/serial ports, IDE drive connector, Floppy drive connector, USB connector, Ps/2 connector

L-1 D 113. Serial ports — rs-232c, ps/2.

L-1 D 114. What is flash memory?

Ans Flash memory is a non-volatile computer memory that can be electrically erased and reprogrammed. It is a technology that is primarily used in memory cards and USB flash drives for general storage and transfer of data between computers and other digital products. It is a specific type of EEPROM

L-1 D 115. Full form of CD-ROM is

Ans Compact Disk-Read Only Memory

L-1 D 116. Character special files

Ans Character special files or character devices relate to devices through which the system transmits data one character at a time. These device nodes often serve for stream communication with devices such as virtual terminals, and serial modems. These devices does not usually support random access.

L-1 D 117. IEEE 1394 is also called

Ans A Firewire port

L-1 D 118. AGP card used for better display and graphical quality is usually of 32 bits

L-1 D 119. Vesa Local Bus VLB is of 32 bits

L-1 D 120. USB — Universal Serial Bus

L-1 D 121. Traces on the motherboards are

Ans Copper circuit paths which connects various components of motherboard.

L-1 D 122. PCI on the motherboard is either 32 or 64 bits

L-1 D 123. SCSI speed is approximately

Ans 160MB/sec

L-1 D 124. A device known as Charged coupled device is used in scanners

L-1 D 125. SCSI is pronounced as scuzzy

L-1 D 126. Components of a sound card are

Ans A digital signal processor, a analog to digital converter ADC, a digital to analog converter ADC, MIDI, ROM, Jack, Game port.

L-1 D 127. ISA Industry Standard Architecture

L-1 D 128. Keys like F1, F5, F7 etc. are called

Ans Function keys

L-1 D 129. What is an auxillary storage device?

Ans Storage devices other than the memory of the computer. Storage of data on these devices is non-volatile

L-1 D 130. The main advantage of Magnetic tapes is

Ans Cheap per bit and removable

L-1 D 131. Light pen has a light sensitive detector

L-1 D 132. Micro Channel Architecture MCA are 16/32 bits

L-1 D 133. Higher the clock speed, faster the processor.

L-1 D 134. On the first 16 blocks of a CDROM, nothing is defined. Data is written only after the 16th block.

L-1 D 135. To place a removable tape or disc into a drive is known as ———— that device.

Ans Mounting

L-1 D 136. IEEE 1394 standard is for packet transfers at speeds up to

Ans 50MB/sec

L-1 D 137. The storage medium often used for backup purpose is

Ans Magnetic Tape

L-1 D 138. Magnetic disks are constant angular velocity drives

L-1 D 139. Any fixed or removable objects that store computer data.

Ans Media

L-1 D 140. Peripheral devices allow people to interact with the CPU

L-1 D 141. Unlike USB, IEEE 1394 does not have a central controller

L-1 D 142. What are advantages and disadvantages of magnetic tapes?

Ans Used to storage huge amounts of data, cheap, easy to handle. Disadvantages are – only sequential access, specialized hardware is required to read which is uncommon

L-1 D 143. What is the main difference between a mouse and a trackball?

Ans Trackball has a ball on the top of the device whereas the ball is situated below the mouse's body.

L-1 D 144. A CPU consists of a Control Unit and Arithmetic Logical Unit

L-1 D 145. In a CD-RW, we can erase the present data and write data again

L-1 D 146. The 8-mm helical-scan tapes have data capacities from 2.5GB to 5GB

L-1 D 147. Any piece of equipment that can be attached to a network or computer is known as a

Ans Device

L-1 D 148. ROM is used for storing an initial program called a bootstrap loader.

L-1 D 149. IDE is the standard type of disk on Pentiums and some other computers.

L-1 D 150. Devices the output as a rectangular grid of points called pixels. This graphical concept is known as

Ans Raster graphics

L-1 D 151. More information can be stored on a disk than a drum of comparable size

L-1 D 152. USB 2.0 standard can theoretically transfer up to 60 megabytes per second

L-1 D 153. A small chip on the board of the computer that loads the hardware settings

Ans BIOS

L-1 D 154. The removable cartridges of a Jaz drive can hold ———————— of data

Ans 1GB-2GB

L-1 D 155. Associative memory is uniquely suited to do parallel searches using data association

L-1 D 156. Primary volume Descriptor in CDROM contains some general information about the CD-ROM

L-1 D 157. The magnetic device which combines the magnetic disk technology with CD-ROM technology is

Ans CD-RW

L-1 D 158. The only device connecting through AGP and to the CPU and system memory is the graphics card.

L-1 D 159. The static RAM consists essentially of internal flip flops that store the binary information.

L-1 D 160. A business card reader is a scanning device used to scan and electronically save and process business cards

L-1 D 161. Input device:- A device used to enter information into a computer or other data processing devices.

L-1 D 162. The graphics card in a modern PC can connect in one of several different ways — onboard, pci, agp

L-1 D 163. Disks may have multiple heads and simultaneous transfer of bits from several tracks at the same time

L-1 D 164. The dynamic RAM offers reduced power consumption and larger storage capacity in a single memory chip.

L-1 D 165. Associative memory is used in applications where the search time is very critical and must be very short

L-1 D 166. IDE devices like CDROM drives or hard disk drives are connected to the motherboard through the IDE connector

L-1 D 167. CD-ROM XA allows CD-Rs to be written incrementally, a few sectors today, a few tomorrow, and a few next month

L-1 D 168. Keyboard which contains buttons named Media, Volume, Internet, Email, Favourites etc on top of it are known as

Ans Multimedia Keyboard

L-1 D 169. The most common types of auxillary storage devices magnetic tapes, magnetic disks, floppy disks, hard disks etc.

L-1 D 170. The dynamic RAM stores the binary information in the form of electrical charges that are applied to the capacitors

L-1 D 171. A device that puts text or images on paper or other print media according to how they look on the computer screen.

Ans Printer

L-1 D 172. A connection socket on a motherboard for a peripheral designed according to the Industry Standard Architecture (ISA)

Ans ISA expansion slot

L-1 D 173. Recordable compact disc. Data can be copied to the CD on more than one occasion; however, data cannot be erased from the CD.

Ans CD-R

L-1 D 174. Source data automation is done using scanners, bar code reader so that data have not to be entered manually through keyboard.

L-1 D 175. ACPI enables the operating system to direct power management on a wide range of mobile, desktop and server Computer and peripherals.

L-1 D 176. Combination of dots form characters and the quality depends on no. of pins since a dmp is an impact printer carbon copies can be printed

Ans Dot Matrix Printer

L-1 D 177. A disk system is addressed by address bits that specify the disk number, the disk surface, the sector number and the track within the sector

L-1 D 178. Associative memory stores both the address and content (Data) of the memory word. This permits any location in cache to store any word from main memory.

L-1 D 179. The cache is used for storing segments of programs currently being executed in the CPU and temporary data frequently needed in the present calculations.

L-1 D 180. A removable device of size similar to that of a debit card, that can be attached into a Personal Computer Memory Card International Association (PCMCIA) slot in a portable computer.

Ans PC Card

L-1 D 181. A magnetic card is a rectangular plastic object of the size of a debit card that contains either a magnetic object embedded within the card or a magnetic stripe on the exterior of the card.

L-1 D 182. AGP uses sideband addressing which allows the graphics card to request and issue addressing info using 8 additional address lines that are separate from the 32 bit path used to transfer data

L-2 D 183. Video Ram

Ans Video RAM (VRAM) means in general all forms of random access memory (RAM) used to store image data for a computer display. All types of video RAM are special arrangements of dynamic RAM (DRAM). Video RAM is really a buffer between the computer processor and the display and is often called the frame buffer.

L-2 D 184. Clock speed

Ans The clock speed of a CPU is defined as the frequency that a processor executes instructions or that data is processed. This clock speed is measured in millions of cycles per second or Megahertz (MHz).

L-2 D 185. Video controller

Ans A chip that pulls the characters or bits out of the video RAM and generates the video signal used to drive the monitor

L-2 D 186. Magneto optical MO drives

Ans A type of disk drive that combines magnetic disk technologies with optical technologies, such as those used in CD-ROMs. An MO disk drive is designed so that an inserted disk will be exposed to a magnet on the label side and to the laser beam on the opposite side

L-2 D 187 SIMM/DIMM are used to house RAM modules

L-2 D 188. What are optical disks and how do they work?

Ans A Optical disc is a flat, generally circular disc which can contain data encoded in microscopic pits (or bumps) on a special material (often aluminum) on one of its flat surfaces. The encoding pattern follows a continuous, spiral path covering the entire disc surface and extending from the innermost track to the outermost track.

L-2 D 189. Firmware is a combination of software and hardware

L-2 D 190. All the USB devices share a Single USB device driver

L-2 D 191. IDE refers to any device which has a built in device controller

L-2 D 192. Universal product code is a unique code assigned to a particular product

L-2 D 193. What is the difference between an impact printer and a non-impact printer?

Ans Impact printers like dot matrix printers have something which hit the paper and this hit causes the print one way or the other.

L-2 D 194. Access time is the total of seek time, rotational time and data transfer time

L-2 D 195. Tracks in CDROMs could be grouped into sessions, leading to multi session CD-ROMs

L-2 D 196. What is the difference between Random access devices and Sequential access devices?

Ans On a random access device, a data can be read immediately irrespective of the location of the data. In sequential access, the data is accessed after recordwise or blockwise parsing from the start of the device to the location of the data.

L-2 D 197. SRS is a sound recording and playback technology that gives sounds acoustical effects

L-2 D 198. Motherboards contains Processor slots, Expansion slots and boards, Ports and connectors

L-2 D 199. ———————————— is a high-capacity floppy disk drive developed by Omega Corporation

Ans Zip drive

L-2 D 200. Disks may have multiple heads and simultaneous transfer of bits from several tracks at the same time

L-2 D 201. A device that is installed in computers to enable the use of smart cards for enhanced security features.

Ans Smart card reader

L-2 D 202. Solid state storage device means that there are no moving parts — everything is electronic instead of mechanical

L-2 D 203. Mangetic disks are organized into cylinders, each one containing as many tracks as there are heads stacked vertically

L-2 D 204. A feature of an uninterruptible power supply (UPS) that removes spikes, surges, sags, and noise from the power supply.

Ans Power conditioning

L-2 D 205. An optical mouse uses a light beam instead of a rotating ball as in the normal mouse to detect the movement of mouse.

L-2 D 206. Rotational time is the rotational delay also called as latency to move the storage medium underneath the read write head.

L-2 D 207. SAM, serial access memory work very well for memory buffers where the data normally stored in the order in which it will be used.

L-2 D 208. A MIDI equipped music instrument can be attached to the sound card so that what is being played could be seen on the computer screen.

L-2 D 209. The data bus of the ROM has only output capability whereas the data bus connected to RAMs can transfer information in both directions

L-2 D 210. Plug and play have the system automatically collect information about the I/O devices, centrally assign interrupt levels and I/O addresses

L-2 D 211. A type of disk-drive interface in which the controller electronics reside on the drive itself, eliminating the need for a separate adapter card.

Ans Intergrated Device Electronics (IDE)

L-2 D 212. Physical dump starts at block 0 of the disk, writes all the disk blocks onto the output tape in order, and stops when it has copied the last one.

L-2 D 213. A device protected in a sealed case. It contains one or more inflexible platters coated with a material in which data can be recorded magnetically with read write heads.

Ans Hard disk

L-2 D 214. Shared bus is for connecting additional components to the computer it is called shared bus because it lets multiple device access the same path to the CPU and system memory

L-2 D 215. The basic function of the device-independent software is to perform the I/O functions that are common to all devices and to provide a uniform interface to the user-level software

L-2 D 216. In electromechanical devices, the access time is sum of seek time required to position the read-write head to the required location and a transfer time required to transfer data to or from the device

L-2 D 217. A volume that you create within an extended partition on a basic master boot record (MBR) disk.

Ans Logical drive

L-2 D 218. A device that draws pictures on paper based on instructions given by the computer system. Plotters draw lines using a pen. So, they can produce continuous lines. Printers only simulate lines by printing a closely spaced dots

L-2 D 219. Also known as CDFS (CD File System), it is a file system used for optical disc media. The idea is that the CD could be run on various platforms. The first 32768 bytes of the disk are unused by ISO 9660 data structure and therefore available for other use.

L-3 D 220. 32-bit In windows refers to the way memory is accessed. 32 bit application access memory in 32-bit chunks.

L-3 D 221. Each mirror of a mirrored volume resides on a different disk. If one disk is unavailabe, windows can use the mirror to gain access to the data.

Ans Mirror

L-3 D 222. Two or more identical printers that are connected to one print server and act as a Single printer. The print job will be sent to the first available printer in the pool.

Ans Printing pool.

L-1 D 223. Block special files

Ans Block devices often support random access and seeking, and generally use buffered input and output routines

L-1 D 224. Capacity of a DVD is

Ans Single-sided, Single-layered can hold 4.7 GB (gigabytes) of data, Single-sided, double-layered can hold 8.5 GB, Double-sided, Single-layered can hold 9.4 GB, Double-sided, double-layered can hold 17 GB

L-1 D 225. Minimum unit of file space on a hard disk or disk partition is known as a ————————

Ans Cluster

L-1 D 226. A device that controls the movement of the cursor or pointer on a display screen is called the ————————

Ans Mouse

L-2 D 227. ———————— points are created when a mounted drive is created

Ans Junction Point

L-1 F 228. In the context of hardware, SCSI is

Ans Small Computer System Interface

L-1 F 229. WORM disks are ————————

Ans Write Once Read Many disks

L-1 F 230. ACPI is ————————

Ans Advanced Configuration and Power Interface

L-1 F 231. Tapes are read on a hardware device called a

Ans Tape Unit

L-1 F 232. SIMM/DIMM slots, PCI slots, AGP slots, SCSI are ————————

A. Expansion slots

L-1 F 233. Aggregate load of all USB devices is approximately ————————

Ans 1.5 MB/sec

L-1 F 234. Any fixed or removable objects that store computer data is called ————————

Ans Media

L-2 F 235. SIMM is

Ans Single Inline Memory Modules

L-2 F 236. EEPROM is ————————

Ans Electronically Erasable Programmable Read Only Memory

L-2 F 237. IDE is ————————

Ans Integrated Drive Electronics

L-2 F 238. Full form of EISA is ——————

Ans Extended Industry Standard Architecture

L-2 F 239. PROM is ——————

Ans Programmable Read Only Memory

L-2 F 240. Motherboards are also called mainboards

Ans Mainboards

L-2 F 241. AGP uses —————— to increase speed

Ans Pipelining

L-2 F 242. PCI bus are successors to ——————

Ans ISA Bus

L-2 F 243. The average time required to reach a storage location in memory and obtain its contents is called ——————

Ans Access time

L-2 F 244. An output device that uses words or messages recorded on a magnetic medium to produce audio response is known as ——————

Ans Voice response unit

L-2 F 245. A socket in a computer, designed to hold expansion boards and connect them to the system bus is known as a ——————

Ans Expansion slot

L-2 F 246. A specification that defines a local bus system that allows up to 10 PCI-compliant expansion cards is known as ——————

Ans Peripheral Component Interconnect (PCI)

L-3 F 247. In the context of CD ROM, CAV is ——————

Ans Constant Angular Velocity

L-3 F 248. In the context of CDROM, CLV is ——————

Ans Constant Linear Velocity

L-2 F 249. In the context of hardware architecture, RISC is ——————

Ans Reduced Instruction set computing

L-1 M 250. The different types of memory units are

A. RAM B. ROM C. PROM D. Memo

L-1 M 251. What are the components of a computer?

A. Keyboard B. CPU C. Printer D. Monitor

L-1 M 252. Printer can be connected to the computer

A. Serially B. On USB port C. PS/2 D. Printer port

L-1 M 253. What are the major auxillary storage devices?

A. Hard disk B. Magnetic tapes C. Pen drive D. Scanner

L-1 M 254. The different types of optical disks are ——————

A. CD ROM B. Worm C. Erasable Optic D. Zip disk

L-2 M 255. What are the different point devices available?
A. Mouse B. Stylus C. Keyboard D. All of the ab
E. Touchpad

L-1 M 256. Special keys
A. Numeric keys B. Function keys C. Alphabetical eye D. Control keys

L-1 M 257. Flash memory examples
A. RAM B. BIOS chip C. Memory stick D. Integrated Circuits E. Memory cards for games

L-1 M 258. USB is commonly used to attach
A. Hard disk B. Pen drive C. Digital camera D. Floppy drive

L-1 M 259. Among the following, which are secondary storage devices
A. RAM B. Magnetic disks C. ROM D. Magnetic Tapes

L-1 M 260. Mouse can be connected to the computer
A. Serially B. Printer port C. PS/2 D. USB port

L-1 M 261. What are the major output devices for a computer?
A. Printer B. Scanner C. Monitor D. Keyboard

L-2 M 262. Two kinds of special files are
A. Block B. Character C. Both of the above
D. None of the above

L-1 S 263. What are the various types of printers?
A. Dot matrix B. Laser C. Optical D. Ink jet

L-2 S 264. A device that connects your computer to a network.
A. Network adapter B. Adapter card C. Ethernet card
D. Connection Card E. Network interface card

L-1 S 265. CPU stands for
A. Central Production Unit B. Central Processing Unit
C. Critical Power Unit D. None of these

L-1 S 266. ROM stores programs and data during the computer operation
A. TRUE B. FALSE

L-1 S 267. The memory unit that holds instructions for starting up the computer is
A. Hard disk B. ROM C. RAM D. Pen drive

L-1 S 268. In magnetic tapes, information is recorded in blocks referred to as ——————
A. Files B. Record C. Field D. Database

L-1 S 269. A semiconductor circuit in which data/program is installed during the manufacturing process
A. RAM B. ROM C. Magnetic disk D. Zip

L-1 S 270. A connection point on a computer where devices that transfer data to and from a computer can be connected
A. Connection B. Port C. Cable D. Hub

L-1 S 271. ________________ is an output technique that records output from a computer as microscopic image on roll or sheet film

A. DCOM B. COM C. Block D. Character

L-2 S 272. Contents of EEPROM are erased by

A. Delete command B. Exposing it to electrical charge
C. Power off D. Chemically

L-2 S 273. Which of the following is a sequential access device?

A. Hard disk B. Magnetic Tape C. Floppy disk D. All of the above

L-2 S 274. The contents of a PROM can be erased by exposing it to ________________

A. Infrared light B. Ultraviolet light
C. Laser D. None of the above

L-2 S 275. Devices which require manual configuration of hardware setting before they can be used

A. Plug and play B. Non-Plug and Play
C. Warm connect D. None of the above

L-2 S 276. Hard disk which can be connect or disconnected even when the system is running are called

A. Hot hard disk B. Hot swapable hard disk
C. Hot replaceable disk D. Hot pluggable hard disk

L-2 S 277. __________ processors means that they can execute more than one instruction per clock cycle

A. Itanium B. Super scaler C. Multifunctional D. Timeless

L-2 S 278. Type of I/O device that delivers or accepts a stream of characters, without regard to any block structure

A. Block device B. Character device
C. Stream device D. None of the above

L-2 S 279. The average time required to reach a storage location in memory and get its contents is known as ________________

A. Read time B. Access time C. Seek time D. Latency time

L-1 S 280. BIOS

A. Basic Input Output System B. Basic Interrupt Output System
C. Benchmark Input Output System D. None of the above

L-1 S 281. RAID

A. Redundant Array of Inexpensive Disk B. Redundant Array Disk
C. Both of the above D. None of the above

L-1 S 282. Non-volatile memory is

A. ROM B. RAM
C. Both of the above D. None of the above

L-1 S 283. What is the function of memory?

A. To store data B. To process data

C. Both of the above D. None of the above

L-1 S 284. Devices that provide backup storage are called

A. Auxillary memory B. Main memory

C. Both of the above D. None of the above

L-1 S 285. Devices that provide backup storage are called

A. Auxillary memory B. Main memory

C. ROM D. None of the above

L-1 S 286. In RAID, ———— different organizations are possible

A. 6 B. 5 C. 8 D. 3

L-1 S 287. A ———— transmits data between various components on the motherboard

A. Bus B. Flash drive

C. Wire D. None of the above

L-1 S 288. Data can be copied to the CD on more than one occasion and can be erased.

A. CD-RW B. CD-W C. CD-R D. CDROM

L-1 S 289 Which of the following memory chip is programmed during the manufacturing process?

A. ROM B. RAM C. EEPROM D. PROM

L-1 S 290. A device that requires manual configuration of hardware settings before it can be used

A. Non-Plug and Play B. USB

C. Plug and Play D. None of the above

L-1 S 291. ———————— a type of magnetic tape that uses the same technology as VCR tapes

A. DAT B. Zip

C. Omega D. None of the above

L-1 S 292. Circuit that provide a communication path between 2 or more devices of a digital computer system

A. Bus B. PCI C. Motherboard D. Port

L-1 S 293. The ———— computers and processes data and delivers the results based on the instructions that are fed to the PC

A. CPU B. RAM C. Display card D. ROM

L-1 S 294. Disks that are permanently attached inside the computer unit and cannot be removed by the occassional user are called

A. Hard disk B. Winchester disk C. Flash disk D. ROM disk

L-1 S 295. A device, such as a disk drive, printer etc. that is connected to a computer. They are controlled by the CPU of the computer

A. Peripheral B. Hardware C. Software D. Parts

L-2 S 296. A storage method in Windows that allows disk and volume management without restarting the system

A. Dynamic storage B. Static storage C. Warm storage D. Cold storage

L-1 S 297. NIC is

A. Network Interaction Card B. Networking Interchange Card
C. New Interface Card D. Network Interface Card

L-1 S 298. The different types of monitors are

A. Monochrome B. Gray-scale C. Colour D. All of the above

L-1 S 299. The capacity of a Single CDROM is ————

A. About 300MB B. Less than 500M C. Over 650MB D. Over 850MB

L-1 S 300. The key in which a box is printed with an arrow is called

A. Ctrl B. Shift C. Context key D. Alt

L-1 S 301. Which of the following is the slowest in accessing data?

A. Zip disk B. Floppy disk C. Hard disk D. Magnetic tape

L-1 S 302. The configuration information of the hardware is stored in

A. RAM B. ROM C. CMOS D. Hard disk

L-1 S 303. CPU contains ———— to hold key variables and temporary results

A. Pointers B. Counters C. Registers D. Variable

L-1 S 304. The input device used mostly for computer games is the ————————

A. Keyboard B. Mouse C. Touch screen D. Joystick

L-1 S 305. A storage medium that loses its contents if power failure occurs or power is switched off

A. Capacitor B. Non-volatile C. Clear RAM D. Volatile

L-1 S 306. CPU can process a number of independent programs concurrently. This is called ————

A. Multi tasking B. Multi processing
C. Threading D. Multi programming

L-1 S 307. Disks that are permanently attached to the computer and cannot be removed by the occassional user

A. Soft disk B. Flash drive C. Hard disk D. Compact disk

L-1 S 308. Each pixel is represented by an 8-bit number. This value is an index into a table of 256 entries, each holding a 24-bit value. This table is called a ———— and often stored in hardware

A. Color range B. RGB C. Color palette D. Pixel density

L-2 S 309. AGP is

A. Advanced Graphics Program B. Advanced Graphics Port
C. Accelerated Graphics Port D. None of the above

L-2 S 310. EEPROM can be erased by exposing it to

A. Sunlight B. Ultraviolet Radiation

C. Magnetic field D. Electrical charge

L-2 S 311. The fastest component of memory hierarchy is

A. RAM B. Flash memory C. Magnetic tape D. Cache

L-2 S 312. The ———————— is a sum of seek time and transfer time

A. Data transfer time B. Access speed

C. Access time D. I/O speed

L-2 S 313. The time elapsed between the instant at which data is called from a storage device and the instant delivery begins

A. Turnaround time B. Response time

C. Access time D. Seek time

L-1 S 314. DAT is a magnetic tape that uses an helical scan to record data

Ans TRUE

L-1 S 315. A semiconductor memory which allows the eraser of the information stored in it by exposure to ultraviolet light. Later new information can be stored in it.

Ans EPROM

L-2 S 316. An input/output connector to which a joy stick is attached. It is typically a 15-pin socket.

Ans game port

L-1 T/F 317. RAM is a secondary storage

A. TRUE B. FALSE

L-1 T/F 318. Plotters cannot draw lines

A. TRUE B. FALSE

L-1 T/F 319. FLASH RAM is volatile memory

A. TRUE B. FALSE

L-1 T/F 320. ROM is not a random access device

A. TRUE B. FALSE

L-1 T/F 321. Flat panel display monitors are analog

A. TRUE B. FALSE

L-1 T/F 322. ROM contains data that can be modified

A. TRUE B. FALSE

L-1 T/F 323. EEPROM can be erased and but cannot rewritten

A. TRUE B. FALSE

L-1 T/F 324. Records on a magnetic tape could only be of fixed length

A. TRUE B. FALSE

L-1 T/F 325. For printing drawings, printers are preferable to plotters

A. TRUE B. FALSE

L-1 T/F 326. Microcomputers can run dos and windows but cannot run unix

A. TRUE B. FALSE

L-1 T/F 327. The access speed of secondary storage devices is higher than that of primary storage

A. TRUE B. FALSE

L-1 T/F 328. The 3.5 inch floppy disks are smaller so they cannot store more data than the 5.25 inch disks

A. TRUE B. FALSE

L-2 T/F 329. ROM is not Random access

A. TRUE B. FALSE

L-2 T/F 330. Dynamic RAM is faster than static RAM

A. TRUE B. FALSE

L-2 T/F 331. Access to disk is faster than access to memory

A. TRUE B. FALSE

L-2 T/F 332. PCI VGA card provides higher performance than AGP

A. TRUE B. FALSE

L-1 T/F 333. ROM is read only memory

A. TRUE B. FALSE

L-1 T/F 334. All colour computers are RGB monitors

A. TRUE B. FALSE

L-1 T/F 335. One can write to a CD-ROM more than once

A. TRUE B. FALSE

L-1 T/F 336. Tapes are generally used only for long-term storage and backup

A. TRUE B. FALSE

L-1 T/F 337. The contents of ROM remain unchanged after power is turned off and on again

A. TRUE B. FALSE

L-1 T/F 338. The contents of RAM remain unchanged after power is turned off and on again

A. TRUE B. FALSE

L-1 T/F 339. The 3.5 inch floppy disks are smaller and can store more data than can the 5.25 inch disks

A. TRUE B. FALSE

L-2 T/F 340. AGP has direct access to system memory for faster performance

A. TRUE B. FALSE

L-2 T/F 341 Accessing data on tapes is much slower than accessing data on disks

A. TRUE B. FALSE

L-2 T/F 342. A 32 bit micro with a 25 MHz processor has more processing ability than a 16 bit micro with a 25 MHz processor

A. TRUE B. FALSE

L-2 T/F 343. In storage devices, DASD is ——————————

Ans Direct Access Storage Device

L-2 T/F 344. A hardware or software component that allows a digital video disc (DVD) drive to "display movies on your computer screen is known as ————————————————

Ans DVD decoder

L-2 T/F 345. For protection against failures, devices, services or connections are duplicated. This is known as ——————

Ans Replication

Hardware

L-2 S 346. A —————— is a fast RAM present between the processor and slower memory such as main memory or a hard disk

A. ROM B. Cache C. PROM D. Processor

History

L-1 D 347. The QWERTY keyboard was designed in the 1800s for mechanical typewriters and was actually designed to slow typists down to avoid jamming the keys

Input/Output

L-1 D 348. CDs are constant linear velocity drive

L-1 D 349. CD-RW

Ans CD-ReWritable

L-1 D 350. DAT — Digital Audio Tape

L-1 D 351 Mounting of an I/O device

Ans Assigning a drive letter to the device for Input output. After mounting a device, it becomes part of the file system

L-1 D 352. DIMM - Dual Inline Memory Modules

L-1 D 353. The disadvantage of Magnetic tape is

Ans Time taken to retrieve the required data because it uses sequential access.

L-1 D 354. CD-ROM stands for ——————————

Ans Compact Disk Read Only Memory

L-1 D 355. The most efficient way to connect peripheral devices to a system is through the use of I/O processors.

L-1 D 356. Com/serial ports are used for connective communication devices like modems or serial devices like mouse

L-1 D 357. Enable to enter drawing and sketches into a computer. it is also called tablet, digitizer, touch tablets, stylus

Ans Digitizing tablet

L-1 D 358. Character special files are used to model printers, modems, and other devices that accepts or output a character stream.

L-2 D 359. SCSI bus is used to connect devices which require

Ans Large bandwidth

L-2 D 360. A backed processor is used to handle data retrieval operations

L-2 D 361. The important characteristics of any device are its access mode, access time, transfer rate, capacity and cost

L-2 D 362. CD - The depressions in the polycarbonate substrate are called pits; the unburnt areas between the pits are called lands

L-2 D 363. Sending traffic through a device whereby the first packet received is the first packet transmitted. No priority is given accept the time of arrival of the packet

Ans First in First out

L-1 D 364. The electronic component in a I/O device is called

Ans Device Controller or Adapter

L-1 D 365. A Single USB port can be used to connect upto 127 peripheral devices

L-2 D 366. CD ROM have a Single continuous spiral containing the bits in a linear sequence

L-1 F 367. ———— is an external bus that supports plug and play installation

Ans Universal Serial Bus (USB)

L-2 F 368. A process for copying data from electronic media on computers onto microfilm — ————

Ans Computer Output Microfilm [COM]

L-1 M 369. Types of printers

A. Laser B. Dot matrix C. Inkjet D. faxJet

L-1 M 370. Which among the following is not the size of a floppy drive?

A. 6 inch B. 5.25 inch

L-1 M 371. Which among the following is not an output device?

A. Printer B. Monitor C. Scanner D. Mouse

E. Keyboard

L-1 S 372. Which is the most common output device?

A. Printer B. Monitor C. Hard disk D. Scanner

E. Tape Drive

L-1 S 373. ———— is an external bus standard that enables data transfer rates of upto 12Mbps

A. Serial port B. USB port

C. Com port D. None of the above

L-1 S 374. You can connect and disconnect devices that connect to ———— without shutting down or restarting your computer

A. IDE devices B. Universal serial

C. SCSI D. None of the above

L-2 S 375. The time interval between the instant at which a read/write command is given to a memory and the instant when the next instruction can be issued

A. Response time B. Cycle time C. Turnaround D. Throughput

L-1 S 376. Which among the following is an Input device?

A. Joystick B. Monitor C. Printer D. Plotter

L-1 S 377. CD-RW stands for

A. CD-Recordable B. CD-Reusuable

C. CD-Rewritable D. None of the above

L-1 S 378. Full form of USB is

A. Unified Serial Bus B. Universal Secondary Bus

C. Universal Serial Bus D. Unified Serial Base

L-1 S 379. Which is the reusable disk?

A. CD-ROM B. CD-R C. WORM D. CD-RW

L-1 S 380. The different types of input devices are

A. Keyboard B. Mouse C. Trackball D. All of the above

L-1 S 381. What is the function of a touch screen?

A. Output B. Processing C. Input D. All of the above

L-1 S 382. Which of the following is an impact device?

A. laser B. Ink-Jet

C. Dot-Matrix D. None of the above

L-1 S 383. Which of the following is a portable computer?

A. Laptops B. Subnotebooks C. PDAs D. All of the above

L-1 S 384. An input device used to convert graphic and pictorial data into binary, numeric inputs for a digital computer

A. Plotter B. Touchpad C. Scanner D. Digitizer

L-2 S 385. An input device that is used widely in supermarkets is

A. Scanner B. Mouse C. Trackball D. Bar code reader

L-2 S 386. Mostly, the minimum quantity of information which can be transferred is a ——

A. Byte B. Track C. Block D. Sector

L-1 T/F 387. Firewire interface is slower than USB 1.1

A. TRUE B. FALSE

L-2 T/F 388. CDROMs have concentric circles

A. TRUE B. FALSE

L-1 T/F 389. You can write data into RAM and read data from ROM

A. TRUE B. FALSE

L-1 T/F 390. A person can write by using a handwriting input device such as graphics tablet

A. TRUE B. FALSE

L-2 T/F 391. Character devices does not have "seek" operation

A. TRUE B. FALSE

L-2 T/F 392. The role of a Device controller is to convert the serial bit stream into a block of bytes and perform any error correction necessary

A. TRUE B. FALSE

Joystick

L-1 D 393. Joysticks are often used to control video games,

L-1 D 394. Joysticks are also used for CAD/CAM systems and other applications.

L-1 D 395. Modern joysticks (as of 2007) mostly use a USB interface for connection to the PC.

L-1 D 396. A joystick is similar to a mouse, except that with a mouse the cursor stops moving as soon as you stop moving the mouse.

L-1 D 397. Joystick Components: 1. Stick, 2. Base, 3. Trigger, 4. Extra buttons, 5. Autofire switch, 6. Throttle, 7. Hat Switch (POV Hat), 8. Suction Cup.

L-1 D 398. A joystick is an input device consisting of a stick that pivots on a base and reports its angle or direction to the device it is controlling

L-1 D 399. Similar to a mouse a joystick has 2 buttons. These are called triggers. The difference is that with a mouse the cursor stops moving as soon as you stop moving the mouse

L-1 D 400. A joystick is generally configured so that moving the stick left or right signals movement along the X axis, and moving it forward (up) or back (down) signals movement along the Y axis.

L-2 D 401. A hat switch is a control on some joysticks. It's also known as a Point of View switch (POV)

Ans Joystick

L-2 D 402. Additionally joysticks often have one or more fire buttons, used to trigger some kind of action.

L-1 S 403. Most joysticks include two buttons called ——————

Ans Buttons B. Triggers C. Lever D. Switch

L-1 S 404. A —————— is a cursor control device used mainly in computer games

Ans Keyboard B. Mouse C. Joystick D. None of the above

Keyboard

L-1 D 405. QWERTY Keyboard

Ans The first few letters of the first line containing the alphabets. They are used to identify any type of keyboard. QWERTY is a kind of keyboard

L-1 D 406. Computer keyboards have a numeric keypad to the right of the alphabetic keyboard.

L-1 D 407. A special key on a computer keyboard or a terminal device keyboard that is used to provide input to the computer

Ans Function Key

L-1 D 408. ____________ is the input device consisting of a set of keys that enable a user to enter data into a computer

Ans Keyboard

L-1 D 409. These keyboards use a continuous membrane that lies beneath the keys pattern printed in the membrane completes the circuit when a key is pressed.

Ans Membrane keyboard

L-1 D 410. The Enter/Return key typically causes a command line, window form or dialog box to operate its default function, which is typically to finish an "entry" and begin the desired process.

L-1 D 411. Metal contact and foam element keyboards less common these days have a spring-loaded key with a strip of metal on the bottom of the plunger. When the key is pressed, the metal strip connects the two parts of the circuit and thus a keypress

L-2 D 412. Modifier keys are special keys that modify the normal action of another key, when the two are pressed in combination.

L-2 D 413. Rubber dome switches use small, flexible rubber domes. The have a hard carbon center. When a key is pressed, a plunger on the bottom of the key pushes down against the dome, and the carbon center presses against a hard, flat surface and thus a keypress is recorded.

L-1 T/F 414. The interpretation of keypresses is done by the hardware

A. TRUE B. FALSE

L-1 T/F 415. Keyboard is the most used input device

A. TRUE B. FALSE

L-1 D 416. The Backspace key deletes the preceding character.

Laser Printer

L-2 D 417. A laser printer is a non-impact printer. It uses electricity, magnetism, optics, heat, chemistry and friction to print

L-2 D 418. Laser printers operate by operating a laser beam on a drum to produce an image on it. The drum is then rolled through a toner, and the electrically charged portions of the drum pick up ink.

L-1 T/F 419. Cost of printing in a laser printer is more than ink jet printer

A. TRUE B. FALSE

L-1 T/F 420. Laser printers make up entire page before printing it

A. TRUE B. FALSE

Light Pen

L-2 D 421 Light pen is an input device that utilizes a light-sensitive detector to select objects on a display screen.

L-2 D 422. A pen shaped device that is used as an input device to computers by writing or sketching on the screen of a cathode ray tube.

Magnetic Ink Character Recognition

L-1 D 423. MICR characters are printed with a magnetic ink or toner, usually containing iron oxide

L-1 D 424. MICR is usually pronounced My-ker. The last line on a check must always be printed in the MICR typeface using a special magnetic ink.

L-1 S 425. Each number or symbol occupies exactly ——— of an inch, but the actual numbers or symbols themselves have one of 5 different widths

A. 1/4 B. 1/8

C. 1/3 D. Each character is of separate width

L-1 S 426. MICR is mainly adopted by

A. Textile industries B. Iron industry C. Banking industry

D. Agriculture industry

L-1 T/F 427. MICR characters are not fixed in width

A. TRUE B. FALSE

L-1 T/F 428. Magnetic scanning is less accurate and reliable than optical character recognition

A. TRUE B. FALSE

Magnetic Tapes

L-1 D 429. Magnetic tape is a magnetically coated strip of plastic on which data can be encoded

L-1 T/F 430. Magnetic tapes are costlier than magnetic disks

A. TRUE B. FALSE

L-1 T/F 431. Magnetic tapes are slower than magnetic disks

A. TRUE B. FALSE

L-2 T/F 432. Magnetic tapes are examples of random access media

A. TRUE B. FALSE

Memory

L-1 D 433. Auxillary storage is long term, non volatile memory

L-1 D 434. Cache memory is placed between the CPU and main memory

L-1 S 435. ROM is

A. Read Only Memory B. Real Only Memory

C. Random Only Memory D. None of the above

L-2 S 436. The two types of auxillary storage devices are

A. Random and Sequential access B. MDIA and MIDI

C. VGA D. None of the above

L-2 S 437. —————— loses its contents when the computer is turned off

A. RAM B. ROM C. PROM D. EEPROM

L-1 S 438. RAM is

A. Permanent memory B. Non-volatile memory

C. Volatile Memory D. None of the above

L-2 S 439. The two types of RAM are

A. Volatile and non-volatile RAM B. Erasable and programmable

C. Static and Dynamic D. None of the above

L-1 T/F 440. Cache memory is

A. Volatile B. Non-volatile

L-1 T/F 441. CMOS is

A. Non-volatile

Memory

L-1 D 442. The storage in a digital computer which is directly under the control of the CPU. Each storage location is accessed using an address.

A. Internal storage

L-1 S 443. The most common auxillary memory devices used in computer systems are

A. Magnetic disks B. Magnetic tapes C. Main memory D. Flash drive

Memory Allocation

L-2 D 444. A portion of computer memory that can be allocated to a device

Ans Memory Address

L-2 D 445. A portion of memory that can be used by one process to pass information to another process.

Ans Named pipe

Memory Card

L-1 D 446 Intelligent Stick memory card, which can plug directly into a USB slot.

L-1 D 447. A magnetic card reader is a device used to scan cards containing magnetic data strips.

L-1 D 448. A memory card reader is a device used for communication with a smart card or a flash memory card.

L-1 D 449. A multi card reader is a device used for communication with more than one type of flash memory card.

L-2 D 450. A punched card reader is a device used to read holes in punched cardboard cards.

L-2 S 451. —————— are used in physical security systems to read a credential and providing access.

A. Credit card B. Access control

C. Debit card D. None of the above

L-1 T/F 452. A memory card reader may accept many types of memories

A. TRUE B. FALSE

L-1 T/F 453. A memory card reader typically is connected to a usb interface

A. TRUE B. FALSE

MICR

L-1 D 454. An MICR code is written on every cheque. This is used for electronic clearance of cheques.

L-1 S 455. MICR

A. Magnetic Ink Character Recognizer B. Magnetic Ink Character Reader

C. Magnetic Input Character Recorder D. None of the above

L-1 S 456. ———————— allows the computer to recognize characters printed using magnetic ink

A. OMR B. OCR C. BCR D. MICR

Microfiche

L-2 D 457. Microfiche is an output device that combines electronic, photo-optical, and electro-mechanical techniques to convert digital computer output to records that can be stored as rolls of microfilm or as frames of microfilm stored on cards called microfiche.

Ans Microfiche

Monitor

L-1 D 458. DIB

Ans Device Independent Bitmap

L-1 D 459. TFT is

Ans Thin Film Transistor

L-1 D 460. SVGA is

Ans Super Video Graphics Array

L-1 D 461. Graphics adapter

Ans Contains special memory called a video RAM, which forms part of the computer's address space and is addressed by the CPU the same way as the rest of the memory

L-1 D 462. Mono monitor means

Ans A black and white monitor.

L-1 D 463. Full form of LCD is

Ans Liquid Crystal Display

L-1 D 464. In the context of monitors, VGA is video graphics array

L-1 D 465. In the context of monitors, CGA colour graphics adapter

L-1 D 466. In the context of monitors, EGA enhanced graphics adapter

L-1 D 467. In the context of monitors, SVGA super video graphics adapter

L-1 D 468. Full page monitors are 16 inch + diagonally

L-1 D 469. Monitor is the display screen of a computer

L-1 D 470. Low-cost digital monitors are often called TTL monitors

L-1 D 471. 2 colours one for background and one for the foreground

Ans Monochrome

L-1 D 472. The number of colors per pixel a monitor and graphics adapter support.

Ans Color depth

L-1 D 473. A card that plugs into a personal computer to give it display capabilities

Ans Video adapter

L-1 D 474. The monitor cannot display graphics. It can display only letters, numbers etc.

Ans Character mode

L-1 D 475. The more bits per pixel, more colours and shades of gray the monitor can display

L-1 D 476. An I/O device which consists of a television-like screen for displaying outputs

Ans Video Display Unit (VDU)

L-1 D 477. A monitor is also known as a video display terminal VDT or visual display unit VDU

L-1 D 478. Given two monitors that offer the same resolution, the one with interlacing will be better

L-1 D 479. A gray-scale monitor is a special type of colour monitor capable of displaying different shadow of gray

L-1 D 480. Display devices that can accept and carry out commands such as drawing points, lines, geometric figures and text

Ans Vector graphics

L-1 D 481. The standard used to measure screen and printer resolution, expressed as the number of dots that a device can display or print per linear inch. The greater the number of dots per inch, the better the resolution

Ans Dots Per Inch (DPI)

L-2 D 482. Digital monitor

Ans Video monitor controlled by a computer circuit that retains settings and resolutions in memory. Subsequent changes in resolutions do not require adjustments. Most computer monitors today are digitally controlled, but still accept analog signals from the display adapter.

L-2 D 483. What is dot pitch?

Ans The distance between a red (or green or blue) dot and the closest red (or green or blue) dot on a color monitor. Also known as "pixel pitch." The smaller the dot pitch, measured in fractions of millimeters, the crisper the image.

L-2 D 484. Degauss a monitor means

Ans To remove unwanted magnetism from a monitor

L-2 D 485. On an LCD the resolution is fixed within each monitor

Ans Native resolution

L-2 D 486. Multi dimensional color space consisting of the red, green, and blue intensities that make up a given color.

Ans RGB Color space

L-2 D 487. A CRT have a electron beam that moves across the back of the screen. Each time the beam makes a pass across the screen, it lights up phosphor dots on the inside of the glass tube which is made of a fluorescent material, thereby illuminating the active portions of the screen

Ans Cathode Ray Tube

L-1 F 488. Picture elements is a ————

Ans Pixel

L-1 F 489. A display mode in which lines and characters on the screen are drawn pixel by pixel is known as ————

Ans Graphics Mode

L-1 S 490. Raster graphics are also known as

A. Vector graphics B. Bitmap graphics
C. Scalar graphics D. None of the above

L-1 S 491. On colour monitors, each pixel is composed of three dots — red, blue and

A. Orange B. Green C. White D. Black

L-2 S 492. CRT stands for ————

A. Critical Ray Tube B. Cathode Ray Tube
C. Cathode Resolution Tube D. Cathode Ray Table

L-2 S 493. Package density of the pixels in a monitor

A. Refresh rate B. Resolution
C. Pixel density D. None of the above

L-2 S 494. The chemical that is painted on the inside of the picture tube is

A. Sodium B. Phosphors
C. Invar D. None of the above

L-2 S 495 Indicates the vertical distance between each pixel on a display screen

A. Resolution B. Dot-pitch
C. Convergence D. None of the above

L-2 S 496. LCD displays use two sheets of ———— with a liquid crystal solution between them

A. Insulating material B. Polarizing mater
C. Charging material D. None of the above

L-2 S 497. The ―――――――― is number of times in a second that display hardware draws the data it is being given.

A. Dot pitch B. Refresh rate C. Resolution D. Frame rate

L-1 S 498. EGA stands for

A. Enhanced Graphics Adapter B. Extreme Graphics Adapter
C. Extra Graphics Adapter D. Enhanced Ground Adapter

L-1 S 499. XGA stands for ――――――――――――――

A. Extended Graphics Array B. Xtra Graphical Array
C. Extra Geometric Array D. Extended Geometric Array

L-1 S 500. The amount of information that appears on the screen, measured in pixels.

A. Screen resolution B. Dot pitch
C. Screensaver D. Refresh rate

L-1 S 501. A ―――――――― is the smallest element that display or print hardware and software can manipulate

A. Pixel B. Bit C. Inch D. Dot

L-1 S 502. The refresh rate of a monitor is measured in

A. Pixels B. Bits C. Hertz D. None of the above

L-1 S 503. How many times per second thė screen is to be refreshed?

A. Draw rate B. Raster rate C. Interlacing rate D. Refresh rate

L-1 S 504. Color monitors are sometimes called ―――――――― monitor

A. New monitors B. XYZ monitor
C. RGB monitor D. VIBGYOR monitor

L-1 S 505. ―――――――― are stored in files as bitmap images and are created by displaying a series of dots on the screen and on paper

A. Bitmap fonts B. Truetype fonts C. Raster fonts D. Picture fonts

L-2 S 506. No. of bits used to represent each pixel

A. Dot pitch B. Resolution C. Bit depth D. Pixel width

L-2 S 507. Vertical distance between each pixel on a display screen

A. Pixel depth B. Clarity C. Resolution D. Dot pitch

L-2 S 508. A metric of sharpness of an individual color pixel on a monitor

A. Resolution B. Dot pitch C. Clarity D. Convergence

L-2 S 509. What is the display technique that enables a monitor to provide more resolution inexpensively

A. Tuning B. Refreshing
C. Interlacing D. None of the above

L-1 T/F 510. VGA uses digital signals rather than analog signals

A. TRUE B. FALSE

L-1 T/F 511. Monochrome graphics adapter can display text as well as graphics

A. TRUE B. FALSE

L-1 T/F 512. CRT are lightweight and compact and have greater resolution than flat panel displays

A. TRUE B. FALSE

L-1 T/F 513. CRT are inexpensive but bulky and have limited resolution

A. TRUE B. FALSE

L-1 T/F 514 The most used output device is

A. Printer B. Flash drive C. Monitor D. Network

Motherboard

L-2 D 515. The video controller is located between the CPU and the monitor. It contains video dedicated memory and other circuitary necessary to send information to the monitor for display on the screen

Mouse

L-1 D 516. Optical mice have no mechanical moving parts

L-1 D 517. Mouse types — mechanical, optomechanical, optical

L-1 D 518. Mechanical mouse requires a special mousepad that have grids drawn on them

L-1 D 519. Mouse was invented by Douglas Engelbart of standard research center in 1963

L-1 D 520. Optical mice illuminate the surface that they track over, using an LED or a laser diode

L-1 D 521. The second mouse button is used to invoke a contextual menu in the computer's software user interface.

L-1 D 522. The laser mouse uses an infrared laser diode instead of an LED to illuminate the surface beneath their sensor

L-1 D 523. Unlike mechanical mice, which can become clogged with lint and dirt, optical mice have no rolling parts, therefore, they do not require maintenance other than removing debris that might collect under the light emitter

L-2 D 524. An optical mouse contains a a light-emitting diode and photodiodes to detect movement relative to the surface beneath the mouse.

L-2 D 525. The scroll wheel is different form of mouse-button, consists of a small wheel that the user can rotate to provide immediate one-dimensional input.

L-1 S 526. A pointing device that functions by detecting 2-dimensional motion relative to its supporting surface

A. Trackball B. Mouse

C. Both of the above D. None of the above

L-1 S 527. A hardware device used by the user to control the cursor

A. Touchpad B. Trackball

C. Mouse D. None of the above

L-1 S 528. The ball mouse utilizes two rollers rolling against two sides of the ball. One roller detects the forward-backward motion of the mouse and other the left-right motion.

A. Optical mouse B. Laser mouse

C. A Mechanical mouse D. None of the above

L-1 T/F 529. A mechanical mouse needs a special mousepad

A. TRUE B. FALSE

Optical Mark Reader

L-1 D 530. OMR optical mark sensor senses presence or absence of a mark such as a pencil mark

L-1 D 531. OMR systems approach one hundred percent accuracy and only take .005 seconds on average to recognize marks

L-1 F 532. ————is used in tests such as aptitude tests

Ans OMR

L-1 S 533. A device which read answers placed on a form

A. Optical character reader B. Optical mark reader

C. Scanner D. None of the above

L-1 T/F 534. The recognition engine is required in OMR as well as OCR

A. TRUE B. FALSE

Plotters

L-1 D 535. A plotter is a vector graphics printing device to print graphical plots.

L-1 D 536. The two basic types of plotters are called flatbed plotters and drum plotters

L-1 S 537. Any device used to draw charts, diagrams, and other line-based graphics.

A. Plotter B. Mouse C. Light pen D. Touch screen

Ports

L-1 T/F 538. Connecting through a parallel port is the fastest common transfer method.

A. TRUE B. FALSE

Printers

L-1 D 539. Print quality depends on dpi (Dots per inch) value of the printer

L-1 D 540. Downloaded font from disk to printers memory

Ans Soft font

L-1 D 541. What are thermal printers and how do they work?

Ans A thermal printer produces a printed image by selectively heating coated thermochromic paper when the paper passes over the thermal print head. The coating turns black in the areas where it is heated, producing an image.

L-1 D 542. The printer windows shows information about any pending print jobs

Ans Printer window

L-1 D 543. A printer that is directly connected to one of the ports of a computer.

Ans Local Printer

L-2 D 544. A print queue is a list of documents waiting to be printed on the printer

L-2 D 545. Printer Control Language (PCL) is a language that enables applications to control printers

L-2 D 546. ———— is the only process which have the permission to use the printers special file, to print the files in the directory

Ans Daemon

L-2 D 547. Solid Ink printers are page printers that use solid wax ink sticks in a "phase-change" process. They work by liquefying wax ink sticks into reservoirs, and then squirting the ink onto a transfer drum, from where it is cold-fused onto the paper as a single operation.

L-2 F 548. An example of a non-impact printer is ————

Ans Laser Printer

L-1 S 549. Examples of non impact printers

A. Laser B. Dot Matrix C. Ink-Jet D. All of the above

L-2 S 550. Documents are stored on a disk until a printer is ready to process them.

A. Buffering B. Storage

C. Spooling D. None of the above

L-2 T/F 551. Duplex printers prints on both sides of the paper at the same time

A. TRUE B. FALSE

L-2 T/F 552. In Inkjet and buble jet printers, the print head sprays drops of liquid ink onto the page

A. TRUE B. FALSE

L-1 D 553. In the context of printing, PPM is ———— and it is used to measure printing speed of a printer.

Ans Pages Per Minute.

L-1 D 554. Fonts that reside in the printer are known as

Ans Device fonts

L-1 D 555. A service on the print server that receives documents (print jobs) from Line Printer

Ans Line Printer Daemon (LPD)

L-1 D 556. Responsible for interacting with the printer driver and ensures that the jobs gets printed correctly

Ans Print processor

L-1 D 557. The input/output connector for a parallel interface device. Printers are generally plugged into a parallel port.

Ans Parallel port

L-1 D 558. A service on the print server that receives documents (print jobs) from Line Printer Remote (LPR) utilities running on client systems.

Ans Line Printer Daemon (LPD)

L-1 D 559. A laser printer is a page printer because the computer's operating system instructs it to print an entire page at a time, rather than a dot at a time

L-2 D 560. Line printer — printer that prints one line at a time.

L-2 D 561. Daisy wheel like a ball head typewriter cannot print graphics

L-2 D 562. In a draft quality printer, a character is formed by arranging dot to resemble it

L-2 D 563. Ink-jets (bubble-jets) printers spray ionized tiny drops of ink onto a page to create an image

L-2 D 564. Thermal printer produce image by pushing electrically heated pins against special heat sensitive papers

L-2 D 565. The purpose of the spooling software is to compensate for the speed differences between the computer and its peripheral devices

L-2 D 566. Both LCD (liquid crystal display) and LED (light emitting diode) printers use a light source instead of a laser to create an image on a drum.

L-2 D 567. Virtual memory in printers

Ans A portion of the physical RAM installed in the printer. It is different from RAM or virtual memory on hard disk of the system

L-2 F 568. The part of memory that stores font information in a postscript printer

Ans Virtual printer memory

L-2 F 569. The memory in PostScript printers is divided into two areas banded memory and

Ans Virtual memory

L-1 M 570. Examples of impact printers are

A. Dmp B. Daisy wheel C. Ink jet D. Line

E. Laser

L-1 M 571. The different types of printers are

A. Daisy wheel B. Dot-matrix

C. Laser and ink-jet D. None of the above

L-1 S 572. It is used as a metric for printer speed

A. RPM B. PPM

C. IPM D. None of the above

L-1 S 573. A printer which has a band on which the characters are embossed. The band rotates at a high, speed and print heads are activated to print characters.

A. Ink-jet printer B. Chain printer C. Dot matrix print D. Plotter

L-1 T/F 574. Line printers can print graphics

A. TRUE B. FALSE

L-1 T/F 575. Color laser printers cannot be used as a regular black and white laser printer.

A. TRUE B. FALSE

L-2 T/F 576. Daisy wheel printers can print graphics

A. TRUE B. FALSE

Processor

L-1 D 577. There are 2 main types of slots for connecting to the motherboard socket 7 and slot 1

L-2 M 578. These companies manufacture processors

A. Intel B. AMD C. Intex D. Microsoft

Programming

L-1 D 579. A computer instruction is a binary code that specifies a sequence of microoperations for the computer

Scanner

L-1 D 580. To edit text read by an optical scanner, an optical character recognition (OCR) system is required

L-1 D 581. Each pixel requires 24 bits to create standard true color and virtually all scanners on the market support this.

L-2 D 582. Evaluation criteria of a scanner includes a metric known as pixels per inch (ppi)

L-2 D 583. Drum scanners capture image information with photomultiplier tubes (PMT)

L-2 D 584. Infrared cleaning is a technique used to remove dust and scratches from film

L-2 D 585. Bit mapped devices allow each individual pixel on the screen to be controlled by the computer.

L-2 D 586. Color depth varies depending on the scanning array characteristics, but is usually at least 24 bits.

L-2 D 587. Handheld scanners are useful for quickly capturing text. These scanners does not provide good image quality.

L-2 D 588. Modern scanners typically use a charge-coupled device (CCD) or a Contact Image Sensor (CIS) as the image sensor.

L-2 D 589. The lamp in scanners can be a cold cathode fluorescent lamp (CCFL), a xenon lamp or a standard fluorescent lamp

L-2 D 590. A high density range means that the scanner is able to reproduce shadow details and brightness details in one scan.

L-2 D 591. Document scanners have document feeders, usually larger than those sometimes found on copiers or all-purpose scanners.

L-2 D 592. Drum scanners are used by the publishing industry to capture incredibly detailed images. They use a technology called a photomultiplier tube (PMT)

L-2 D 593. An application accesssing a scanner does not need to know the specific details of it. This is possible because an api presents a uniform interface to the scanner.

L-2 D 594. Most scanners speak a common language known as ——————. It acts as an interpreter between any application that supports its driver standard and the scanner.

Ans TWAIN

L-2 D 595. The core component of a scanner is the CCD array. It is a collection of tiny light-sensitive diodes, which convert photons (light) into electrons (electrical charge).

L-1 F 596. ________________ is a process that the scanning software uses to increase the normally apparent resolution of an image.

Ans Interpolation

L-2 F 597. Most commonly used scanners are ________________

Ans Flatbed scanners

L-2 F 598. ________________ is the number of colors that the scanner is capable of reproducing on screen

Ans Bit depth or color depth

L-2 F 599. An scanner's true resolution is known as optical resolution. But manufacturers show ________________, achieved via software as the resolution power of the scanner

A. Interpolated resolution

L-1 M 600. A scanner in which the document is placed on a glass window for scanning

A. Hand held B. Desktop
C. Flat bed D. None of the above

L-1 M 601. In addition to the scanning utility, these softwares are also usually supplied with the scanner

A. Optical character recognition B. Excel
C. Photoshop D. Accounting

L-1 S 602. The device which is used to input images into the computer is

A. Mouse B. Scanner
C. Joystick D. None of the above

L-1 S 603. An input device which can read text or graphics printed on a paper and transit it into a form a computer can use

A. Bar code reader B. Plotter
C. Graphics tablet D. Scanner

L-1 T/F 604. Scanned image of a text page is not editable

A. TRUE B. FALSE

L-1 T/F 605. In sheet fed scanners, the scan head is mobile

A. TRUE B. FALSE

L-2 T/F 606. Handheld scanners provide better image quality in comparison to flat bed scanners

A. TRUE B. FALSE

L-2 T/F 607. Most scanners use the TWAIN API

A. TRUE B. FALSE

L-2 T/F 608. Flatbed scanners are also known as desktop scanners

A. TRUE B. FALSE

Sound card

L-1 D 609. A sound file contains information that Windows uses to play sounds on your computer. Extension of sound files is .wav.

L-1 T/F 610. A sound card can only play sound it cannot record audio

A. TRUE B. FALSE

Touch screen

L-1 D 611. A type of display screen that has a touch-sensitive transparent panel covering the screen and is used as an input device as well as output device

Ans Touchscreen

L-2 D 612. In a touch screen, there is a microwave beam emanating from the bottom and the side of the screen, When a user presses a finger on the screen, the infrared beam is broken at an intersection point of microwave beam from the side and bottom of the screen. This intersection point denotes the location of the touch and is used to determine the input

Touchpad

L-2 S 613. The special screen where we input information by touching the screen is

A. Touch pad B. Touch screen

C. Mouse mat D. None of the above

L-2 S 614. The input device that uses a light sensitive detector to select objects on a display screen is

A. Touch pad B. Light pen

C. Touch screen D. None of the above

L-2 S 615. Pointing device used in portable computers. It is a small sensitive pad.

A. Touch pad B. Touch screen

C. Mouse mat D. None of the above

Trackball

L-1 D 616. A trackball takes more space to use it than a mouse.

L-1 D 617. Trackball is a pointing device

L-1 D 618. A pointing device. Essentially, a trackball is a mouse lying on its back.

L-1 D 619. People with a mobility impairment use trackballs as an assistive technology input device.

L-1 S 620. The cursor is moved by the thumb and fingers and the device is held on the palm.

A. Trackball B. Touch ball C. Mouse D. Touch screen

L-1 T/F 621. A trackball is a pointing device.

A. TRUE B. FALSE

Types of computers

L-2 F 622. RISC is ______________

Ans Reduced Instruction Set Computer

L-2 F 623. CISC is ______________

Ans Complex Instruction Set Computer

Webcam

L-1 D 624. Video capturing devices connected to computers
Ans Webcam

L-1 D 625. They combine a camera and a VCR or other recording device in one unit.
Ans Camcorders

L-1 D 626. For streaming video, the camera should take atleast 15 frames per second
Ans Webcam

L-1 D 627. A video camera is a camera used for electronic motion picture acquisition

L-1 D 628. A simple Webcam setup consists of a digital camera attached to a computer

L-1 D 629. Webcams typically include a lens, an image sensor, and some support electronics

L-1 D 630. In a webcam there is an aperture or iris to regulate the exposure and to control depth of field.

L-1 D 631. ____________ indicates the number of pictures the software can grab and transfer in one second
Ans Frame Rate

L-1 D 632. This Axis camera can be connected directly to a network or the Internet, via an RJ45 connector on its rear

L-1 D 633. Closed circuit television cameras are generally used for security and surveillance as well as for monitoring purposes

L-1 D 634. Digital cameras convert the signal directly to a digital output; are smaller than CCTV security cameras, and are often used as webcams

L-2 D 635. An archive can be created that saves all of your Webcam images or only certain images at pre-set intervals.
Ans Image Archiving

L-2 M 636. A Camcorders has 3 major components
A. Imager B. Disk C. Lens D. Recorder

L-2 S 637. The webcam takes a new picture when it detects motion. This is known as
A. Buzz effect B. Motion sensing C. Photograph programing
D. Sensors

L-1 T/F 638. Videoconferencing cannot be done using webcam
A. TRUE B. FALSE

L-1 T/F 639. Some instant messenger softwares support webcam
A. TRUE B. FALSE

Zip Disk

L-1 T/F 640. Capacity of a Zip disk is about 100 MB
A. TRUE B. FALSE

Answers

Q. No.	Answer	Q. No.	Answer
15	A	252	A B D
19	B	253	A B C
21	A	254	A B
26	B	255	A B E
27	B	256	B D
28	B	257	B C E
29	B	258	B C
37	A C	259	B D
38	C	260	A C D
39	A	261	A C D
40	B	262	C
66	A B C	263	A B D
67	B	264	A B C E
68	B	265	B
69	B	266	B
70	B	267	B
71	B	268	B
72	B	269	B
73	A	270	B
74	A	271	B
75	A	272	B
76	A	273	B
77	C	274	B
78	C	275	B
79	C	276	B
80	D	277	B
81	B	278	B
82	B	279	B
83	B	280	A
84	B	281	A
85	A	282	A
86	A	283	A
87	A	284	A
250	A B C	285	A
251	A B D	286	A

Q. No.	Answer	Q. No.	Answer
287	A	324	B
288	A	325	B
289	A D	326	B
290	A	327	B
291	A	328	B
292	A	329	B
293	A	330	B
294	A	331	B
295	A	332	B
296	A	333	A
297	D	334	A
298	D	335	A
299	C	336	A
300	C	337	A
301	D	338	B
302	C	339	A
303	C	340	A
304	D	341	A
305	D	342	A
306	D	343	A
307	C	344	A
308	C	345	A
309	C	346	B
310	D	369	A B C
311	D	370	A
312	C	371	C D
313	C	372	B
314	A	373	B
315	A	374	B
317	B	375	B
318	B	376	A
319	B	377	C
320	B	378	C
321	B	379	D
322	B	380	D
323	B	381	C

Q. No.	Answer	Q. No.	Answer
382	C	456	D
383	D	490	B
384	D	491	B
385	D	492	B
386	D	493	B
387	B	494	B
388	B	495	B
389	A	496	B
390	A	497	B
391	A	498	A
392	A	499	A
403	B	500	A
404	C	501	A
414	B	502	C
415	A	503	D
419	B	504	C
420	A	505	C
425	B	506	C
426	C	507	D
427	B	508	D
428	B	509	C
430	B	510	B
431	A	511	B
432	B	512	B
435	A	513	A
436	A	514	C
437	A	526	B
438	C	527	C
439	C	528	C
440	A	529	A
441	A	533	B
443	A	534	B
451	B	537	A
452	A	538	B
453	A	549	A C
455	A	550	C

Q. No.	Answer	Q. No.	Answer
551	A	606	B
552	A	607	A
570	A B D	608	A
571	A B C	610	B
572	B	613	B
573	B	614	B
574	B	615	A
575	B	620	A
576	B	621	A
578	A B	636	A C D
600	C	637	B
601	A C	638	B
602	B	639	A
603	D	640	A
604	B		
605	B		

3

INTERNET

Address Resolution Protocol

L-2 M 1. ————————— searching of table is done in table lookup method of address resolution protocol.

A. Sequentially B. Using hash C. Using Indexing D. Inverted

Communication

L-2 D 2. The integration of Windows NetMeeting with Microsoft Office allows you to share and make changes to a document with people at different sites in real time.

Ans Online meetings

L-1 M 3. Using Yahoo messenger we can

A. Text chat B. Blog

C. Voice Chat D. None of the above

L-1 S 4: Yahoo messenger is used for

A. Instant Chat B. Email

C. Gaming D. Software development

E-Commerce

L-1 D 5. Electronic Wallet

Ans Instead of giving credit card number every time a payment has to be made, electronic wallets allows to store the credit card information in encrypted form and access it easily and securely

L-1 D 6. The business to business kind of e commerce refers to a company selling to or buying from other companies

L-1 D 7. What is electronic commerce?

A. E-commerce (electronic commerce or EC) is the buying and selling of goods and services on the Internet, especially the World Wide Web

L-1 D 8 What is business to business e commerce?

A. Companies doing business with each other such as manufacturers selling to distributors and wholesalers selling to retailers. Pricing is based on quantity of order and is often negotiable.

L-1 D 9. What is business to customer e commerce?

A. Businesses selling to the general public typically through catalogs utilizing shopping cart software. By volume and value, B2B is greater.

L-2 D 10. Digital cash is a series of secure numbers. These digits mean real cash to insuing banks.

L-1 D 11. What is consumer to business e commerce?

A. A consumer posts his project with a set budget online and within hours companies review the consumer's requirements and bid on the project. The consumer reviews the bids and selects the company that will complete the project.

L-1 D 12. What is consumer to consumer e commerce?

A. There are many sites offering free classifieds, auctions, and forums where individuals can buy and sell and use online payment options, Eg., E-bay auction site

L-1 M 13. What are different types of electronic commerce?

A. B2B B. B2C C. C2B D. A2C

E. C2C

Email

L-1 D 14. In the context of email, CC means

Ans Carbon Copy

L-1 D 15. List of contacts in a email client is known as a ____________

Ans Address book

L-1 D 16. Why we should use email?

Ans To send and receive messages

L-1 D 17. What is a file attachment?

Ans An attachment is a text, image or any other file which is sent within an email

L-1 D 18. What are email service providers?

Ans Companies which provide email services to the users who register with them, e.g., Hotmail, gmail. Yahoo etc.

L-1 D 19. What is email forwarding service?

Ans Sending a received mail to other user(s)

L-1 D 20. What is a mail enabled application?

Ans An application which could be used to send email messages

L-1 D 21. What is the structure of an email address?

Ans name@server-name.com

L-1 D 22. What is an address book ? What is its advantage?

Ans Contact information of acquitances are stored in the address book. This information can be received later.

L-1 D 23. ——— identifies a person for the purpose of exchanging mail messages

Ans Email address

L-1 D 24. In its simplest form, a mail enabled application is a windows program that has a "Send" command in the "File" menu

L-2 D 25. MIME

Ans Multipurpse Internet Mail Exploration

L-2 D 26. Post office protocol

Ans An application-layer protocol used by local email clients to retrieve e-mail from a remote server over a TCP/IP connection. Other such protocol is IMAP (Internet Message Access Protocol)

L-1 M 27. Name some email service providers

A. Yahoo B. Hotmail C. IN D. Snail
E. Times of India

L-1 S 28. One way of protecting the email message is

A. Caching B. Encryption C. Mirroring D. Shadowing

L-1 S 29. ——————— is an electronic message sent from one computer to another

A. M-mail B. E-mail C. Snail mail D. Telegram

L-2 S 30. The default priority of an email message is

A. High B. Normal C. Low D. None

L-2 S 31. A mailing list is a way to share information via ———————

A. Instant message B. Email
C. Blog D. None of the above

L-1 S 32. BCC means

A. Blind Carbon Copy B. Barred Carbon Copy
C. Blind Console Copy D. None of the above

L-1 S 33. Junk mails usually reaches to ——— folder

A. Spam B. Inbox C. Outbox D. Compose

L-1 S 34. In a@yahoo.com ——— is yahoo id

A. a@yahoo.com B. yahoo C. a D. com

L-1 S 35. ——————— is an email program that lets a user exchange mail.

A. Pop B. Internet explorer C. Outlook express D. Email

L-1 S 36. Among the following, ——————— does not provide web email services

A. Yahoo B. Hotmail C. Compaq D. Indiatimes

L-1 S 37. In an email system, ——— allows to store the information about people

A. Index B. Folders
C. Address Book D. None of the above

L-1 S 38. If we have to send an email to many addresses at once, we type those addresses separated by

A. Full stop B. Dash C. Hypen D. Comma

L-1 S 39. If we have to send a text file or a picture with the email message we have to —— ——— those files with the email message

A. Link B. Bind C. Attach D. Hook

L-1 T/F 40. One can send an email to many users simultaneously

A. TRUE B. FALSE

L-1 T/F 41. Email messages can be personalised by using emoticons and smileys.

A. TRUE B. FALSE

L-1 T/F 42. In addition ot the default folders in email, new folders can also be created.

A. TRUE B. FALSE

L-2 T/F 43. One can search emails stored in selected folders at once

A. TRUE B. FALSE

L-2 T/F 44. You can set priority to a mail message that you are sending

A. TRUE B. FALSE

L-2 T/F 45. Most email service providers automatically blocks malicious content

A. TRUE B. FALSE

L-2 T/F 46. In yahoo mail, messages can be typed as rich text as well as plain text

A. TRUE B. FALSE

L-2 T/F 47. The recipients mentioned in "To" do not know that the recepients metioned in "Bcc" also received the email

A. TRUE B. FALSE

L-2 T/F 48. Store the information that you want to attach at the end of the messages as your — ————————————

Ans Signature

General

L-1 D 49. Full form of WWW

Ans World Wide Web

L-1 D 50. What is extranet?

Ans An extranet is a private network that uses Internet technology and the public telecommunication system to securely share part of a business's information or operations with suppliers, vendors, partners, customers, or other businesses. An extranet can be viewed as part of a company's intranet that is extended to users outside the company

L-1 D 51. What is internet?

Ans Is a network of networks. The constituent networks are heterogeneous

L-1 D 52. What is signature ?

Ans The text which is written after a message usually in a email to identify the sender

L-1 D 53. What are emoticons?

Ans Small animated icons which one can send in a chat message or in a email message

L-1 D 54. What are newsgroups?

Ans A newsgroup is a place (website) on the internet where people can exchange information and ideas in a special forum or area.

L-1 D 55. What are search engines?

Ans Website that provides the service to search for webpages containing information relating to a particular topic.

L-1 D 56. What is a web-enabled application?

Ans Any application program which can be run over a network using usually an internet Web browsers.

L-1 D 57. What are benefits of using hypermedia?

Ans Many media in one, one can jump from a page to another and does'nt have to access pages sequentially

L-1 D 58. TurboGopher is a Gopher client application

L-1 D 59. What are mailing lists ? How do they work?

Ans Mailing lists are websites which are used to post and see messages which would be visible to every other user registered with the website. They are used to organize discussions on topics of group interest and sending to messages to every one registered.

L-1 D 60. What is difference between Intranet and internet?

Ans Internet is a global network and intranet limits to an organization

L-1 D 61. A protocol used to transfer information on the www.

Ans Hyper Text Transfer Protocol (HTTP)

L-1 D 62. What are hypertext links? And where they are used?

Ans Hypertext links or hyperlinks are text or image which when clicked opens the webpage or file specified under that link. Hyperlinks are used in webpages so that a user can open a web page and surf across websites

L-1 D 63. Hypertext includes text, images, videos, graphics etc.

L-1 D 64. What are the advantages of mail-enabled applications?

Ans A document created in a mail enabled application can be sent directly from within the application

L-1 D 65. A simple markup language used to create hyper text documents.

Ans Hyper text Markup Language (HTML)

L-1 D 66. Followed hyperlinks appear as purple and underlined by default.

L-1 D 67. A company that provides access to the Internet and the World Wide Web.

Ans Internet service provider (ISP)

L-1 D 68. The process of stabilizing a system after changes occur in the network

Ans Convergence

L-1 D 69. Two or more network segments connected by routers. Another term for internetwork.

Ans internet

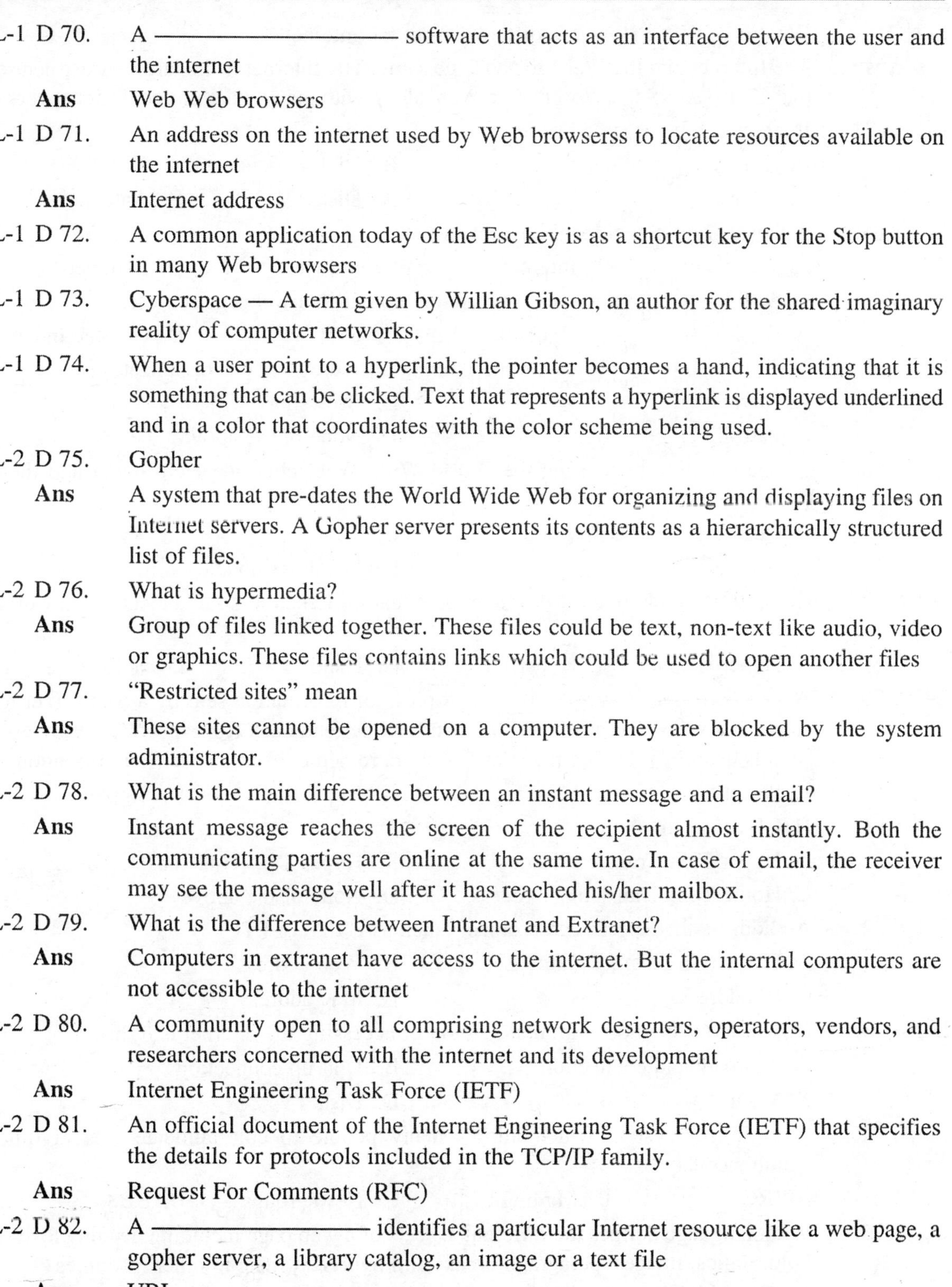

L-1 D 70. A —————————— software that acts as an interface between the user and the internet

Ans Web Web browsers

L-1 D 71. An address on the internet used by Web browserss to locate resources available on the internet

Ans Internet address

L-1 D 72. A common application today of the Esc key is as a shortcut key for the Stop button in many Web browsers

L-1 D 73. Cyberspace — A term given by Willian Gibson, an author for the shared imaginary reality of computer networks.

L-1 D 74. When a user point to a hyperlink, the pointer becomes a hand, indicating that it is something that can be clicked. Text that represents a hyperlink is displayed underlined and in a color that coordinates with the color scheme being used.

L-2 D 75. Gopher

Ans A system that pre-dates the World Wide Web for organizing and displaying files on Internet servers. A Gopher server presents its contents as a hierarchically structured list of files.

L-2 D 76. What is hypermedia?

Ans Group of files linked together. These files could be text, non-text like audio, video or graphics. These files contains links which could be used to open another files

L-2 D 77. "Restricted sites" mean

Ans These sites cannot be opened on a computer. They are blocked by the system administrator.

L-2 D 78. What is the main difference between an instant message and a email?

Ans Instant message reaches the screen of the recipient almost instantly. Both the communicating parties are online at the same time. In case of email, the receiver may see the message well after it has reached his/her mailbox.

L-2 D 79. What is the difference between Intranet and Extranet?

Ans Computers in extranet have access to the internet. But the internal computers are not accessible to the internet

L-2 D 80. A community open to all comprising network designers, operators, vendors, and researchers concerned with the internet and its development

Ans Internet Engineering Task Force (IETF)

L-2 D 81. An official document of the Internet Engineering Task Force (IETF) that specifies the details for protocols included in the TCP/IP family.

Ans Request For Comments (RFC)

L-2 D 82. A —————————— identifies a particular Internet resource like a web page, a gopher server, a library catalog, an image or a text file

Ans URL

L-3 D 83. What is WWW? How it is different from the internet?

Ans The Internet and the Web are NOT the same. The Internet is the large infrastructure that CONTAINS the World Wide Web, along with many other protocol subnetworks

L-1 M 84. Internet can be accessed using

A. A broadband connection B. Dial-up connection
C. V-sat D. Dish-TV E. Antenna

L-1 S 85. A world wide networks of computers

A. World net B. Internet C. Intranet D. Extranet

L-1 S 86. Underlined text or some text in different colour in a webpage represents

A. Bookmarks B. Hyper Text Links C. FTP D. Graphic Images

L-1 S 87. Visiting different websites on the Internet hosted by various organizations.

A. Navigation B. Browsing
C. Patrolling D. None of the above

L-1 S 88. To learn more about using the World Wide Web, click the Help menu and then click

A. Customer feedback option B. Tour
C. About us D. Windows update

L-1 S 89. Colored and underlined text or a graphic that is clicked to go to a location on world wide web

A. Hyperterminal B. Hyperlink C. Hand D. Network

L-2 S 90. A —————————— is a small piece of information sent by a web server to store on a web Web browsers so it can later be read back from that Web browsers. This is useful for having the Web browsers remember some specific information

A. Script B. Cookie C. Batch file D. Snippet

L-1 S 91. HTTP refers to

A. Hyper Text Transfer Protocol B. Hyper Text Transfer Procedure
C. Home Text Translating Process D. None of the above

L-1 S 92. An address that specifies a protocol (such as HTTP or FTP)

A. URLs (Uniform Resource Locator) B. Web address
C. IP address D. Mac address

L-1 S 93. Now-a-days the most common method of accessing the internet is by using

A. A broadband connection B. Dial-up connection
C. V-sat D. Dish-TV

L-1 S 94. A multiuser system which allows many people to communicate in real time simultaneously

A. IRC B. Mailing List C. Newsgroups D. BBSs

L-1 S 95. What language defines the different aspects of a web page including heading levels, bold, italics, images, paragraph breaks and hypertext links to other resources?

A. HTML B. HTRL C. HTTL D. HTPL

L-2 S 96. ———————— refers to the number of times the condition of the line changes. This is equal to bits per second only if each signal corresponds to one bit of transmitted data.

A. Band rate B. Bit rate C. BPS D. KBPS

L-1 S 97. "At the rate of" is

A. # B. % C. & D. @

L-1 S 98. What is netscape ?

A. Is an antivirus B. Is a system file

C. Is a internet Web browser D. Is a disk manager

L-1 S 99. The owner of internet is

A. Microsoft B. Sun C. No body owns internet

D. Oracle

L-1 S 100. To open a website ———— program is used

A. Windows Explorer B. FTP Client

C. Internet Explorer D. All of the above

L-1 S 101. ———————— are virtual locations on IRC networks where users meet to talk to one another

A. Web space B. WWW

C. Chat rooms D. None of the above

L-1 S 102. ———————— files are simple text files with codes embedded to denote formatting and hypertext links

A. FTP B. HTTP

C. HTML D. None of the above

L-1 D 103. With the introduction of the Internet, organization can communicate with each other irrespective of the size and type of internal network they have

L-1 T/F 104. HTML documents are not portable in terms of the operating system

A. TRUE B. FALSE

L-2 T/F 105. The '.com' extension in a website address indicates that the website belongs to an educational institution

A. TRUE B. FALSE

L-1 T/F 106. If we click on a hyperlink on a word document, internet explorer is opened and the url on the hyperlink is displayed

A. TRUE B. FALSE

Instant Messenger

L-1 D 107. Full form of IRC

Ans Internet Relay Chat

L-1 D 108. An ———————— lets a user communicate with people from all over the world, in real-time

Ans Instant messenger

Internet

L-1 D 109. Public discussion forums where the participants post their messages to be seen by all readers of the newsgroup

Ans Newsgroups

L-1 S 110. User-friendly view of the internet through the use of many protocols is

Ans A. Telnet B. HTTP C. FTP D. WWW

L-1 S 111. WWW is

Ans World Wide Web

L-1 T/F 112. Multimedia cannot be used in WWW

A. TRUE B. FALSE

Internet Explorer

L-2 D 113. Record of all the webpages visited

Ans Log

Internet Explorer

L-1 D 114. Marquee

Ans The marquee tag is a non-standard HTML markup element type which causes text to scroll up, down, left or right

L-1 D 115. In internet explorer, Refresh button is pressed to

Ans Reload a page

L-1 D 116. Home page of internet explorer means

Ans When internet explorer is opened, it tries to display the document as per the URL specified as home page

L-1 D 117. We can set a webpage as home page by

Ans Tools → Internet Options → General → Home page

L-1 D 118. To view the source code of a web page

Ans View → Source code

L-1 D 119. Working offline in the internet explorer

Ans means that user's system is not connected to the internet and he/she is viewing locally stored copy of pages that where visited previously

L-1 D 120. "Home page" of the internet explorer means

Ans When internet explorer is opened, the home page is the page that appears by default

L-1 D 121. To increase/decrease text size in the internet explorer window

Ans View → Text size

L-1 D 122. Internet security properties can be quickly accessed by double clicking

Ans Internet/local internet icon appearing on the status bar

L-1 D 123. To see how any Web page was coded, right-click in the page, and then click

Ans View Source

L-1 D 124. If you use Netscape, you can learn about differences in Internet Explorer by clicking the Help menu and then clicking

Ans For Netscape Users

L-1 D 125. It is usually located at the bottom of a window. It's a line of information related to the current program. Not all windows have it.

Ans Status bar

L-2 D 126. Security levels in Internet Explorer

Ans Medium, medium high, high. Low security levels which defines the kind of protection a system while browsing the internet

L-2 D 127. View→ Encoding

Ans Most web pages contain information that tells the web browsers what language and character set to use when displaying the page. This type of information is referred to as language encoding. Internet Explorer can usually determine the correct language encoding, even if the webpage does not include language encoding information.

L-2 D 128. Advanced tab of internet properties of the internet explorer has.

Ans Accessibility options, java options, security options etc.

L-2 D 129. What are helper applications and why are they important?

Ans A helper application is an external viewer program launched to display content retrieved using a web Web browsers. E.g. Windows Media Player for playing streaming content. Unlike a plugin (whose full code is included into Web browsers code), a small line is added to the Web browsers code to tell it to open a certain helper application in case it encounters a certain file format.

L-2 D 130. There are ——— content zones in the security tab of the Internet properties

Ans 4

L-2 D 131. There are ——— security levels specified in security settings of the internet explorer

Ans 4

L-2 D 132. Install more Internet Explorer components by clicking the Tools menu and then clicking

Ans Windows Update

L-2 D 133. Quickly put a shortcut to any Web page on your desktop by right-clicking in the page and then clicking

Ans Create Shortcut

L-1 D 134. Home page of a website means

Ans The first page that appears when the site is opened by using its basic address

L-2 F 135. "Accessability" settings can be accessed using ——— tab of the internet properties

Ans General

L-2 M 136. "Internet Properties" can be accessed using

A. Internet explorer B. Control Panel C. www.internet.com D. Modem

L-2 M 137. Security levels in the security settings of the internet explorer

A. High B. Medium C. Medium-low D. Low
E. Very High

L-1 M 138. In the Address bar, quickly move the cursor between parts of the address by pressing

A. CTRL+LEFT ARROW B. Winkey + D
C. Escape D. CTRL+RIGHT ARROW

L-1 S 139. Cookies can be deleted using ———— tab of the internet properties

A. General B. Programs C. Connections D. L-3

L-1 S 140. "Language" settings can be accessed using ———— tab of the internet properties

A. Connections B. General C. L-3 D. Privacy

L-1 S 141. We can save the links and latter use them to quickly open mostly visited pages/ websites using

A. History B. Favourites C. Quick launch D. Links

L-2 S 142. To set ratings that help control the internet content that can be viewed on a computer

A. Content Utility B. Content Advisor C. Set Restriction D. All of the above

L-2 S 143. ———— set up how windows connects to windows update for drivers.

A. Win connect B. Windows update
C. Security center D. None of the above

L-2 S 144. "Certificate" settings can be accessed using ———— tab of the internet properties

A. General B. Content C. Privacy D. L-3

L-2 S 145. If there are error(s) in the scripts written in the web page, the error indication appears

A. Via a message box B. On the status bar
C. On the title bar D. None of the above

L-2 S 146. The ———— option on the tools menu of the internet explorer updates all offline content

A. Windows messenger B. Synchronize
C. Windows update D. Options

L-1 S 147. "Show the Tools menu (Tools button)

A. ALT+L B. Ctrl+T C. ALT+7 D. Alt+T

L-1 S 148. The cross icon in the toolbar of internet explorer is used to

A. Stop the loading of a page B. Close the intern
C. Do nothing D. None of the above

L-1 S 149. Current window of the internet explorer can be closed by using ———— keys

A. Ctrl+W B. Ctrl+X C. Alt+W D. Alt+X

L-1 S 150. We can set the font for the internet explorer using ———— tab of the internet properties dialog box

A. General B. Content C. Privacy D. L-3

E. Connect-ions

L-2 S 151. To display a list of the Internet addresses already typed in the Address bar,

A. press F4. B. press F5 C. press F1 D. press Ctrl+H

L-2 S 152. Add-ons of internet explorer could be managed using manage add-ons option in the

A. Tools menu B. File C. View D. Help

L-2 S 153. To change setting for pop-up blocker we can use the pop-up blocker menu on the ———— menu of the internet explorer

A. Tools B. File C. Help D. View

L-1 S 154. A web page can be refreshed by using ———— function key

A. F10 B. F1 C. Esc D. F5

L-1 S 155. ———— are used to access pages of the world wide web

A. Control Panel B. Word

C. Command pro D. Internet explorer

L-1 S 156. The bar that appears in the bottom of the internet explorer window is

A. Toolbar B. Quick bar C. Status bar D. Navigation bar

L-1 S 157. In internet explorer press ———— to view the website in full screen

A. F10 B. F1 C. F11 D. F12

L-1 S 158. "Temporary Internet files" can be deleted using ———— tab of the internet properties

A. L-3 B. Privacy C. Programs D. General

L-1 S 159. "Home page" settings of the internet explorer can be accessed using ———— tab of the internet properties

A. Programs B. Privacy C. General D. Contents

L-2 S 160. Tip of the day option is located in ———— of the internet explorer

A. View B. File C. Help menu D. Favourites

L-2 S 161. "Color" settings can be accessed using ———— tab of the internet properties

A. Content B. L-3 C. General D. Privacy

L-2 S 162. Sun java console could be accessed from the ———— menu of the internet explorer

A. View B. File C. Help D. Tools

L-2 S 163. Windows update option could be accessed from ———— menu of the internet explorer

A. File B. View C. Tools D. Update

L-2 S 164. "Autocomplete" settings can be accessed using ———— tab of the internet properties

A. Privacy B. L-3 C. General D. Content

L-2 S 165. Version of the internet explorer can be seen from ———— → ———— of the internet explorer

A. File → Properties B. Tools → Internet
C. Help → about D. View → Enconding

L-2 S 166. Updates the network copy of materials that were edited offline such as documents, calendar and email messages

A. Windows messenger B. Copy
C. Windows update D. Synchronize

L-2 T/F 167. One cannot block any website on a particular system

A. TRUE B. FALSE

L-2 T/F 168. Preventing Pop-ups from appearing when a particular site loads could be done

A. TRUE B. FALSE

Programming

L-1 D 169. What is a script?

Ans A script is a program or sequence of instructions that is interpreted or carried out by another program.

L-1 D 170. A container that can be resized and positioned anywhere on the page

Ans Frame

Security

L-1 D 171. What is a spam?

Ans Spam is flooding the Internet with many copies of the same message, in an attempt to force the message on people who would not otherwise choose to receive it. Most spam is commercial advertising, often for dubious products.

L-2 D 172. Cipher strength being used by the internet explorer can be seen in

Ans About Internet explorer message box

L-2 D 173. A secure version of HTTP which provides general transaction security over the web

Ans S-Http

L-2 D 174. The ———— frame contains options for setting ssl states, certificates and publishers

Ans Certificate

L-2 F 175. A ———— is a password that does not change, or is rarely altered. It is also called weak authentication

Ans Static password

Web Browsers

L-1 D 176. Lynx is a graphical Web browsers

L-1 F 177. Web browsers ———— add functionality to the Web browsers to make browsing more attractive

Ans Add-ons

L-1 S 178. The most widely used web browsers are

A. Netscape navigator B. Internet explorer

C. Google chrome D. MSN explorer

L-1 S 179. Which of the following is a graphical Web browsers ?

A. Mosaic B. Netscape

C. Internet Explorer D. All of the above

L-1 T/F 180. A web browsers cannot play sound or video files

A. TRUE B. FALSE

Web Designing

L-1 S 181. The ability of an application to display an accurate representation of the printed output on the screen

A. Rendering B. What you see is What you get C. Display D. Monitor

L-1 S 182. The documents in World Wide Web are created using a language known as

A. HTML B. URL C. HTTL D. HTRL

L-1 S 183. WYSIWYG means

A. The page would appear wrongly

B. The page would be printed in a computer named WYSIWYG

C. The page would appear on the screen in similar fashion as it would be printed/published

D. None of the above

WWW

L-1 D 184. A system for exploring the Internet by using hyperlinks.

A. World Wide Web

L-2 D 185. Microsoft Passport is a service that provides security and convenience when using many online services. Instead of having a user name and password for each server, Passport lets you have a S user name and password for many sites

L-1 F 186. A ———————— is a tool that enable a user to search information in the www

A. Search engine

L-1 S 187. A URL for www is preceded with

A. C: B. http://

C. utp:// D. None of the above

L-1 S 188. ____________ is the process of visiting different websites on the internet

A. File transfer
B. Web surfing
C. Resource sharing
D. None of the above

L-1 S 189. Internet explorer, Netscape Navigator, MSN explorer are examples of

A. Web Web browsers
B. Application software
C. Utilities
D. Instant messenger

L-1 S 190. An address that uniquely identifies a location on the internet

A. Ip address
B. Hyperlink
C. Address
D. Uniform Resource Locator (URL)

L-1 S 191. ________________ is the world's largest computer network, the network of networks, scattered all over the world

A. Intranet
B. Extranet
C. WAN
D. Internet

L-2 S 192. This computer is present at the ISP and responds to requests from a user's Web browsers

A. WWW
B. Internet server
C. File server
D. Web server

L-2 S 193. The tool that provides a single interface that enables users to search many different search engines, indexes and databases simultaneously

A. Web Index
B. Search Engines
C. Meta-search Engines
D. None of the above

Answers

Q. No.	Answer	Q. No.	Answer
1	A B C	37	C
3	A C	38	D
4	A	39	C
13	A B C E	40	A
27	A B C	41	A
28	B	42	A
29	B	43	A
30	B	44	A
31	B	45	A
32	A	46	A
33	A	47	A
34	C	48	A
35	C	84	A B C
36	C	85	B

Q. No.	Answer	Q. No.	Answer
86	B	147	A C
87	B	148	A
88	B	149	A
89	B	150	A
90	B	151	A
91	A	152	A
92	A	153	A
93	A	154	D
94	A	155	D
95	A	156	C
96	A	157	C
97	D	158	D
98	C	159	C
99	C	160	C
100	C	161	C
101	C	162	D
102	C	163	C
104	B	164	D
105	B	165	C
106	A	166	D
110	D	167	B
111	A	168	A
112	B	178	B
136	A B	179	D
137	A B C D	180	B
138	A D	181	B
139	A	182	A
140	B	183	C
141	B	187	B
142	B	188	B
143	B	189	A
144	B	190	D
145	B	191	D
146	B	192	D
		193	C

4

MS OFFICE

Autocorrect

L-2 D 1. AutoCorrect capitalizes the first letter in each sentence. This is one among many features of AutoCorrect.

L-2 T/F 2. AutoCorrect does not capitalize the first letter in the names of days
A.TRUE B. FALSE

L-2 T/F 3. AutoCorrect capitalizes the first letter in table cells
A.TRUE B. FALSE

Excel

L-1 D 4. In Excel, the names of ranges are case-sensitive

L-1 D 5. In Excel 97, database are limited to the number of rows in a worksheet which is
Ans 64k

L-1 D 6. The cell situated at the 3rd row and 2nd column is B3. This naming style is known as
Ans A1 naming style

L-2 D 7. A pivot table report is an interactive table

L-1 D 8. In Excel 97, a worksheet contains —————— columns
Ans 256

L-2 D 9. The —————————— lists all the files that were recovered.
Ans Document recovery window

L-1 D 10. Features of Excel — Worksheet and graphics, data lists and databases, data exchange with other applications, standardized user interface

L-1 D 11. Shortcut Ctrl+Home is used to reach
Ans First cell of the worksheet

L-1 D 12. Cell pointer

Ans A rectangular highlight that indicates the active cell in a spreadsheet program.

L-1 D 13. When deleting a cell/cells, the new position of the adjacent cells is asked through a dialog box (such as Shift row up, shift cell left etc.)

L-1 D 14. AutoSum button in the standard toolbar of Ms-Word

Ans An icon in which there is a picture of summation is used for autosum

L-1 D 15. Following are the Edit → Clear menu option

Ans All, formats, content, comment

L-1 D 16. Comma style button

Ans Used to format numerical data in comma style notation

L-1 D 17. Vertical alignment is a measure of

Ans How far the text is placed from the top and the bottom of a cell

L-1 D 18. Shift cell right/left

Ans When deleting a cell/cells, specifying the new position of the adjacent cells

L-1 D 19. Advanced filter option in excel are used

Ans to see data based on conditions on all/one column of a worksheet

L-1 D 20. Merge and Center button is used

Ans To merge two or more adjacent cells and place the text in the center of combined cell area

L-1 D 21. Presents format cells dialog box in Excel

Ans Ctrl+1

L-1 D 22. Select the entire worksheet.

Ans CTRL+A

L-1 D 23. For protection against macro viruses

Ans Disable macros

L-1 D 24. In Excel 97 Maximum Colors in a workbook 56

L-1 D 25. Paste a defined name into a formula.

Ans F3

L-1 D 26. Centering vertically and horizontally of content in a cell.

Ans Using format cell menu

L-1 D 27. Cell pointer points to the current selected cell

L-1 D 28. = (equal sign) is used to start a formula

L-1 D 29. In Ms Excel 97, Number precision 15 digits

L-1 D 30. Point and click method of entering formula

Ans Addresses of cells which constitutes the formula can be entered by just clicking on them

L-1 D 31. The sheet tab in the page setup dialog box

Ans Define print area, specify the rows to repeat at top etc.

L-1 D 32. Increase decimal and decrease decimal buttons

Ans To increase or decrease decimal places on numeric data which is selected for such change

L-1 D 33. Current or active cell contains the cell pointer

L-1 D 34. Hold down SHIFT and press an arrow key repeatedly

Ans Extend a selection to adjacent cells

L-1 D 35. To get time in an excel cell use ——————

Ans Ctrl+;

L-1 D 36. Anything such as text, number and formula can be entered in a cell

L-1 D 37. When a menu is selected, display the list of commands.

Ans SHIFT+DOWN ARROW

L-1 D 38. ENTER (in a cell with a hyperlink) to activate a hyperlink.

L-1 D 39. With multiple cells selected, select only the active cell.

Ans SHIFT+BACKSPACE

L-1 D 40. Excel uses rules to check whether the formula entered is correct

L-1 D 41. An —————— is a place where two ranges come together or overlap

Ans Intersection

L-1 D 42. The merge cells check box merges two or more cells into one cell

L-1 D 43. This default option aligns text to the left of a cell and numbers to the right

Ans General

L-1 D 44. Edit the active cell and position the insertion point at the end of the cell contents.

Ans F2

L-1 D 45. A defined name in a formula can make it easier to understand the purpose of the formula. For example sum(English) is more understandable than sum(a2:a10).

L-1 D 46. Applications of Electronic spreadsheets — Inventory management, Sales analysis, Costing etc

L-1 D 47. 0 (zero) displays insignificant zeros if a number has fewer digits than there are zeros in the format.

L-1 D 48. CTRL+' (apostrophe) "Copies a formula from the cell above the active cell into the cell or the Formula Bar."

L-1 D 49. Cell pointer is a rectangular highlight that appear once cell in the worksheet and identifies it as the current cell

L-1 D 50. Microsoft Excel works with several types of forms so that the user can perform data entry tasks efficiently and correctly.

Ans TRUE

L-1 D 51. In Excel 97, open workbooks are limited by available memory and system resources. Worksheet size 65,536 rows by 256 columns

L-1 D 52. Shows the macro recorder status. Double-click REC to turn the macro recorder on or off. When the recorder is off, REC appears dimmed.

Ans REC

L-1 D 53. Excel contains many built-in number formats to choose from. To access them, click Cells on the Format menu, and then click the Number tab.

L-1 D 54. A Microsoft Excel workbook is a file that contains one or more worksheets, which you can use to organize various kinds of related information.

L-1 D 55. By importing data, it have not to be retyped. One can also update your Excel reports and summaries automatically from the original source database

L-1 D 56. Excel automatically links charts to the source data used to create them, so whenever the worksheet data is altered, the chart is updated automatically.

L-1 D 57. The name of a range must begin with either a letter or the underscore character. You cannot use spaces, commas, exclamation points or other special characters

L-1 D 58. The Formula Auditing toolbar is used to graphically display the relationships between cells and formulas with blue arrows. Both the precedent cells or the dependent cells can be traced.

Ans Trace precedent and dependent cells with Formula Auditing

L-1 D 59. When a workbook that was created in a earlier version of Excel is opened, all the formulas in the workbook — those that depend on cells that have changed and those that do not — are recalculated.

L-1 D 60. Create a workbook that contains the sheets, default text (such as page headers and column and row labels), formulas, macros, styles, and other formatting you want in new workbooks based on the template.

Ans Workbook template

L-1 D 61. If you have worksheets with specified column widths, you can paste information from another worksheet without losing that formatting by clicking the Paste Options button, and then clicking Keep Source Column Widths.

Ans Retain column widths

L-1 D 62. Excel's default margins are 0.75 inch on each side and 1 inch on top and bottom with a 0.5 inch header and footer margin. Headers and footer print in 0.5 inch of space between the header/footer margin and the regular margin

L-1 D 63. When excel is loaded two windows appear that are nested one within the other. The larger window is called the application window, which covers the entire screen. The application window is used to communicate with excel program. The smaller window is called document window

L-2 D 64. ALT+END to reach

Ans Last cell in a row

L-2 D 65. In excel, press ALT+ENTER to

Ans Start a new line in the same cell.

L-2 D 66. Fill handle

Ans So that data can be filled in columns/rows based on values on two cells. These two cells are selected and fill handle on the latter one is dragged on the target cells

L-2 D 67. Copying formulae

Ans Changes the constituents of the formula as per the location of the source and target cells. Doesn't do that if paste special is used with "Paste values" option

L-2 D 68. Mixed cell references

Ans Cell addresses that contain both relative and absolute references. An example of this is: $A3, B$4 and $A5:B$4

L-2 D 69. Paste vs paste special

Ans Paste special presents the option about pasting data, such as past all, paste formats, paste values only, paste formulae etc

L-2 D 70. Absolute cell reference

Ans An address that does not change even if copied elsewhere

L-2 D 71. In Excel use, CTRL+SHIFT+C to Copy formats

L-2 D 72. In Excel 97, Max Data series in one chart

Ans 225

L-2 D 73. IN excel 97, Number of available worksheet functions

Ans 329

L-2 D 74. In Excel 2002, Largest allowed negative number

Ans -10.00E-308

L-2 D 75. In Excel 2002, Largest allowed positive number

Ans 1.79769313486231E308

L-2 D 76. Max Data points in a data series for 3-D charts

Ans 4,000

L-2 D 77. Maximum Data points in a data series for 2-D charts

Ans 32,000

L-2 D 78. CTRL+PAGE DOWN Move to the next sheet in the workbook.

L-2 D 79. Restore the window size of the selected workbook window.

Ans CTRL+F5

L-2 D 80. Use ———————————— to move to the previous sheet in the workbook.

Ans CTRL+PAGE UP Move to the previous sheet in the workbook.

L-2 D 81. In Excel 2002, Largest amount of time that can be entered

Ans 9999:99:99

L-2 D 82. A formula can contain up to seven levels of nested functions

L-2 D 83. Maximum no. of Data points for all data series in one chart

Ans 256,000

L-2 D 84. In Excel 2002, largest number allowed to be typed into a cell

Ans 10.00E+307

L-2 D 85. Excel can suggest a function based on a natural language query.

Ans Recommended functions in the function wizard

L-2 D 86. In Excel, fields are columns and each record is an individual row

Ans TRUE

L-2 D 87. A reference to a range that spans two or more worksheets in a workbook

Ans 3-D reference

L-2 D 88. On ——————————, one can see various parts of a nested formula

Ans Formula evaluator

L-2 D 89. To get refreshable data from the Web into Excel for viewing and analysis.

Ans Querying data from Web pages

L-2 D 90. The amount a person periodically receives from an investment or are paid on a loan

Ans Payment pmt

L-2 D 91. Using Worksheet protection, elements of a worksheet can be protected for user access

L-2 D 92. Pivot tables are excellent tools for working with data in a three dimensional manner

L-2 D 93. Copy the value from the cell above the active cell into the cell or the Formula Bar.

Ans CTRL+SHIFT+" (quotation mark)

L-2 D 94. Excel's —————————— feature lets a user automatically fill a range of cells with data

Ans AutoFill

L-2 D 95. Click to place the cursor into the formula bar so that an equation or function can be edited.

L-2 D 96. CTRL+F11 Inserts a Microsoft Excel 4.0 macro sheet. Work with multiple national languages

L-2 D 97. When a formula is copied, the cell references may change based on the type of reference used.

L-2 D 98. A Pivot table summarizes the columns of information in a database in relationship to each other

L-2 D 99. To copy data to a different sheet press ctrl + alt while dragging the selection to the sheet's tab

L-2 D 100. Because dates and times are values, they can be added, subtracted, and included in other calculations

L-2 D 101. CTRL+' (Single left quotation mark) – Alternate between displaying cell values and displaying formulas.

L-2 D 102. In excel, field names must be the tops of columns, each be in a single cell and unique within a worksheet.

Ans. TRUE

L-2 D 103. Excel has three types of add-in programs: Excel add-ins, custom Component Object Model (COM) add-ins (COM)

L-2 D 104. In page setup, specifying rows to repeat at top ensures that heading is printed in every page of the document

L-2 D 105. To copy, first select the cells to be copied, hold down the CTRL key and drag the border of the selected range

L-2 D 106. In a pivot table report, a category field provides the individual categories for which data points are charted.

A. Category field

L-2 D 107. In a pivot table, use the refresh button to refresh the values if the values within the database have been changes

L-2 D 108. Ranges are defined by addresses of two opposite or diagonally paired corner cells separated by a colon or two dots

L-2 D 109. In Excel 2002, Length of cell contents (text) 32,767 characters. Only 1,024 display in a cell; all 32,767 display in the formula bar.

L-2 D 110. Microsoft Office provides a PivotTable list, an interactive Web component, which is similar to excel PivotTable report

L-2 D 111. Data table calculations Data tables recalculate whenever a worksheet is recalculated, even if they have not changed.

L-2 D 112. To drag selected cells to a different sheet, hold down the ———————— and drag the selected area onto the sheet label

Ans. Alt key

L-2 D 113. A file you create on your hard disk or a network share to store OLAP source data for a PivotTable or "PivotChart report.

Ans. Offline Cube File

L-2 D 114. To select from a list of entries already in the column, right-click the cell, and then click Pick from List on the shortcut menu.

L-2 D 115. Workbook-level protection: A user can apply protection to workbook elements and you can protect a workbook file from viewing and changes.

L-2 D 116. You can add data to embedded charts by dragging new source data from the worksheet onto the chart. The chart then automatically updates.

L-2 D 117. To create a reference to a range which has been named previously, press F3, select the name in the Paste name box, and click OK. Press ENTER.

L-2 D 118. It calculates the net preset value of an investment. It uses a discount rate and a series of future payments and income to calculate the result

Ans NPV

L-2 D 119. To move a sheet within a workbook, drag the selected sheet along the row of sheet tab. To copy the selected sheet, hold down the Ctrl key while doing the same

L-2 D 120. An interactive, crosstabulated Excel report that summarizes and analyzes data, such as database records, from various sources including one's external to Excel

Ans PivotTable report

L-2 D 121. A ———————————— identifies a cell or a range of cells on a worksheet and tell microsoft excel where to look for the values or data you want to use in a formula

Ans Reference

L-2 D 122. If you want to delete a data series from a chart but leave the corresponding data intact in the worksheet, select the data series on the chart, then press the delete key

L-2 D 123. Solver is part of a suite of commands sometimes called what-if analysis tools. With Solver, you can find an optimal value for a formula in one cell — called the target cell — on a worksheet.

L-2 D 124. A PivotChart report provides a graphical representation of the data in a PivotTable report. You can change the layout and data displayed in a PivotChart report just as you can in a PivotTable report.

L-2 D 125. Keep track of cells and their formulas on the Watch Window toolbar, even when the cells are out of view. This moveable toolbar tracks cell properties including workbook, worksheet, name, cell, value, and formula.

Ans Watch window

L-2 D 126. Microsoft Excel stores dates as sequential numbers which are called serial values. By default, January 1, 1900 is serial number 1, and January 1, 2008 is serial number 39448 because it is 39,448 days after January 1, 1900.

L-2 D 127. Anyone who frequently publishes Excel data to the Web will appreciate additional Web publishing features that allow you to automatically republish items to Web pages whenever you save a workbook with previously published items.

Ans Autorepublish

L-2 D 128. A mixed reference has either an absolute column and relative row, or absolute row and relative column. An absolute column reference takes the form $A1, $B1, and so on. An absolute row reference takes the form A$1, B$1, and so on.

L-2 D 129. In Excel, safeguards are provided against viruses that can be transmitted by macros. If a user shares macros with others, she can certify them with a digital signature so that other users can verify that they are from a trustworthy source.

Ans Macro security

L-2 D 130. Formula being copied "Reference (Description) — Changes to "A1 (*absolute column and absolute row*) — A1 "A$1 (*relative column and absolute row*) — C$1 "$A1 (*absolute column and relative row*) — $A3 "A1 (*relative column and relative row*) — C3

L-2 D 131. In computer spreadsheet programs, a Cell address that indicates the position of a cell relative to another cell. If the reference is copied to another location, the reference will be changed to refer to the cell in the same position relative to the new location.

Ans Relative references

L-3 D 132. Maximum no. of worksheets that can be referred by a chart

Ans 225

L-3 D 133. Scenarios are part of a suite of commands sometimes called what-if analysis

L-3 D 134. Data fields Excel PivotTable reports have data fields instead of total fields.

L-3 D 135. Scaling is used to enlarge or reduce the printed worksheet. Ms Excel can scale a worksheet even for printers that do not support scaling.

L-3 D 136. Determining formatting options - The Paste Options button appears just below your pasted selection after you paste text. When you click the button, a list appears that has options for formatting of the newly pasted text.

L-3 D 137. The 3-D reference style - If you want to analyze data in the same cell or range of cells on multiple worksheets within the workbook, use a 3-D reference. A 3-D reference includes the cell or range reference, preceded by a range of worksheet names.

L-1 D 138. A list is a series of worksheet rows that contain related data

L-1 D 139. The ———————— option repeats cell contents across a cell or a range of cells

Ans Fill

L-1 D 140. A cell can hold a number, a text string or a formula that performs a calculation using one or other cells

L-2 D 141. The time is added to the date serial number as a decimal fraction of a 24hr day

L-2 D 142. A formula can also contain any or all of the following: functions, references, operators, and constants.

L-2 D 143. When the desired result is known but not the input value to the formula and it needs to be determined, you can use the Goal Seek feature

L-1 F 144. There are ———— kinds of data that can be entered into an excel worksheet

Ans 3

L-1 F 145. Move to a task pane from another pane in the program window.

Ans F6

L-2 F 146. Shortcut key Ctrl+‘, shows the ‘formula layer’ of the worksheet. Pressing Ctrl+‘ again, toggles the view back to normal.

Ans Formula auditing mode

L-3 F 147. ———————————— category of formula searches for and returns values from a range, creates hyperlinks to network or internet documents

Ans Lookup and reference

L-1 M 148. Chart types in excel

A.Bar B. Line C. Pie D. Square

L-1 M 149. Insert a new worksheet.

A.ALT+SHIFT+F1 B. SHIFT+F11 C. SHIFT+SPACE D. SHIFT+TAB

L-1 M 150. Creates a chart of the data in the current range.

A.F11 B. ALT+F1 C. F10 D. Alt

L-2 M 151 Following calculations can be done using the autosum button

A.Sum B. Average

C.Mean D. Count E. Max

L-1 S 152. By using the ———————— feature located under Window in the menu bar, you can view different areas of your worksheet simultaneously

A. Split Panes B. Freeze Panes

C. Both of the above D. None of the above

L-1 S 153. Chart wizard step 1 is

A. Chart source data B. Chart Type

C. Chart location D. Chart option

L-1 S 154. Display a shortcut menu

A. SHIFT+ENTER B. SHIFT+F10

C. SHIFT+SPACE D. SHIFT+TAB

L-1 S 155. The shortcut for format cells dialog box

A. Ctrl+0 B. Ctrl+1 C. Ctrl+2 D. Alt+1

L-1 S 156. Insert an AutoSum formula with the SUM function.

A. = B. ALT+ = C. Ctrl+ = D. Ctrl+A

L-1 S 157. Complete a cell entry and select the cell below.

A. Tab B. ENTER C. Shift D. Ctrl

L-1 S 158. By default there are ———— worksheets in a workbook

A. 1 B. 3 C. 2 D. 5

L-1 S 159. Move to the rightmost nonblank cell in the current row.

A. Ctrl+Enter B. END+ENTER C. Enter+Right arrow

D. None of these

L-1 S 160. The set of coordinates that a cell occupies on a worksheet

A. Cell address B. Cell reference

C. Cell pointer D. none of the above

L-1 S 161. Data forms can display a maximum of —— fields at one time.

A. 10 B. 32 C. 64 D. 50

L-1 S 162. In Ms Excel 97-2003 maximum column width is ———— characters

A. 128 B. 255 C. 100 D. 150

L-1 S 163. A ———— identifies a cell or a range of cells on a worksheet

A. Address B. Reference C. Location D. Pointer

L-1 S 164. In Excel 2000, the clipboard can hold upto ———— items at once

A. 10 B. 12 C. 16 D. 14

L-1 S 165. ———— key is used to bring excel to edit mode for the current cell

A. Esc B. F2 C. Shift D. Alt

L-1 S 166. There is a square box in the lower right corner of the cell pointer. It is called

A. Selection handle B. Fill handle C. Cross point D. Hourglass

L-1 S 167. Switch to the next pane in a worksheet that has been split (Window menu, Split command).

A. F10 B. F6 C. F5 D. F8

L-1 S 168. View of an Ms-Excel sheets which shows where pages start and end. Helps to set pages for printing

A. Print preview B. Page break view C. Page end preview D. Page start view

L-1 S 169. A bar at the top of the excel window which is used to enter or edit values or formulas in cells or charts

A. Edit bar B. Formula bar C. Calculation bar D. Text bar

L-1 S 170. Each cell on the spreadsheet has a ———————— that is the column letter and the row number

A. Cell name B. Cell address C. Cell path D. All of the above

L-1 S 171. The column is not wide enough to display the results of the calculation. Then ——— ———— is displayed

A. Overflow B. ######

C. !Div D. None of the above

L-1 S 172. The ———————— reduces the size of the contents of selected cells so that they fit the width of the column

A. Wrap text B. Shrink to fit C. Multiline cell D. All of the above

L-1 S 173. By using the ———————— feature located under Window in the menu bar, the headings can be visible at all times

A. Split windows B. Freeze Panes

C. Both of the above D. None of the above

L-1 S 174. The———————— check box show the content of a cell in the next line if the cell content is too large to be fit in column width

A. Shrink to fit B. Wrap text

C. Multiline cell D. None of the above

L-1 S 175. A small black square in the lower-right corner of the selection. When you point to the fill handle, the pointer changes to a black cross.

A. Fill button B. Fill handle C. Fill icon D. None of these

L-2 S 176. Use CTRL+D to

A. Deselect B. Fill down.

C. Insert date D. None of the above

L-2 S 177. For new workbook,

A. CTRL+N B. CTRL+F3

C. Alt+N D. None of the above

L-2 S 178. Create AutoText

A. ALT+I B. ALT+F3

C. ALT+PAGE D D. ALT+PAGE UP

L-2 S 179. Enter the date in a cell

A. Ctrl+D B. CTRL+; (semicolon)

C. Alt+D D. CTRL+: (colon)

L-2 S 180 In excel worksheet, Hide the selected rows.

A. Alt+H B. Ctrl+9 C. Ctrl+F9 D. Ctrl+H

L-2 S 181. Select the entire column in excel

A. Ctrl+C B. Ctrl + Spacebar C. Ctrl+E D. Ctrl+A

L-2 S 182. Hiding a column in an excel worksheet

A.Ctrl+1 B. Ctrl+0 C. Alt+0 D. Ctrl+Alt+0

L-2 S 183. Max no. of Items in a PivotTable report

A. 5000 B. 8000 C. 1000 D. 10000

L-2 S 184. In Ms Excel 97-2003 Arguments in a function

A. 20 B. 30 C. 36 D. 64

L-2 S 185. Cells that can be highlighted in a shared workbook

A. 65256 B. 32767

C. 256 D. None of the above

L-2 S 186. High security level to reduce macro virus infection

A.No macros can be run B. Macros can be run if they are digitally signed

C.Macros that are specified previously can only run D. All macros can run

L-2 S 187. Copy a picture of the selected window to the Clipboard.

A. ALT+I B. ALT+PRINT SC

C. ALT+PAGE D D. ALT+PAGE UP

L-2 S 188. Function that use a function as one or more of the arguments

A.Recursive function B. Nested function

C.Call-in function D. Branched functions

L-2 S 189. ________________ shows the value represented by each chart marker

A.Legend B. Data labels C. Title D. Bars

L-2 S 190. Using ____________, the absolute cell references could also be created

A.F1 B. F4 C. F3 D. F10

L-2 S 191. A formula in which 1 or more arguments depends on the result of this formula

A.Recursive formula B. Circular reference

C.Fence reference D. None of the above

L-2 S 192. What a loan or investment will be worth at a future time when all payments have been made?

A.Present value B. Future value

C.Break even value D. None of the above

L-2 S 193. The process of examining a worksheet for errors in formulas is referred to as ——

A.Checking B. Auditing C. Debugging D. All of the above

L-2 S 194. A reference to a range that spans two or more worksheets in a workbook is called ________________

A.2D reference B. 3D reference C. Simple reference D. Formula

L-2 S 195 ____________ is a very small program that allows a user to automate tasks that are programmable and frequently used

A.Snippet B. Macro C. Script D. Module

L-2 S 196. An ———————— in a formula always refer to a cell in a specific location. If the position of the cell that contains the formula changes, the ———————— remains the same.

A. Relative B. Absolute reference C. Random D. Formula

L-2 S 197. The ———————— command can filter a list in place like the A utoFilter command, but it does not display drop-down lists for the columns. Instead, you type the criteria

A. Autofilter B. Advanced filter
C. AutoQuery D. Advanced Query

L-3 S 198. A format, such as cell shading or font color, that Excel automatically applies to cells if a specified condition is true.).

A. Toggle formatting B. Conditional formatting
C. Autoformatting D. None of the above

L-1 S 199. Move between panes

A. F2 B. F1 C: F6 D. Shift

L-1 S 200. Chart wizard step 2 is

A. Chart source data B. Chart Type C. Chart location D. Chart option

L-1 S 201. Previous cell in a row

A. SHIFT+TAB B. Tab C. Ctrl D. Scroll

L-1 S 202. Complete a cell entry and select the previous cell above.

A. SHIFT+ENTER B. SHIFT+F10 C. SHIFT+SPACE D. SHIFT+TAB

L-1 S 203. The intersection of each row and column is called a ————————

A. Cell B. Value C. Formula D. Address

L-1 S 204. To enter the same data into some cells, select all of them and on the active cell type the data. Then press ————————

A. Ctrl+Enter B. Alt+Enter C. Ctrl+Esc D. Ctrl+F1

L-2 S 205. In a cell, Enter the time

A. CTRL+SHIFT+: (colon) B. Ctrl+T
C. Ctrl+Shift+’ D. None of the above

L-2 S 206. Open insert menu

A. ALT+I B. ALT+F3
C. ALT+PAGE D D. ALT+PAGE UP

L-2 S 207. Displays the Macro dialog box.

A. ALT+F8 B. Ctrl+M C. Alt+M D. Ctrl+A

L-2 S 208. Remove the document window split

A. ALT+SHIFT+C B. ALT+F3
C. ALT+PAGE D D. ALT+PAGE UP

L-2 S 209. Display the window shortcut menu (Control menu).

A. ALT+SPACEBAR B. ALT+F3

C. ALT+PAGE D D. ALT+PAGE UP

L-2 S 210 A ———————— is all cells in two separate ranges

A. Union B. Intersection C. Collection D. Group

L-1 S 211. In excel, Chart wizard step 3 is

A. Chart source data B. Chart type C. Chart location D. Chart option

L-1 S 212. In excel, Chart wizard step 4 is

A. Chart source data B. Chart Type

C. Chart location D. Chart option

L-1 S 213. In excel, Select the entire row.

A. SHIFT+ENTER B. SHIFT+F11

C. SHIFT+SPACE D. SHIFT+TAB

L-1 S 214. A collection of excel sheets is called a

A. Worksheet B. Grid

C. Workbook D. None of the above

L-1 S 215. The initial value of an investment or loan

A. Fixed value B. Past value

C. Present value D. Future value

L-1 S 216. A Formula always begins with ——— sign

A. ' B. " C. $ D. =

L-1 S 217. The extension of an Excel template file is

A. ext B. tmp C. xls D. xlt

L-1 S 218. Auto sum or automatic adding icon is available on

A. Tools toolbar B. Formatting Toolbar C. Standard toolbar

D. View toolbar

L-1 S 219. To enter today's date in a cell, press CTRL+; (semicolon).

A. Ctrl+: B. Alt+: C. Ctrl+; D. Alt+;

L-1 S220. A ———————— is an excel file where the data is stored

A. Grid B. Column C. Table D. Workbook

L-1 S221. Complete a cell entry and select the previous cell to the left.

A. SHIFT+ENTER B. SHIFT+F11

C. SHIFT+SPACEBAR D. SHIFT+TAB

L-1 S222. You can use ———————— to add shading to your worksheets

A. Colour B. Format

C. Patterns D. None of the above

L-1 S223. To cancel an entry in the cell before pressing the enter key press

A. Home B. Escape key C. Alt D. Ctrl

L-1 S224. —————— refers to the position of cell contents within a cell

A. Height B. Margin

C. Alignment D. None of the above

L-1 S225. An application package which displays a table consisting of rows and column

A. Word processor B. Presentation package

C. Both of the above D. Spreadsheet package

L-1 S226. Excel columns are slightly more than —————— characters wide

A. 6 B. 10 C. 7 D. 8

L-1 S227. In charts, —————— show the value represented by each chart marker

A. Title B. Legend

C. Data labels D. None of the above

L-1 S228. The column letter followed by the row number is called a ——————

A. Cell array B. Relative address C. Absolute address D. Cell reference

L-1 S229. Name of ranges can be upto —————— characters long and can include letters, numbers, underscores or periods

A. 128 B. 8 C. 255 D. 100

E. 64

L-1 S230. A box formed by the intersection of a row and column in a worksheet or a table, in which information is entered.

A. Workcell B. Box

C. Cell D. None of the above

L-1 S231. If you move the mouse toward the border of the active cell, the mouse pointer will change to an ——————

A. Hand B. Different pointer C. Arrow D. Hourglass

L-1 S232. Use —————— so that you can see the heading of the excel document even after scrolling down to next pages.

A. Lock heading B. Split window

C. Freeze panes D. None of the above

L-1 S233. The —————— option divides the text in a cell into lines and spreads the text out so that it is as wide as the cell

A. Right align B. Wrap text C. Justify D. Shrink to fit

L-1 S234. To enter nonconsecutive cells into the function, hold the —————— and click on the cell(s) you want to include in the total

A. Alt B. Shift C. Winkey D. Ctrl key

L-2 S235. Goal seek is

A. A how it happens tool B. a game

C. A graphical chart utility D. A what if analysis tool

L-2 S236. Naming Ranges
A. Name could not be a cell reference
B. Name cannot have spaces in it
C. Names cannot begin with a number
D. Names cannot use certain special characters
E. All of the above

L-2 S237. Fields in a data form
A. 15 B. 16 C. 30 D. 32

L-2 S238. Goto Last cell in a column
A. ALT+I B. ALT+F3
C. ALT+PAGE DOWN D. ALT+PAGE UP

L-2 S239. Goto First cell in a column
A. ALT+I B. ALT+F3
C. ALT+PAGE DOWN D. ALT+PAGE UP

L-2 S240. A note that is attached to a cell
A. Endnote B. Footer C. Comment D. Note

L-2 S241. Displays the Visual Basic Editor.
A. ALT+F1 B. Ctrl+F11 C. ALT+F10 D. ALT+F11

L-2 S242. Shortcut to get now's time in a cell is
A. Ctrl+T B. Ctrl+P C. Ctrl+Y D. Ctrl+Shift+;

L-2 S243. Pick from list command can also be accessed using
A. Ctrl+down arrow key B. Alt+Page down
C. F1 D. Alt+ "Down arrow key"

L-2 S244. A ―――――― is a grid that appears below a chart
A. Legend table B. Label list
C. Data table D. None of the above

L-2 S245. A series of worksheet rows that contain related data
A. Group B. Record C. List D. All of the above

L-2 S246. Fill the selected cell range with the current entry.
A. ALT+F B. CTRL+F C. CTRL+E D. CTRL+ENTER

L-2 S247. ―――――― a way to find and work with a subset of data
A. Sorting B. Grouping C. Filtering D. Summarizing

L-2 S248. In Excel 2002, Maximum no. of characters displayed in a cell
A. 2048 B. 256 C. 512 D. 1024

L-2 S249. Users who can open and share a shared workbook at the same time
A. 12 B. 128 C. 256 D. 512

L-2 S250. ―――――― can answer to "what if" questions involving numbers
A. Help B. Wordpad C. Word D. Excel

L-2 S251. References to cells in other workbooks are called ——————

A.Hyperlink B. Attachment C. Links D. Reference

L-2 S252. It counts the number of cells within a range that meet the given criteria

A.If then B. Conditional counter

C.CountIf D. None of the above

L-2 S253. Stats with an equal sign an return a value based on the value of other cells

A.Macro B. Subroutine C. Function D. All of the above

L-2 S254. A formula that contains references to other worksheet is called a ———— formula

A.1-D B. 2-D C. 3-D D. Referencing

L-2 S255. —————————— the name of the sheet in the tab at the bottom and type the new name

A.Click B. Triple click

C.Double click D. None of the above

L-2 S256. —————————— the name of the sheet in the tab at the bottom and type the new name

A.Click B. Double Click

C.Triple Click D. None of the above

L-2 S257. —————————— could be used to get a graphical display of the constituents of the formula.

A.Formula palette B. Formula verification tool

C.Formula tracer D. Formula auditing toolbar

L-2 S258. A word or string of characters that represents a cell, range of cells, formula, or constant value

A.Identifier B. Number C. Name D. All of the above

L-2 S259. It returns the internal rate of return for a series of cash flows represented by the numbers in values

A.Compound Int B. Break even C. FV D. IRR

L-2 S260. A filter is used to select records that meet a specific criterion and temporarily hide all the other records.

A.Sorting B. Deleting C. Filtering D. Selection

L-2 S261. It returns the future value of an investment based on periodic, constant payments and a constant interest rate

A.Break even B. FutVal C. FV D. IRR

L-2 S262. An environment in which you can edit macros that you've recorded and write new macros and Visual Basic for Applications programs

A.Notepad B. C# editor

C.Java D. Visual Basic Editor

L-2 S263. When you double click a cell with a formula to open it for editing, excel paints each cell address or range address in the formula a different color and places a border of the same color, called a ——————————— around the cell or range

A.Path finder B. Source finder C. Both of the aboveD. Range Finder

L-3 S 264. Max Data fields in a PivotChart report

A.128 B. 512 C. 256 D. 1024

L-1 S 265. To enter todays date in a cell, move to that cell and type

A.=today()

L-1 T/F 266. Workbooks and sheets cannot be hidden

A.TRUE B. FALSE

L-1 T/F 267. Data from other sources cannot be imported in excel

A.TRUE B. FALSE

L-1 T/F 268. Headers and Footers are visible in normal excel screen

A.TRUE B. FALSE

L-1 T/F 269. The name of a range could also be valid cell addresses

A.TRUE B. FALSE

L-1 T/F 270. Change in formatting of a cell changes its contents too

A.TRUE B. FALSE

L-1 T/F 271. In the formula bar, the content as well as formatting of a cell can be seen

A.TRUE B. FALSE

L-1 T/F 272. In excel, one cannot search for a specific string in all the worksheets of a workbook

A.TRUE B. FALSE

L-1 T/F 273. Changing a default font in an Ms-Word document also changes the font in existing files

A.TRUE B. FALSE

L-1 T/F 274. The right most cell of the merged cells becomes the cell reference of the newly formed cell

A.TRUE B. FALSE

L-1 T/F 275. In electronic spreadsheet, one has to recalculate a result of a formula if the values which constitutes the formula changes

A.TRUE B. FALSE

L-1 T/F 276. If on a print dialog box, you specify "All" as page range, everything in the file even that excluded in the print area is printed

A.TRUE B. FALSE

L-2 T/F 277. You cannot import excel data into access database

A.TRUE B. FALSE

L-2 T/F 278. Autocomplete shows a list from data entered in whole sheet

A.TRUE B. FALSE

L-2 T/F 279. Hidden data is removed from the workbook if the workbook is closed

A.TRUE B. FALSE

L-2 T/F 280. Numbers stored as text are sorted first, and then numbers stored as numbers

A.TRUE B. FALSE

L-2 T/F 281. Shortcut key through which a macro is activated is created by the macro itself

A.TRUE B. FALSE

L-2 T/F 282. When a filter is applied, all the records not included in the subset are deleted

A.TRUE B. FALSE

L-2 T/F 283. In excel's data form, autocomplete feature can be used to do work more efficiently

A.TRUE B. FALSE

L-2 T/F 284. When a cell containing a formula is mode, the cell references within the formula also changes

A.TRUE B. FALSE

L-2 T/F 285. Once an excel sheet is split or freeze paned, the rows or column specified are printed on every page of the excel sheet

A.TRUE B. FALSE

L-2 T/F 286. If some data from a workbook is hidden and the workbook is closed then on opening the workgroup again, the hidden data appears

A.TRUE B. FALSE

L-3 T/F 287. Formula cannot be used as a criteria in a query

A.TRUE B. FALSE

L-1 T/F 288. GUI is available in MS Excel

A.TRUE B. FALSE

L-1 T/F 289. XML files could be used in excel

A.TRUE B. FALSE

L-1 T/F 290. Cell references may be used in formulas

A.TRUE B. FALSE

L-1 T/F 291. A formula always begins with an equal (=) sign

A.TRUE B. FALSE

L-1 T/F 292. A cell's content does not change if the formatting is changed

A.TRUE B. FALSE

L-1 T/F 293. Transpose rows to columns or columns to rows - can be done in excel

A.TRUE B. FALSE

L-1 T/F 294. Sheets can be renamed to make it easier to remember what each one contains

A.TRUE B. FALSE

L-1 T/F 295. Headers and footers do not appear or print in Web documents displayed in browsers.

A.TRUE B. FALSE

L-1 T/F 296. Maximum number of sheets in a workbook is limited by available memory of the computer

A.TRUE B. FALSE

L-2 T/F 297. Autocomplete only works for text data

A.TRUE B. FALSE

L-2 T/F 298. To insert ampersand character & type &&

A.TRUE B. FALSE

L-2 T/F 299. A formula can contain functions and references

A.TRUE B. FALSE

L-2 T/F 300. Excel edits text as needed to make valid names

A.TRUE B. FALSE

L-2 T/F 301. In excel, dates are displayed in 2 digit years

A.TRUE B. FALSE

L-2 T/F 302. Customised autofill entries can be added to excel

A.TRUE B. FALSE

L-2 T/F 303. A range can also include cells from adjacent sheets

A.TRUE B. FALSE

L-2 T/F 304. In excel, it is also possible to present graphical data

A.TRUE B. FALSE

L-2 T/F 305. Excel stores dates as sequential numbers known as serial values

A.TRUE B. FALSE

L-2 T/F 306. A user cannot both split a worksheet and freeze parts of a worksheet at the same time.

A.TRUE B. FALSE

L-2 T/F 307. If a cell contains a formula that references other cells, its value automatically change as other cell values referenced in the formula change

A.TRUE B. FALSE

General

L-3 D 308. Microsoft Office Safe Mode allows to fix the problem associated with its or isolate them using safe mode

L-1 M 309. ______________ is an spreadsheet application

A.Lotus 123 B. Excel C. Word D. Outllook

L-1 S 310. A box which a user can type some data or text

Ans Text box

Ms Word

L-1 T/F 311 While typing a paragraph in Ms Word "Enter key" have to be pressed after every line

A.TRUE B. FALSE

Photo Editor

L-2 D 312. Its easy and fast to get photos from your hard disk drive, scanner, or digital camera into a presentation. Special layout options for photo albums include oval frames, captions under each picture, and more.

Ans Photo album

Powerpoint

L-1 D 313. CTRL+M Insert a new slide

L-1 D 314. CTRL+A (in slide sorter view) Select All slides

L-1 D 315. One can copy slides using the slide finder

L-1 D 316. One can automate PowerPoint to perform repetitive tasks to reduce keystrokes.

L-1 D 317. Use the pen option to be able to draw or write on the slide during the slide show

L-1 D 318. Presentation viewer could be added to the package using the Pack and Go Wizard in PowerPoint.

L-1 D 319. ————— can be used to run a powerpoint presentation on a system which do not have powerpoint installed

Ans Powerpoint viewer

L-1 D 320. Microsoft PowerPoint records the amount of time you take on each slide.

Ans Automatic slide timings

L-1 D 321. Use the title master to make changes to slides that use a Title Slide layout. The Title Slide layout is available in the Slide Layout task pane and is the first layout shown.

Ans Title Master

L-1 D 322. Thumbnails of slides in normal view: When you want to navigate your presentation visually, click the slides tab in normal view. Use the thumbnail representations of each slide to quickly find the slide you want to work on.

L-2 D 323. CTRL+D Make a copy of the selected slide

L-2 D 324. Slide sorter view is an exclusive view of the slides in thumbnail form.

Ans Slide sorter view

L-2 D 325. A slide master is added to a presentation when a design template is applied.

L-2 D 326. The slide master and title master for a design template are called slide-title master pairs

L-2 D 327. See a presentation as a thumbnail sized images. Order of slides could be easily changed in this view.

Ans Slides tab

L-2 D 328. A gradual progression of colors and shades, usually from one color to another, or from one shade to another of a similar color

Ans Gradient

L-2 D 329. Select the Display speaker notes with presentation check box if you want to automatically view speaker notes during the broadcast.

Ans Speaker notes

L-2 D 330. Animation schemes are a pre-designed set of animation and transition effects that can be applied to the entire presentation at once.

L-2 D 331. Every slide in a presentation must be in same orientation. Different orientation can be set for notes pages, handouts, and the outline.

L-2 D 332. To add a slide number or date and time to every slide, on the View menu, click Header and Footer, and then select the appropriate options.

L-2 D 333. Insert an equation : To insert an equation in a presentation, use the characters and commands that are available in Microsoft Equation Editor.

L-2 D 334. Microsoft PowerPoint gives you many ways to deliver your presentation, including on-screen, online, overhead transparencies, paper printouts, and 35mm slides.

Ans Delivering presentations

L-2 D 335. Slide show view takes up the full computer screen, like an actual slide show presentation. In this full-screen view, you see your presentation the way your audience will.

Ans Slide show view

L-2 D 336. A powerpoint presentation could be printed as notes pages for the use of the presenter during the presentation. Notes pages could also be given to the audience as hand outs

Ans Notes pages

L-2 D 337. A "smart tag" is a type of button in Microsoft PowerPoint 2002 that appears after certain actions, such as an automatic text correction or a copy-and-paste, have taken place.

L-2 D 338. With the current slide shown in this large view, a user can add text, insert pictures and cliparts, tables, charts, drawing objects, text boxes, movies, sounds, hyperlinks, and animations.

Ans Slide pane

L-2 D 339. A color scheme consists of the eight colors used in the design of the slide — background color, color of text and lines, color of shadows, title text color, color of fills, color of accents, and hyperlink color

L-2 D 340. A file that contains the styles in a presentation, including the type and size of bullets and fonts; placeholder sizes and positions; background design and fill; color schemes and a slide master and optional title master

Ans Design Template

L-2 D 341. When a presentation is packaged, any linked file can be included. TrueType fonts if used can be embedded as well. Embedding fonts guarantees that the fonts will be available when the presentation is run on a different computer which may not have that truetype font.

L-1 M 342. Presentation programs

A.Powerpoint B. Irfanview C. Lotus freelance D. Show manager

L-1 S 343. ———— is the way things are arranged on a slide.

A.View B. Layout C. Order of appearance D.Look

L-1 S344. Run a presentation

A.F10 B. F1 C. F5 D. F8

L-1 S345. PowerPoint is an example of a ———— software

A.Text processor B. Presentation maker

C.Spreadsheet D. Office manager

L-1 S 346. ———— view gives an overall picture of a presentation

A.Outline view B. Slide layout view C. Slide sorter view D. All of the above

L-1 S 347. ———— can be used to apply a bitmaped image over a surface

A.Background B. Foreground

C.Desktop D. Texture Mapping

L-1 S 348. Program used to run Powerpoint presentation if Ms Powerpoint is unavailable

A.Internet explorer B. Ms Word

C.Image viewer D. Powerpoint viewer

L-2 S 349. If a change is made to this slide, It will be reflected in all the slides

A.Main slide B. Parent slide

C.Master slide D. None of the above

L-2 S 350. Printing a powerpoint presentation is such a way that the printout can be used as notes pages.

A. Print out B. Hard copy C. Hand out D. All of the above

L-1 S 351. A Title Slide layout contains placeholders for a title, subtitle, and headers and footers.

A.TRUE

L-1 T/F 352. A presentation can not be broadcasted over the web

A.TRUE B. FALSE

L-1 T/F 353. Once started, a presentation could not run by itself

A.TRUE B. FALSE

L-1 T/F 354. More than one template could not be used in a powerpoint presentation

A.TRUE B. FALSE

L-1 T/F 355. Pictures can be rotated in powerpoint

A.TRUE B. FALSE

Security

L-2 D 356. Depending on macro security setting, when a macro is opened, a warning is displayed and the macro may be disabled.

Word

L-1 D 357. Pictures and scanned objects could not be part of a word document

L-1 D 358. The ———————— shows the line, column and page that your insertion point is on

Ans Standard toolbar

L-2 D 359. In a mail-merge in Word, the document that contains the text and graphics that are the same for each record of the data source

Ans Merge document

L-2 D 360. A non printing symbol inserted automatically by Ms Word when enter key is pressed at the end of a paragraph. It stores the formatting applied to the paragraph

Ans Paragraph registry

L-2 D 361. Author name of the file can be changed by using the properties option on the ———————— menu

Ans Tools

L-1 D 362. Ruler

Ans Is available on the left and top of the typing area which helps in setting the page margin of the page as well as placing tabs at appropriate places

L-1 D 363. Annotations

Ans An annotation is an addition made to information in a book, document, online record, video, or other information

L-1 D 364. Increase indent

Ans Increase the space which is left before a line in Ms Word

L-1 D 365. To clear all tab stops

Ans Format → tab

L-1 D 366. Inserting manual page breaks

Ans So that the page ends where the manual page break is inserted and the next page is started immediately

L-1 D 367. Newspaper style columns can be set in ms word

L-1 D 368. To see the font size in the formatting toolbar

Ans Ctrl+Shift+P

L-1 D 369. By default, Word numbers every line in a document

L-1 D 370. There are ———— basic areas on the Word screen

Ans 3

L-1 D 371. Replace all replaces every occurrence in the document

L-1 D 372. Press ALT+U to choose AutoShape on the Drawing toolbar.

L-1 D 373. A view of a document as it will appear when it would be printed

Ans Print preview

L-1 D 374. Before and after spacing is related to the space between paragraphs

L-1 D 375. In a table, to select: a cell Click the left edge of the cell.

L-1 D 376. The use of computers to create, edit, view, and print text materials

Ans Word processing

L-1 D 377. By default, Word numbers every line in a document (except those in tables.

L-1 D 378. Go to a page, bookmark, footnote, table, comment, graphic, or other location

Ans CTRL+G

L-1 D 379. Resize handle in a table is used to increase or decrease the size of the column row

L-1 D 380. Headers and footers are areas in the top and bottom margins of each page in a document.

L-1 D 381. By default, Word keeps track of how much text can fit on a document page and makes page breaks automatically

L-1 D 382. Flowcharts are created using different autoShapes on the Drawing toolbar, including flowchart shapes and connectors.

L-1 D 383. Use autocorrect to quickly insert symbols that are included in the built-in list of AutoCorrect entries

L-1 D 384. Misspelled or misused words are underlined and alternatives appear, eliminating the need to check spelling and grammar

Ans Automatic spelling and grammer checking

L-1 D 385. Word links and integrates with —————— so that documents created in Ms Word can be sent as email from Ms Word itself

Ans Ms-Outlook

L-1 D 386. When a document with a file name extension other than the default extension .doc is saved, Word adds the default extension to the file name entered.

L-1 D 387. This shows the position of the first line of a paragraph, or, in a bulleted or numbered list, the position of the bullet or number for an item in the list.

Ans First line indent marker

L-1 D 388. A view of a document as it will appear when printed. For example, items such as headers, footnotes, columns, and text boxes appear in their actual positions

Ans Print layout view

L-1 D 389. To turn on or show the Office Assistant, press ALT+H to open the Help menu, and then press O. With the Assistant visible, press F1 to display the Assistant balloon.

L-1 D 390 A mark to show the end of a section. A section break stores the section formatting elements, such as the margins, page orientation, headers and footers, and sequence of page numbers.

Ans Section break

L-1 D 391. To create a screentip when one rest mouse on a hyperlink, click ScreenTip in the Insert Hyperlink dialog box, then type the text you want. If you do not specify a tip, a default tip is used.

Ans Screentip

L-1 D 392. Microsoft Word can automatically count the lines in a document and display the appropriate number beside each line of text. This is useful if you need to refer to specific lines in a document

Ans Line numbers

L-1 D 393. A format that makes lowercase text appear as capital letters in a reduced font size. Small caps formatting does not affect numbers, punctuation, nonalphabetic characters, or uppercase letters

L-1 D 394. To turn on or off the spelling checker corrections, select the Replace text as you type check box, and then select or clear the Automatically use suggestions from the spelling checker check box

L-2 D 395. Ctrl+Up arrow

Ans Move the insertion point to the beginning of the next paragraph

L-2 D 396. A page break

Ans CTRL+SHIFT+ENTER

L-2 D 397. Ctrl+Right arrow

Ans Move the insertion point to the beginning of the next word

L-2 D 398. Justify a paragraph

Ans CTRL+J

L-2 D 399. Set 1.5-line spacing

Ans CTRL+5

L-2 D 400. In Word, Use CTRL+1 for Single-spacing

L-2 D 401. In Word, Use CTRL+2 Double-space lines

L-2 D 402. To select a series of words

Ans Click on the first word and then while holding down Shift key click on the second word

L-2 D 403. In Ms-Word, to Left align a paragraph, Use

Ans CTRL+L

L-2 D 404. In Ms-Word, Create a nonbreaking hyphen

Ans CTRL+HYPHEN

L-2 D 405. In Ms-Word, to indent a paragraph from the left

Ans CTRL+M

L-2 D 406. CTRL+SHIFT+SPACEBAR is used to Create a nonbreaking space in Ms-Word

L-2 D 407. In Ms-Word, Use CTRL+SPACEBAR to Remove paragraph or character formatting

L-2 D 408. CTRL+0 (zero) Add or remove one line space preceding a paragraph

L-2 D 409. ———— are used to customize the content of individual documents.

Ans Mail merge fields

L-2 D 410. Word indicates possible inconsistent formatting using blue wavy underlines

L-2 D 411. A cross-reference refers to an item that appears in another location in a document

L-2 D 412. A mark that shows where a deletion, insertion, or other editing change has been made in a document.

Ans Tracked change

L-2 D 413. Click and Type is not available in the following views: normal view, outline view, and print preview.

L-2 D 414. The name of the resultant new document created in mail merge is ———— by default for form letters

Ans Form letters

L-2 D 415. The AutoFit Options button appears when PowerPoint resizes text you're typing to make it fit the current placeholder.

L-2 D 416. A footnote or an endnote consists of two parts which are inter-linked-the note reference mark and the corresponding note text.

L-2 D 417. To automatically add AutoCorrect exceptions, select the Automatically add words to list check box in the AutoCorrect Exceptions dialog box.

L-2 D 418 By using wild cards (an asterisk), word can search for text that matches what has been entered into the Find window, not counting the wild card

L-2 D 419. Shows the track changes status. Double-click TRK to turn the Track Changes feature on or off. When changes are not being tracked, TRK appears dimmed.

Ans TRK

L-2 D 420 In print layout view or Web layout view, markup balloons show markup elements, such as comments and tracked changes, in the margins of the document.

L-2 D 421 This macro enables you to change some Word settings, such as the colors used for wavy underlines and smart tags and the paths for some file locations.

Ans Registry Options

L-2 D 422 When the Track Changes feature is enabled, TRK appears on the status bar at the bottom of your document. When you turn off change tracking, TRK is dimmed.

L-2 D 423 When Microsoft Word finishes checking spelling and grammar, it can display information about the reading level of the document, including the following

Ans Readability scores

L-2 D 424 A field is a set of codes that insert text, graphics, page numbers, and other material into a document. For example, the DATE field inserts the current date.

L-2 D 425 Capitalization options - AutoCorrect can capitalize the first word in a sentence, the names of days of the week, the first letter of text in a table cell, and so on.

L-2 D 426 A view that shows the headings of a document intended to represent their level in the document's structure. Outline view could also be used to work with master documents.

Ans Outline view

L-2 D 427 You can quickly insert text, graphics, tables, or other items in a blank area of a document by using Click and Type. Just double-click in a blank area, and Click and Type.

Ans About Click and Type

L-2 D 428. If the drop down list of merge fields is too large to be displayed on screen, ——— ——— have to be pressed to display the merge fields in a "Insert merge field" dialog box

Ans Alt+Shift+F

L-2 D 429. Reveal formatting - On the Format menu, click Reveal Formatting. Select the text whose formatting you want to review. The formatting information will appear in the Reveal Formatting task pane.

L-2 D 430. The AutoCorrect Options button first appears as a small, blue box when the mouse pointer is rested near text that was automatically corrected. The box changes to a button icon when you point to it.

L-2 D 431. You can save time by using smart tags to perform actions in Microsoft Word that you'd normally open other programs to do. The purple dotted lines beneath text in your document indicate the smart tags.

L-2 D 432. Footnotes and endnotes are used in printed documents to explain, comment on, or provide references for text in a document. Usually, footnotes are used for detailed comments and endnotes for mentioning sources.

L-2 D 433. Click and Type is not available in multiple columns, bulleted and numbered lists, next to floating objects, to the left or right of pictures with top and bottom text wrapping, or to the left or right of indents.

L-2 D 434. When the autocomplete feature scans a column, it compiles a list of the entries in that column. This list can be accessed to quickly insert data that has already been entered in that column. This helps in typing quickly

L-2 D 435. In a shared workbook, information that is maintained about changes made in past editing sessions. The information includes the name of the person who made each change, when the change was made, and what data was changed.

Ans Change history

L-3 D 436. A hyphen that prevent a hyphenated text from breaking if it falls at the end of a line.

Ans Non-breaking hyphen

L-3 D 437. This feature senses the language and determine how the language is written and accordingly changes the keyboard layout

Ans Automatic keyboard switching

L-3 D 438. To turn on the click and type option, on the Tools menu, click Options, click the Edit tab, select the Enable click and type check box, and then click OK.

L-3 D 439. Use a gutter margin to add extra space to the side or top margin of a document you plan to bind. A gutter margin ensures that text isn't obscured by the binding.

L-3 D 440. One can save multiple versions of a document within the same document. No overhead of disk space occurs because this information is saved within the file itself.

L-3 D 441. The (invisible) selection bar is the left-hand margin of the document, next to the ruler. When the cursor is moved into this area, it changes to a right-pointing arrowhead

L-3 D 442. When you use the Legal blackline option (Tools menu, Compare and Merge Documents command), Word compares the documents and displays only what changed between the two documents. That is, previous tracked changes in the documents are not displayed

L-1 D 443. To select a sentence

Ans Hold the Ctrl key and click the sentence

L-1 D 444. In Ms-office, use —————— to extend a selection

Ans SHIFT+RIGHT ARROW

L-1 D 445. In a table to select a row, click to the left of the row

L-1 D 446. In a table, to select a column, click the column's top gridline or border

L-2 D 447. For Double space use

Ans Ctrl-+2

L-2 D 448. On the left or right border of text than contains tracked changes, vertical bars appear. These are called

Ans Changed lines

L-1 M 449. Four paragraph alignments are

A. Left B. Right C. Top D. Center

E. Justify

L-1 M 450. Standard toolbar contain these icons

A. Copy B. Font C. Table D. Justifcation

L-2 M 451. Mail merge uses

A. Form letters B. Labels C. Data entry D. Envelops

L-2 M 452. In mail merge data source could be

A. Access database B. Excel worksheet C. Query D. Internet website

L-1 M 453. Quick access to the help system in Ms Word could be obtained using

A. Esc key B. F1 key

C. F10 key D. The Office Assistant

L-1 M 454. If a word is spelled correctly and you prefer not to see the wavy red line for every such occurrence of this word, choose —————— from the spell-check pop up menu

A. Stop spell check B. Ignore all

C. Add to dictionary D. All of the above

L-1 M 455. Type of Text alignment

A. Left B. Right C. Middle D. Center

E. Justify

L-1 M 456. The following gets automatically capitalized in Word

A. First letter of text in table cells B. Name of a person

C. Names of days D. First letter of every word

L-1 S 457. Subscript

A. A^{Test} B. A_{Test} C. ~~A Test~~ D. Test

L-1 S 458. ________ are used to display data

A. Chart B. Tables C. Columns D. Grid

L-1 S 459. The extension of a Ms Word document file is

A. txt B. doc

C. word D. None of the above

L-1 S 460. For pointwise text, ________ can be used.

A. Table B. Bullets and numbering

C. Columns D. Auto-formatting

L-1 S 461. Default vertical alignment in a Ms Word document is

A. Center B. Top C. Bottom D. Justify

L-1 S 462. Spell check button is available on the ________ toolbar

A. Drawing B. Standard

C. Formatting D. None of the above

L-1 S 463. First letter of a paragraph is bigger in size and may have special style

A. Bold Cap B. Drop cap C. Drop letter D. Bold Parastart

L-1 S 464. Word uses ________ wavy underlines to indicate possible spelling errors

A. Purple B. Red C. Green D. Orange

L-1 S 465. The option which would be used to get to page 19 if page 2 is on screen is ________

A. Ctrl+P B. Ctrl+G

C. Ctrl+J D. None of the above

L-1 S 466. To close the print preview view and get back to normal view ________ key is pressed

A. Alt B. Escape C. F1 D. Home key

L-1 S 467. AutoText entries must be at least —— characters long if you want to insert the entry by using AutoComplete.

A. 4 B. 5 C. 3 D. 6

L-1 S 468. Position the cursor at the beginning of each new paragraph and press ________. This inserts a page break

A. Ctrl+P B. Ctrl+Enter

C. Ctrl+B D. Ctrl+Down arrow key

L-1 S 469. A combination of formatting characteristics, such as font, font size, and indentation that is named and stored as a set to be applied anytime

A. Autoformatting B. Style C. Trend D. Template

L-1 S 470. To select vertically, hold down the ——— key and drag down and across the text you want to select. This is useful for editing data in tabular form

A. Ctrl B. Alt
C. Esc D. None of the above

L-2 S 471. In Ms-Word, Use CTRL+E to

A. Goto the end of the document B. Center a paragraph
C. Insert endnote D. None of the above

L-2 S 472. Turn track changes on or off

A. CTRL+E B. CTRL+SHIFT+E
C. Alt+SHIFT+E D. None of the above

L-2 S 473. Conversion of normal language text into speech

A. Speech recognition B. Speech synthesis
C. Both of the above D. None of the above

L-2 S 474. ——— can be used to display data based on some criteria

A. Fill B. Autofill
C. Autocorrect D. None of the above

L-2 S 475. Newly inserted text is marked as ——— when the track change feature is used.

A. Bold B. Underline C. Italic D. Strike-through

L-2 S 476. By default, left aligned tab stops are set every ——— across the page

A. 1 inch B. 1/2 inch
C. 0.75 inch D. None of the above

L-2 S 477. ——— is used for merging a table of names and addresses with a standard letter to create personalized letters

A. Formatting B. Mail Merge C. Syclstyle D. Table

L-1 S 478. WYSIWYG is

A. What you see is what you get B. What your system is where you get
C. What you is is where you get D. Where you see is where you get

L-1 S 479. Superscirpt

A. A^{Test} B. A_{Test} C. ~~A Test~~ D. Test

L-1 S 480. Distance between lines of text is known as

A. Line spacing B. Line displacement
C. Gap area D. None of the above

L-1 S 481. "Font size" could be changed by using the standard toolbar

A. TRUE B. FALSE

L-1 S 482. Select the menu bar, or close an open menu and submenu at the same time.
A. F10 B. Fl C. Esc D. Alt

L-1 S 483. The ———— feature lists possible matches from entries that were typed before
A. Autocomplete B. Autotext
C. Autotype D. None of the above

L-2 S 484. To select a paragraph
A. Triple click in the paragraph B. Double Click the paragraph C. Double Click in the selection bar

L-2 S 485. For fancy text effects one can use ————
A. Word art B. Word effects C. Fancy Design D. Clip art

L-2 S 486. In mail merge, ———— is the document that contains the data to be merged into the main document
A. Data source B. Result document C. Main Document D. None of the above

L-1 S 487. Strikethrough
A. A^{Test} B. A_{Test} C. ~~A Test~~ D. Test

L-1 S 488. Select to the beginning of the document
A. Ctrl+Home B. Ctrl+Shift+Home C. Alt+Shift+Home D. Alt+Home

L-1 S 489. Spell and grammer option is available under
A. Format menu B. Insert menu C. Tools menu D. View menu

L-1 S 490. A place which is marked for reference purpose
A. Tick mark B. Footnote C. Header D. Bookmark
E. Endmark

L-1 S 491. The Office Clipboard can hold up to —— items.
A. 25 B. 12 C. 24 D. 14

L-1 S 492. To go to the end of a line ———— is used
A. Alt+Right arrow key B. Ctrl+Right arrow key C. End D. Ctrl+End

L-1 S 493. To stop numbering, one has to press ———— twice
A. Ctrl B. Shift C. Winkey D. Enter key

L-1 S 494. To use the Goto command, one can press ————
A. Ctrl+P B. Alt+G C. Ctrl+shift+G D. F5

L-1 S 495. As the text is typed, automatically correct common typos
A. Thesaurus B. Spell check C. AutoCorrect D. Autotype

L-1 S 496. A ———— under a word indicates a possible spelling mistake
A. Blue wavy line B. Underline
C. Red wavy line D. None of the above

L-1 S 497. These are the common methods of indicating a list and the items in it

A. Bullets only B. Numbers or letters only

C. Numbers followed by letters or bullets D. All of the above

L-1 S 498. Copy, cut and paste options are available in ———— menu in Ms Word

A. View B. Insert C. Edit D. File

L-1 S 499. The filename suggested by Ms Word when a file is saved for the first time is

A. Document1 B. Text1 C. The first heading or sentence in a document D. The page header of the document

L-1 S 500. Word uses ———— wavy underlines to indicate possible grammatical errors

A. Purple B. Red C. Green D. Orange

L-1 S 501. If office assistant is turned on, Press ———— to open the assistant button

A. Win key B. Home key C. F1 D. F10

L-1 S 502. The ———— key deletes the character to the left of the insertion point

A. Delete B. End C. Backspace D. Alt

L-1 S 503. A ———— identifies a location in a file for future reference and quick access

A. URL B. Goto mark C. Header D. Bookmark

L-1 S 504. To format a document automatically ———— option in the tools menu could be used

A. Autodesign B. Self-format

C. Autoformat D. Style and format

L-1 S 505 To set your own tab stops, you can use the Tabs selection from the ———— menu

A. Tools B. Insert C. View D. Format

L-1 S 506. If the computer finds a word which is not available in the dictionary it ———— that word

A. Deletes B. Make the word Bold

C. Underlines D. None of the above

L-1 S 507. To start a new line of text at a specific point, click where you want to break the line, and then press

A. Ctrl+E B. Alt+N C. ALT+ENTER D. Ctrl+Enter

L-1 S 508. To search for a word in a Ms Word document, ———— option is used which is located in ———— menu

A. Alt+F B. Ctrl+SC. Both of the above D. Find, Edit

L-1 S 509. The ———— provides meaning of words, and highlights the one that is closest to what you have typed.

A. Grammer B. WordPerfect C. Thesaurus D. Dictionary

L-1 S 510. The function which allows you to type continuously without thinking about where one line will end and the next one begins

A. Word scroll B. Hyphenation

C. Word wrap D. None of the above

L-1 S 511. The mode which denotes that if cursor is in between some text and this mode is on, then typing would replace the already typed characters

A. Insert mode B. Replace mode C. Rollover mode D. Overtype mode

L-1 S 512. A storage location for text or graphics which is used frequently such as name of the office or address of a regular customer. Each selection of text or graphics is recorded and is assigned a unique name.

A. Auto entry B. Auto type C. Auto Punch D. Auto text

L-2 S 513. CTRL+H

A. Hyphenation on B. Hide text

C. Creates a hyperlink D. Replace text

L-2 S 514. Insert a hyperlink

A. Alt+Spacebar B. Ctrl+I C. Ctrl+H D. Ctrl+K

L-2 S 515. In Ms Word, Mail merge option is available on the

A. File menu B. Insert menu C. Format menu D. Tools menu

L-2 S 516. A ———————— is displayed in blue colour and is underlined by default

A. Shortcut B. PIF C. Hyperlink D. Explorer

L-2 S 517. To insert a manual page break, click in the document and then press ———————

A. Alt+Enter B. Ctrl+Esc C. Alt+Enter D. Ctrl+Enter

L-2 S 518. The ———————— on the standard toolbar is used for applying an existing format to other parts of document

A. Font B. Format copier C. Copy D. Format Painter

L-2 S 519. By default, page numbers will be positioned ———— inch form the top (header) or bottom (footer) of the page

A. 0.75 B. 0.4 C. 1/2 D. 1

L-2 S 520. When you open a new document, by default Word uses a template called ————, which contains several default styles

A. System template B. Auto template C. Default template D. Normal

L-2 S 521. Instead of deleting a word and then adding another one, one can also simply type right over the unwanted word(s). This is called

A. Insertion B. Overlapping

C. Typing Over D. none of the above

L-2 S 522. In mail merge, ———— is the column heading in the first row of a table in the Data source, which Dribes the related data, record by record, in the column

A. Files B. Record C. Field D. Database

L-2 S 523. In mail merge, —————————— is the document that contains the text, graphics and merge fields into which the data from the fields located in the data source will be merged

A. Data source B. Result document

C. Main Document D. None of the above

L-1 S 524. There are two components for mail merge

Ans Main document and data source

L-1 S525. Shows the line of text where the insertion point is located. No measurement is displayed if the insertion point is not in the window.

Ans Ln

L-2 S 526. AutoCorrect can use a list of built-in corrections to detect and correct typos, misspelled words, and common symbols

Ans Autocorrect entries

L-2 S 527. It is a macro which backs up the autocorrect list. This could be used it autocorrect list has to be copied to another computer

Ans AutoCorrect Backup

L-1 T/F 528. Ms Word cannot check grammer

A. TRUE B. FALSE

L-1 T/F 529. Once cannot work in Ms-Office safe mode

A. TRUE B. FALSE

L-1 T/F 530. A header can contain graphics but a footer cannot

A. TRUE B. FALSE

L-1 T/F 531. More than one font cannot be used in a word document

A. TRUE B. FALSE

L-1 T/F 532. Portable documents cannot be created using Ms Word

A. TRUE B. FALSE

L-1 T/F 533. More than one page could not be seen on the screen at a time

A. TRUE B. FALSE

L-1 T/F 534. The waved red underline which marks spelling mistakes get printed

A. TRUE B. FALSE

L-1 T/F 535. To replace the automatically entered characters, continue typing. If overtype mode is off

A. TRUE B. FALSE

L-1 T/F 536. If a document has not been saved and the close button is pressed, Word closes without saving the document

A. TRUE B. FALSE

L-2 T/F 537. One cannot add words to the Ms Word dictionary

A. TRUE B. FALSE

L-2 T/F 538. Microsoft Word even corrects words contained in hyperlinks

A.TRUE B. FALSE

L-2 T/F 539. Word does not check spelling and grammer automatically by default

A.TRUE B. FALSE

L-2 T/F 540. Headers and footers appear in outline view where they can be edited

A.TRUE B. FALSE

L-2 T/F 541. Reviews by multiple users on separate copies of the same document cannot be merged and viewed in a single file

A.TRUE B. FALSE

L-2 T/F 542. Footer cannot be modified by double clicking the dimmed text in the footer area. It has to accessed from the menu

A.TRUE B. FALSE

L-1 T/F 543. A word processor could check the spellings

A.TRUE B. FALSE

L-1 T/F 544. There are four types of paragraph alignment

A.TRUE B. FALSE

L-1 T/F 545. By default, any document created will be single-spaced

A.TRUE B. FALSE

L-1 T/F 546. By default, Microsoft Word inserts characters they are typed

A.TRUE B. FALSE

L-1 T/F 547. Ms word underlines spelling mistakes by a waved red underline

A.TRUE B. FALSE

L-1 T/F 548.Word inserts an autocomplete entry only after 4 characters are typed

A.TRUE B. FALSE

L-1 T/F 549. In MS Word, spell checking occurs automatically as the text is typed

A.TRUE B. FALSE

L-1 T/F 550. In Ms Word, fonts of selected text or complete document can be changed.

A.TRUE B. FALSE

L-1 T/F 551. In Justify setting of paragraph alignment both right and left margins are even

A.TRUE B. FALSE

L-1 T/F 552. If a word is too long to fit on the end of a line, Microsoft Word moves the word to the beginning of the next line instead of hyphenating it

A.TRUE B. FALSE

L-2 T/F 553. Header and Footers can contain page numbers

A.TRUE B. FALSE

L-2 T/F554 You can insert text or graphics in headers and footers

A.TRUE B. FALSE

L-2 T/F 555. Ms Word has default option of auto-save every 10 minutes

A.TRUE B. FALSE

L-2 T/F 556. Header can be modified by double-clicking the dimmed text in the header area

A.TRUE B. FALSE

L-2 T/F 557. To open the page setup dialog box, double click any gray portion of the ruler bar

A.TRUE B. FALSE

L-2 T/F 558. Tools → Language → Set language option is used to set the language for the document

A.TRUE B. FALSE

L-2 T/F 559. In the Font dialog box, if you want to restore the default font settings, click in the Normal font check box

A.TRUE B. FALSE

L-2 T/F 560.To recover work after a power failure or similar problem, you must have turned on the autorecover feature before the problem occurred

A.TRUE B. FALSE

L-3 T/F 561. AutoCorrect entries are limited to 255 characters

A.TRUE B. FALSE

L-3 T/F 562. The autotext entries are available to all documents if they are stored in the normal template.

A.TRUE B. FALSE

Word

L-2 D 563. In Ms-Word, Click on the selection bar

Ans To select a entire paragraph

L-1 D 564. Move handle in a table

Ans Point from which a table in a word document can be dragged and placed to another location

L-1 D 565. Move to the beginning of the line.

Ans HOME

L-1 D 566. Ms Word is a paragraph oriented program

L-1 D 567. A combination of character and paragraph formatting characteristics that are named and stored as a set.

Ans. Paragraph style

L-1 D 568. In word processing, a paragraph that has all lines but the first indented. A hanging indent is also known as a hanging paragraph.

L-2 D 569. A view of a document as it will appear in a Web browser.

Ans Web layout

L-2 D 570. Click and drag the contents of the selected cell to move the content to the other cell

L-2 D 571. AutoFit, which resizes text as type, if necessary, to fit the text into a placeholder.

L-2 D 572. ——————— means that the second and subsequent line single of a paragraph are indented, as in bibliography

Ans Hanging Indent

L-2 D 573. A graphic or other object that is inserted in the drawing layer so that it can be positioned precisely on the page or in front of or behind text or other objects.

Ans Floating Object

L-1 S 574. Insert a comment

A. Alt+Ctrl+C B. ALT+CTRL+M C. Alt+C D. Ctrl+C

L-1 S 575. Open the thesaurus

A. Shift+F1 B. Shift+F7 C. Alt+F7 D. Ctrl+F7

L-2 S 576. In this view, text and tables wrap to fit in the window

A. Outline B. Web layout C. Page layout D. Print layout

L-2 S 577. The default margin setting for any new document is ——————— for top, bottom, left and right respectively

A. 0.75,1,1,1 B. 1,1,1.25,1.25 inch

C. 0.75, 0.25, 1.25, 1 D. 1.25,1,1.25,1

L-2 S 578. To copy text (insert a duplicate of the text instead of moving it) using dragging, hold ——————— key while you drag

A. Shift B. Ctrl C. Alt D. Delete

L-1 S579 The default font in Ms Word is

A. Arial B. Courier C. Lucida Console D. Times New Roman

L-1 S 580. Hold down the ——————— key, then hit Enter key to move up to the above row

A. Alt B. Backspace C. Insert D. Shift

L-1 S 581. Ms Word highlights grammatical errors by a ——————— line, which is not printed

A. Black waved line B. Red waved line C. Blue waved line D. Green waved line

L-1 S 582. Strikethrough, superscript and subscript options are available in the ——————— section of the Format cells—>Font dialog box

A. Font style B. Format style C. Special effects D. Effects

L-2 S 583. In this view, the documents appears as one long page without page breaks

A. Page layout B. Outline

C. Web layout D. None of the above

L-1 T/F 584 Shrink to fit is not available in Ms Word

A. TRUE B. FALSE

L-2 T/F 585. Separate Headers and Footers can be specified for even and odd numbered pages

A. TRUE B. FALSE

Word, Excel

L-2 D 586. The ruler can be used to change margins

A.TRUE

L-2 D 587. "What's this ?" in the help menu changes the mouse pointer to a question mark, then clicking on a topic opens a bubble text box with the help on that topic

Ans TRUE

L-1 D 588. Use Edit → Clear option and then click on formats

L-2 D 589. Changing the default page setup

Ans On page setup dialog box, check and change various settings and the click on default button

L-2 D 590. This template is located in Program Files\Microsoft Office\Office10\Macros

L-2 D 591. Recently used symbols list is available in symbol dialog box. From there, a symbol recently used could be quickly inserted.

L-2 D 592. Shows the extend selection mode status. Double-click EXT to turn the mode on or off. When selection mode is off, EXT appears dimmed.

Ans EXT

L-2 D 593. AutoSummarize identifies the key points in a document for you to share with others or quickly scan. AutoSummarize works best on well-structured documents

L-2 D 594. A minimum width for page margin is required by most printers. They cannot print to the edge of the page. If an improper margin is set, Microsoft word says that "One or more margins are set outside the printable area of the page"

L-1 M 595. ——————— allows a user to use the mouse to move to parts of the document currently not on screen

Ans Scroll bar B. Page up C. Backspace D. Page dn

L-1 S 596. Change case

A.Shift+F5 B. Shift+F3 C. Shift+C D. Ctrl+C

L-1 S 597. Spelling errors are corrected by ——— feature

A.Autoformat B. Autocorrect C. Autostyle D. Autorun

L-1 S 598. ——————— key could also be used for selecting text in a MS Word document

A.Esc B. Shift

C.Alt D. None of the above

L-1 S 599. A temporary copy of the file being worked on is saved periodically by ——— feature

A.Autoformat B. Autocorrect C. Autorecover D. Autorun

L-1 S 600. Ctrl+A is used to

A.Select all B. Select a line

C.Select a paragraph D. Select a section

L-1 S 601. ——————— is used to get to the last position in Ms Word

A.Shift+F5 B. Shift+F3 C. Shift+C D. Ctrl+C

L-1 T/F 602. The Find What and Replace With boxes do not save latest entries

A.TRUE B. FALSE

L-1 T/F 603. One cannot specify different headers for even and odd numbered pages

A.TRUE B. FALSE

L-1 T/F 604. The 'Delete key' removes the character to the left of the insertion point

A.TRUE B. FALSE

L-2 T/F 605. A block of text could not be moved to another location in a word processing software

A.TRUE B. FALSE

L-1 T/F 606. Text can be inserted anywhere in MS Word

A.TRUE B. FALSE

L-1 T/F 607. Still and motion graphics could be used as bullets in a word document

A.TRUE B. FALSE

L-1 T/F 608. The icons beside the font names in the font box identify the font types

A.TRUE B. FALSE

L-1 T/F 609. One could find or find and replace one by one occurrence or find and replace all at once

A.TRUE B. FALSE

L-2 T/F 610.A modified template can be saved by another name to be used for later use as a new template

A.TRUE B. FALSE

L-2 S 611. Paste formats

A.CTRL+V B. Ctrl+P C. CTRL+SHIFT+V D. Ctrl+C

L-2 S 612. Copy a format already applied to text and apply it to other text

A.Format copy B. Style copy C. Style painter D. Format painter

Word, Excel, Powerpoint

L-2 D 613. Microsoft Office —————— allows you to safely use an Office program that has encountered certain startup problems. When a problem is detected at startup, Office either fixes the problem or isolates it, allowing the program to star

Ans Normal mode

L-1 D 614. Full form of OLE is

Ans Object linking and embedding

L-1 D 615. Automatic backup copies

Ans Ms-Office documents are also backed up when worked on, if the option for automatic backup is enabled

L-1 D 616. Use CTRL+S to save a document in Ms-Office

L-1 D 617. Use CTRL+W to Close a document in Ms-office

L-1 D 618. Move backward through tabs

Ans Ctrl+SHIFT+TAB

L-1 D 619. To Apply or remove bold formatting, press Ctrl+B

L-1 D 620. To Apply or remove underlining use Ctrl+U

L-1 D 621. Ctrl+Shift with any of the arrow keys

Ans Highlight a block of text

L-1 D 622. CTRL+C Copy the selected text or object

L-1 D 623. Searches for a text string in a file or files.

Ans FIND

L-1 D 624. Move counterclockwise among panes of normal view

Ans CTRL+SHIFT+TAB

L-1 D 625. A place where the most common tasks in Office are displayed

Ans Office Task Panes

L-1 D 626. An embedded object becomes a part of the destination file.

L-1 D 627. Page margins are the blank space around the edges of the page.

L-1 D 628. clip: A single media file, including art, sound, animation, or movies.

L-1 D 629. CTRL+N Create a new document of the same type as the current or most recent document

Ans Create a new document of the same type as the current or most recent document

L-1 D 630. Office task panes. The most common tasks in Microsoft Office are organized in panes

L-1 D 631. To see the name of a toolbar button, rest the pointer over the button until the name appears

L-1 D 632. Press ALT to select the menu bar. Press CTRL+TAB repeatedly to select the toolbar or task pane which is required

L-1 D 633. Open the list if it is closed and move to that option in the list. ALT+ the underlined letter in an option

L-1 D 634. When the Assistant is turned on, program and system messages are displayed in the Assistant balloon by default.

L-1 D 635. Microsoft office shortcut bar could be used to get Single click access to msoffice programs and opening a blank msoffice document

L-1 D 636. To undo or redo multiple actions at once, select the drop down arrow next to either button and select the number of steps to undo or redo

L-1 D 637. Shows the distance from the top of the page to your insertion point. No measurement is displayed if the insertion point is not in the window.

Ans On the status bar of the document window.

L-1 D 638. A window within an Office application that provides commonly used commands. Its location and small size allow you to use these commands while still working on your files.

Ans Task pane

L-1 D 639. The Microsoft Office Clipboard allows the user to collect text and graphic items from any number of Office documents or other programs and then paste them into any Office document.

L-1 D 640. If the —————— mode is on and we type in a line where text already exists, the text we type would be placed at the insertion point and previous text would move to the right

Ans INSERT

L-2 D 641. In Ms-Office, CTRL+5 is used to

Ans Apply or remove strikethrough.

L-2 D 642. In Ms-Office, CTRL+I

Ans Apply or remove italic formatting.

L-2 D 643. In Ms-Office, CTRL+F5

Ans Restore the size of the active window after it is maximized

L-2 D 644. CTRL+F3

Ans Cut to the Spike

L-2 D 645. In Ms-Office, use CTRL+SHIFT+< Decrease font size

L-2 D 646. In Ms-Office, use CTRL+SHIFT+> Increase font size

L-2 D 647. CTRL+TAB Switch to the next tab

L-2 D 648. To compare two versions of a document

Ans Compare and merge on tools menu

L-2 D 649. In Ms-Office, use CTRL+A (on the Outline tab) All text

L-2 D 650. In Ms-Office, use CTRL+DELETE Delete one word to the right

L-2 D 651. In Ms-Office, use CTRL+F10 Maximize or restore a selected window

L-2 D 652. In Ms-Office, use CTRL+Move between a master document and its subdocuments

L-2 D 653. In Ms-Office, use CTRL+F10 Maximize or restore the selected workbook window.

L-2 D 654. When more than one window is open, switch to the next window

Ans CTRL+F6

L-2 D 655. Damaged files can be opened using this and text could be recovered

Ans File recovery converter

L-2 D 656. CTRL+DOWN ARROW Display the full set of commands on the task pane menu.

L-2 D 657. In OLE, the information can be copied either as a linked object or as a

Ans Embedded object

L-2 D 658. An electronic, encryption-based, secure stamp of authentication on a document.

Ans Digital signature

L-2 D 659. CTRL+DOWN ARROW When a shortened menu is open, display the full set of commands.

L-2 D 660. A supplemental program that adds custom commands or custom features to Microsoft Office

Ans Add-In

L-2 D 661. The transferred information changed in the word document is also changed at the excel source

Ans Linking

L-2 D 662. Ms-Office also supports handwriting input through handwriting input device (graphics tablet or a tablet PC

L-2 D 663. Mirror margins, is used if pages will be duplicated or printed double sided and then binding (or hole punching) them

Ans Changes "Left" and "Right" settings to "Inner" and "Outer" and makes any gutter you've set as inner margin offset.

L-2 D 664. The diagramming tool on the drawing toolbar could be used to display hierarchical relationships such as organization chart

Ans Organization Chart

L-2 D 665. One can password protect an Ms-Office documents in two levels. One to open the document and another for modification rights

L-2 D 666. Set margins for facing pages. Use mirror margins to set up facing pages for double-sided documents, such as books or magazines

Ans Mirror Margins

L-2 D 667. Use from among the following to find? (question mark) Any Single character. For example, smith finds "smith" and "smyth" * (asterisk) Any number of characters

L-2 D 668. When you use Search, the Search task pane is displayed on the right side of the page. Each Office application can have its own instance of the Search task pane.

Ans Search task pane

L-2 D 669. To select the text that is not next to each other, select the first item and then hold down the Ctrl key and then select other items without releasing the Ctrl key

L-2 D 670. A folder where a collection of files is shared and the files often use the same template. Each file in a library is associated with user-defined information that is displayed in the content listing for that library.

Ans Document Library

L-2 D 671. When an object is linked, information is updated only if the source file is modified. Linked data is stored in the source file. The destination file stores only the location of the source file and displays a representation of the linked file.

Ans Linked objects

L-3 D 672. Control paste options and automatic changes with smart tags Smart tags let you immediately adjust how information is pasted or how automatic changes occur in Office programs.

L-3 D 673. If a Microsoft Office program encounters a problem and stops responding, the files in use/opened at that time are analyzed for errors, and information in them is recovered as far as possible.

Ans Document recovery and autorecover

L-3 D 674. When a user save changes to a shared workbook, another person who's currently editing the workbook might have saved changes to the same cells. In this case, the changes conflict, and a conflict resolution dialog box appears

Ans Resolving conflicts

L-1 D 675. "Help" option is available on the ———— menu

Ans Help

L-2 D 676. It allows the user to change the information within the cells of the word document but not withing the original excel source

Ans Embedding

L-2 F 677. OLE stands for ————————

Ans Object Linking and Embedding

L-2 F 678. Information created in another program that has been pasted inside another document. That information becomes part of the document in which it is pasted. This is called an ————————

Ans Embedded object

L-3 F 679. A supplemental program that extends the capabilities of a Microsoft Office program by adding custom commands and specialized features.

Ans COM add-in

L-3 F 680. During startup, Office checks for problems such as an add-in or extension that won't start, or a corrupted resource, file, registry, or template. A message is displayed the next time the program is started

Ans Automated safe mode

L-1 M 681. Msoffice package contains

A. Word B. Powerpoint C. Access

D. Internet explorer E. Excel

L-1 M 682. The ———————— gives access to commands

A. Status bar B. Toolbar C. Menu bar D. All of the above

L-1 M 683. The ———————— is an area in Ms-Office that stores text and objects. These can be moved and inserted to different parts in a document by copying, different documents, and even different applications

A. Task pane B. Cache C. Clipboard D. Temp

L-1 S 684. CTRL+Y

A. Undo an action B. Redo or repeat an action

C. Select a document D. None of the above

L-1 S 685. Check spelling

A. F6 B. F7 C. F5 D. F8

L-1 S 686. Insert a hyperlink

A. Alt+K B. CTRL+K

C. Ctrl+L D. None of the above

L-1 S 687. Turn extend mode on

A. F1 B. F8 C. F7 D. F10

L-1 S 688. Shows a shortcut menu

A. Shift+F1 B. Shift+F10 C. Ctrl+F10 D. Alt+F10

L-1 S 689. Go to the beginning of a document

A. Home B. Ctrl+Home

C. Ctrl+Up arrow key D. All of the above

L-1 S 690. Shortcuts for the print dialog box

A. Alt+P B. Ctrl+P C. Ctrl+Y D. Ctrl+Shift+F12

L-1 S 691. To select the entire document press

A. Ctrl+E B. Ctrl+A C. ALT+ENTER D. Alt+A

L-1 S 692. Find text, formatting, and special items

A. Alt+FB. Ctrl+FC. Shift+FD. None of the above

L-1 S 693. The information at the bottom of a document.

A. Tail B. Footer C. Endnote D. End mark

L-1 S 694. Copy option is available in ——— toolbar

A. Format B. Standard

C. Drawing D. None of the above

L-1 S 695. The folder in which documents appear when opened or saved

A. Default folder B. Working folder

C. Document folder D. None of the above

L-1 S 696. The keyboard shortcut to apply or remove the bold style is

A. Ctrl+SB. Ctrl+B C. Alt+B D. Ctrl+Alt+B

L-1 S 697. The keyboard shortcut to apply or remove the italic style is

A. Alt+I B. Ctrl+I C. Ctrl+Alt+I D. Ctrl+Shift+I

L-1 S 698. The clipboard provided by office 2000 can store upto ——— copy/cut

A. 5 B. 12 C. 9 D. 3

L-1 S 699. If any dialog box is open and you want to get help about any of its content, click ——— and then click the sentence/word in the dialog box for which help is required

A. Help B. Question mark

C. Exclamation mark D. All of the above

L-2 S 700. CTRL+BACKSPACE

A. Move to previous page B. Delete one word to the left

C. Delete a paragraph D. Delete a line

L-2 S 701. Display the Open dialog box

A. F1 B. CTRL+F12 C. Ctrl+O D. Alt+F,O

L-2 S 702. —————————— a word to select it

A. Click B. Double Click C. Triple Click D. Press backspace

L-2 S 703. A note or annotation that an author writes to clarify a particular thing in a document

A. Documentation B. Comment C. Footnote D. Tracked change

L-2 S 704. A mark that shows where a deletion, insertion, or other editing change has been made in a document

A. Documentation B. Comment C. Footnote D. Tracked change

L-2 S 705. A way to transfer and share information between applications by pasting information created in one application into a document created in another

A. Hyperlink B. OLE

C. Both of the above D. None of the above

L-3 S 706. Pasting a document created in Ms Word in a excel spreadsheet.

A. Insert Document B. OLE C. Clipart

D. Com E. None of the above

L-1 S 707. Ctrl+C

A. Copy B. Cut

C. Insert column D. None of the above

L-1 S 708. Undo an action

A. CTRL+Z B. Ctrl+U

C. Ctrl+A D. None of the above

L-1 S 709. Paste text or an object

A. CTRL+V B. Ctrl+P

C. Ctrl+O D. None of the above

L-1 S 710. Change or resize the font

A.CTRL+SHIFT+FB. CTRL+ALT+FC. ALT+SHIFT+FD. None of the above

L-2 S 711. When the source file is changed, the ———— copy of the document does not change

A. Embedded B. Linked

C. Both of the above D. None of the above

L-1 S 712. CTRL+P

A. Paste from clipboard B. Pause an event

C. Prints a document D. None of the above

L-1 S 713. Shortcut to save

A.Ctrl+SB. Ctrl+P C. Ctrl+Y D. Ctrl+Shift+F12

L-1 S 714. Shortcut for Redo is

A.Ctrl+R B. Ctrl+P C. Ctrl+Y D. Ctrl+Shift+;

L-1 S 715. Go to the end of a document

A.Alt+F10 B. Ctrl+Page down

C.Ctrl+down arrow key D. Ctrl+End

L-1 S 716. Display the Save As dialog box

A.F1 B. F10 C. Home D. F12

L-1 S 717. Cut selected text to the Clipboard

A.Ctrl+SB. B. Ctrl+C

C.CTRL+X D. None of the above

L-1 S 718. Move clockwise among panes of normal view

A.Alt+Shift B. Shift+F1 C. Ctrl+Shift D. SHIFT+F6

L-1 S 719. In Ms-Office, You can Undo and Redo last ——————— actions

A.150 B. 10 C. 100 D. 50

L-1 S 720. To go to the beginning of a line ——————— is used

A.Page up B. Ctrl+Home C. F1 D. Home key

L-1 S 721. Template file '———————' is convenient for most editing and formatting tasks

A.Typing B. Outline C. Print D. Normal

L-1 S 722. A ——————— is a preformatted document to which a user can add text of its own

A.Shell B. Normal

C.Template D. Sample document

L-1 S 723. To see what the document will look like when printed, click the ——————— button

A. Export file B. Dry Print

C. Print Preview button D. Print

L-1 S 724. Copies the format from a selected object or text and applies to the object or text that is clicked

A.Autoformat B. Autostyle C. Format paster D. Format painter

L-1 S 725. ——————— can be used as an outline document to create a new document. It contains suitable style. Layouts etc as per the requirement of the document under consideration

A.Skeleton B. Format C. Template D. Base design

L-1 S 726. A line break

A.Ctrl+Pause break B. Alt+Enter C. CTRL+ENTER D. Shift+Enter

L-1 S 727. A skeleton document for frequently used formats is called

A.Shell B. Base file C. Normal D. Template

L-2 S 728. Shortcut for "What's this ?" option is

A.Ctrl+W B. Ctrl+P C. Ctrl+Y D. Shift+F1

L-2 S 729. Find documents that are automatically recovered

A.Use windows search feature B. Use dos prompt

C.Both of the above D. File—>Open—>Tools option

L-2 S 730. —————— sets a page offset. This setting is used if binding of the printed document is required

A.Left margin B. Top margin C. Both of the above D. Gutter

L-2 S 731. ———— the text or pictures that appear behind the document text. They are intended only for printed documents

A. Background B. Scene C. Watermark D. Bitmap

L-2 S 732. ———— helps to recover Ms Word file, if a file is open and either Ms Word stops responding or power is switched off

A.Backup manager B. Autorecover

C.Autotype D. None of the above

L-2 S 733. Work done can be further protected by using the —————— feature. This feature periodically save a temporary copy of the file you're working on

A.Autosave B. Autobackup

C.Autorecover D. None of the above

L-1 S 734. You can position some items in the margins — for example, headers, footers, and page numbers.

A.TRUE

L-1 T/F 735. Hiding the office assistant is same as disabling it

A.TRUE B. FALSE

L-1 T/F 736. Office Clipboard do not work with the standard Copy and Paste commands.

A.TRUE B. FALSE

L-2 T/F 737. Text included in hyperlinks is automatically corrected

A.TRUE B. FALSE

L-2 T/F 738. In recording a macro, sequence of instructions is not important

A.TRUE B. FALSE

L-2 T/F 739. A password cannot be used to protect MS Word document against reading and/or modifying

A.TRUE B. FALSE

L-2 T/F 740. When an object is embedded, information stored in the destination file change if the source file is modified.

A.TRUE B. FALSE

L-1 T/F 741. Microsoft hosts an online clip art gallery

A.TRUE B. FALSE

L-1 T/F 742. One can type in the document in Print Preview mode

A.TRUE B. FALSE

L-1 T/F 743. Wild cards can be used in the Find option in Ms Word

A.TRUE B. FALSE

L-1 T/F 744. WordPerfect alows the user to see the formatting codes

A.TRUE B. FALSE

L-1 T/F 745. Icons present on the toolbar gives direct access to commands

A.TRUE B. FALSE

L-1 T/F 746. For a document which is not saved, Ms Word suggests a file name

A.TRUE B. FALSE

L-1 T/F 747. Word documents can be sent as email, instead of attaching them to an email

A.TRUE B. FALSE

L-1 T/F 748.Clip art is built in gallery in Ms-Office which contains hundreds of images

A.TRUE B. FALSE

L-1 T/F 749. The office assistant automatically appears, whenever it thinks that some help is need, If it is not disabled.

A.TRUE B. FALSE

L-1 T/F 750. Except for a specific menu in each application, the menus in the main menu bar of excel, word and powerpoint are identical

A.TRUE B. FALSE

L-2 T/F 751. Autorecover periodically save a temporary copy of the file being worked on

A.TRUE B. FALSE

L-2 T/F 752."Office on the web option" in help menu of Ms Word/Excel takes to online help

A.TRUE B. FALSE

L-2 T/F 753. When an object is linked, information is updated only if the source file is modified

A.TRUE B. FALSE

L-2 T/F 754. Press shift+F5 to return to the place where you were before closing the document previously

A.TRUE B. FALSE

L-2 T/F 755. When you copy multiple items to the Office Clipboard, the last item copied is always copied to the system Clipboard.

A.TRUE B. FALSE

L-3 T/F 756. If a Ms-Office program is started in safe mode, no templates can be saved, but files can be

A.TRUE B. FALSE

Answers

Q. No.	Answer	Q. No.	Answer
2	B	180	B
3	A	181	B
148	A B C	182	B
149	A B	183	B
150	A B	184	B
151	A B D E	185	B
152	A B	186	B
153	B	187	B
154	B	188	B
155	B	189	B
156	B	190	B
157	B	191	B
158	B	192	B
159	B	193	B
160	B	194	B
161	B	195	B
162	B	196	B D
163	B	197	B
164	B	198	B
165	B	199	C
166	B	200	A
167	B	201	A
168	B	202	A
169	B	203	A
170	B	204	A
171	B	205	A
172	B	206	A
173	B	207	A
174	B	208	A
175	B	209	A
176	B	210	A
177	B	211	D
178	B	212	C
179	B	213	C

Q. No.	Answer	Q. No.	Answer
214	C	250	D
215	C	251	C
216	D	252	C
217	D	253	C
218	C	254	C
219	C	255	C
220	D	256	B
221	D	257	D
222	C	258	C
223	B	259	D
224	C	260	C
225	D	261	C
226	D	262	D
227	C	263	D
228	D	264	C
229	C	266	B
230	C	267	B
231	C	268	B
232	C	269	B
233	C	270	B
234	D	271	B
235	D	272	B
236	E	273	B
237	D	274	B
238	C	275	B
239	D	276	B
240	C	277	B
241	D	278	B
242	D	279	B
243	D	280	B
244	C	281	B
245	C	282	B
246	D	283	B
247	C	284	B
248	D	285	B
249	C	286	B

Q. No.	Answer	Q. No.	Answer
287	B	354	B
288	A	355	A
289	A	449	A B D E
290	A	450	A B D
291	A	451	A B D
292	A	452	A B C
293	A	453	B D
294	A	454	B C
295	A	455	A D E
296	A	456	A C
297	A	457	B
298	A	458	B
299	A	459	B
300	A	460	B
301	A	461	B
302	A	462	B
303	A	463	B
304	A	464	B
305	A	465	B
306	A	466	B
307	A	467	B
309	A B	468	B
310	A	469	B
311	B	470	B
342	A C	471	B
343	B	472	B
344	C	473	B
345	B	474	B
346	C	475	B
347	D	476	B
348	D	477	B
349	C	478	A
350	C	479	A
351	A	480	A
352	B	481	A
353	B	482	A D

Q. No.	Answer	Q. No.	Answer
483	A	519	C
484	A C	520	D
485	A	521	C
486	A C	522	C
487	C	523	C
488	C	524	A
489	C	525	A
490	D	526	A
491	C	527	A
492	C	528	B
493	D	529	B
494	D	530	B
495	C	531	B
496	C	532	B
497	D	533	B
498	C	534	B
499	C	535	B
500	C	536	B
501	C	537	B
502	C	538	B
503	D	539	B
504	C	540	B
505	D	541	B
506	C	542	B
507	C	543	A
508	D	544	A
509	C	545	A
510	C	546	A
511	D	547	A
512	D	548	A
513	D	549	A
514	D	550	A
515	D	551	A
516	C	552	A
517	D	553	A
518	D	554	A

Q. No.	Answer	Q. No.	Answer
555	A	611	C
556	A	612	D
557	A	681	A B C E
558	A	682	B C
559	A	683	C
560	A	684	B
561	A	685	B
562	A	686	B
574	B	687	B
575	B	688	B
576	B	689	B
577	B	690	B D
578	B	691	B
579	D	692	B
580	D	693	B
581	D	694	B
582	D	695	B
583	C	696	B
584	B	697	B
585	A	698	B
595	A B D	699	B
596	B	700	B
597	B	701	B C D
598	B	702	B
599	B C	703	B
600	A	704	B D
601	A	705	B
602	B	706	B
603	B	707	A
604	B	708	A
605	B	709	A
606	A	710	A
607	A	711	A
608	A	712	C
609	A	713	A
610	A	714	C

Q. No.	Answer	Q. No.	Answer
715	D	736	B
716	D	737	B
717	C	738	B
718	D	739	B
719	C	740	B
720	D	741	A
721	D	742	A
722	C	743	A
723	C	744	A
724	D	745	A
725	C	746	A
726	C	747	A
727	D	748	A
728	D	749	A
729	D	750	A
730	D	751	A
731	C	752	A
732		753	A
733	C	754	A
734	A	755	A
735	B	756	A

5

OPERATING SYSTEM

L-1 D 1. Full form of BCR

Ans Bar Code Reader

L-1 D 2. A barcode reader (or barcode scanner) is an electronic device for reading printed barcodes

Administration

L-2 D 1. Operating system cannot use a hardware device without installing a driver for it

L-2 D 2. A representation of a stored state of a computer system is known as a ———

Ans Restore point

L-2 D 3. By default, members in this group have no right to install programs

Ans Guests

L-2 D 4. Supports managing system resources through common interfaces

Ans Windows Management Instrumentation (WMI)

L-1 D 5. A computer configuration that runs two or more operating systems

Ans Multiple boot

L-1 D 6. Files used by Windows to load, configure, and run the operating system.

Ans System files

L-1 D 7. An area of storage on a hard disk drive. It is formatted by using a file system

Ans Volume

L-1 D 8. A service used for managing removable media (such as tapes and discs) and storage devices (libraries).

Ans Removable storage

L-1 D 9. Lock your computer if you are connected to a network domain, or switch users if you are not connected to a network domain

Ans Win key + L

L-1 D 10. To access the setting about how a computer can be used from another location — ———————— tab of system properties could be used.

Ans Remote

L-2 D 11. In the context of system administration, GID is

Ans Group Identification Device

L-2 D 12. Superuser

Ans On many computer operating systems, the superuser, or root, is a special user account used for system administration

L-2 D 13. Power users

Ans Members of the Power Users group can create user accounts, but can modify and delete only those accounts they create. They cannot modify the Administrators or Backup Operators groups, nor can they take ownership of files, back up or restore directories, load or unload device drivers, or manage the security and auditing logs

L-2 D 14. System state data is also known as

Ans SYSVOL

L-2 D 15. Each person authorized to use a system is assigned a certain ——— which denotes its identity on that system.

Ans UID

L-2 D 16. Logging of certain types of events for auditing purpose

Ans Event logging

L-2 D 17. The smallest amount of disk space that can be allocated to hold a file.

Ans Allocation unit

L-2 D 18. Windows Product Activation - Activation of Windows operating system for use.

L-2 D 19. A type of partition that can be created only on basic master boot record (MBR) disks.

Ans Extended partition

L-2 D 20. In Task Manager, the amount of virtual memory, or address space, committed to a process.

Ans Virtual Memory Size

L-2 D 21. ———————— make sure that the installed drivers are compatible with windows

Ans Driver signing

L-2 D 22. In Task Manager, the total processor time, in seconds, used by a process since it started.

Ans CPU Time

L-2 D 23. A user belonging to a ———————— has all the rights and permissions granted to the group

Ans Group account

L-2 D 24. To be able to boot from the hard disk, one partition must be marked as ———— ———— in the partition table

Ans Active

L-2 D 25. System calls are provided by the operating system which acts as interface between the operating system and user

Ans System calls

L-2 D 26. Permissions on an object that are automatically inherited from its parent object. Inherited permissions cannot be modified.

Ans Inherited permissions

L-2 D 27. A set of routines that an application uses to request and carry out lower-level services performed by a computer's operating system.

Ans Application Programming Interface (API)

L-2 D 28. Disk quota is a limit set by a system administrator that restricts certain aspects of file system usage on modern operating systems.

Ans Disk quota

L-2 D 29. In Task Manager, the percentage of time that a process used the CPU since the last update. On the Task Manager Process tab, the column heading is CPU.

Ans CPU Usage

L-2 D 30. An NTFS system file on NTFS-formatted volumes that contains information about each file and folder on the volume. The MFT is the first file on an NTFS volume.

Ans Master File Table

L-2 D 31. ———————————— prevents the replacement or removal of protected system files. It runs in the background and protects the files installed by the windows setup program

Ans Windows File Protection

L-2 D 32. A built-in account used to log on to a computer running Windows when a user does neither have an account on the computer nor on the domain and even not on any domain trusted by the computer's domain.

Ans Guest account

L-2 D 33. When an attempt is made to access a file, the permissions are checked before read or write operation could be performed. If access is permitted, the system returns a ———————— which is a small integer to use in subsequent read and write operations

Ans File Descriptor

L-3 D 34. A security or distribution group that can be used anywhere in the domain tree or forest.

Ans universal group

L-3 D 35. A volume that is created within an extended partition on a basic master boot record (MBR) disk.

Ans Logical drive

L-2 D 36. Latency is also known as

Ans Propagation delay

L-2 D 37. Volumes that span multiple disk

Ans Spanned volume

L-2 D 38. Restore point is created by System Restore at specific intervals and when System Restore detects the beginning of a change to your computer.

L-1 D 39. A server-based user profile that is downloaded to the local computer when a user logs on and that is updated both locally and on the server when the user logs off

Ans Roaming user profile

L-2 D 40. A partition consisting of disk space on one or more physical disks.

Ans Volume set

L-2 D 41. A numerical identifier that uniquely distinguishes a process while it runs.

Ans Process Identifier Device (PID)

L-2 D 42. It tracks changes to a computer and creates a restore point when it detects the beginning of a change

Ans System Restore

L-2 D 43. In Active Directory replication, the delay between the time an update is applied to a given replica and the time it is applied to some other replica.

Ans Latency

L-2 D 44. System is put in ____________ mode after a preset amount of idle time. In this mode, system consumes less power and it is available for immediate use

Ans Stand-by

L-2 D 45. This directory is shared and it stores the server copy of the domain's public files. These public files are replicated among all domain controllers in the domain

Ans SYSVOL

L-2 S 46. If we have to set the virtual memory of a system, we have to open

A. My Computer Icon B. Control Panel

C. Internet explorer D. None of the above

L-1 S 47. A user's right to perform a specific task

A. Right B. Privilege

C. Both of the above D. None of the above

L-1 S 48. Default Location of operating system files

A. C:\program files B. C:\Windows

C. C:\temp D. none of the above

L-1 S 49. ____________ is used to switch between accounts without having to restart the computer

A. It is not allowed B. Fast user switch

C. User logoff and logon D. User swap

L-2 S 50. This Operating System has process hierarchy

A. Windows B. UNIX

C. Dos D. None of the above

L-2 S 51. This table gives the starting and ending addresses of each partition

A. File allocation table B. Partition table

C. Both of the above D. None of the above

L-2 S 52. If we have to change date and time format of a system we have to go to

A. Date and Time icon of control B. Regional Setting Control

C. Folder Icon of control D. Administrative tools icon of the control panel

L-2 S 53. A program that allows a hardware device to communicate with the operating system

A. Function B. Device driver

C. API D. Utility

L-2 S 54. The process to determine what a user is permitted to do on a computer or network

A. Rights evaluation B. Auditing

C. Patrolling D. Authorization

L-2 S 55. New fonts could be installed on the system using ———— applet of the control panel

A. Add remove programs B. Font

C. Both of the above D. None of the above

L-2 S 56. This process logs events of some selected kind thereby tracking the activities of the user

A. Logging B. Auditing

C. Checking D. Evaluating

L-2 S 57. If we have to create a password or change if we use ———— applet in the control panel.

A. Administrative task B. User Accounts

C. Add or remove D. None of the above

L-2 S 58. New programs can be installed on the computer using ———— option of the control panel

A. Add or remove hardware B. Add or remove program

C. Administrative tools D. Folder options

L-2 S 59. In dual-boot or multiple-boot systems, the configuration settings that specify which system service to start and how each system service should be started

A. System environment B. Startup configuration

C. Boot setting D. None of the above

L-3 S 60. ASR is

A. Automated Software Recovery B. Automated System Recovery

C. Analysis of System Recovery D. Automated System Rollback

L-2 S 61. "Power Option" can be accessed using

A. Control Panel B. CPU

C. Internet explorer D. None of the above

L-2 S 62. Users can be members of groups, each group has

A. GID B. UID
C. Group password D. None of the above

L-2 S 63. This volume represents a duplicate of the original volume taken at the time the copy began

A. Volume shadow copy B. Replica
C. Duplicate D. Backup

L-2 S 64. For making changes to most of the settings on the Advanced tab of System properties, one should be logged on as

A. Administrator B. User
C. Guest D. None of the above

L-2 S 65. In a Windows environment, the person who controls how permissions are set on objects and can grant permissions to others.

A. Owner B. Judge
C. Third party D. None of the above

L-2 S 66. Computer name, Network Id, Workgroup name, Domain name can be viewed and specified in ——————— tab of the System properties

A. Computer Name B. Network
C. Workgroup D. Domain

L-2 S 67. If we have to set our system so that every icon is opened when we click it only once, we have to do this setting using ———————

A. Folder options B. Display option
C. Desktop proper D. System properties

L-1 S 68. Magic number in a file format is used to identify the file as

A. Read only B. Execute only
C. Executable D. Readable

L-1 S 69. A rule associated with an object to regulate which users can gain access to the object and in what manner.

A. Right B. Policy
C. Strategy D. Permission

L-1 S 70. Removing program files and folders from the hard disk and related registry data so that the software is no longer available

A. Delete B. Undo
C. Uninstall D. None of the above

L-2 S 71. What is true about a Device driver ?

A. Is a part of the operating system B. A Single device driver is enough for a system
C. Is a software that runs hardware D. Is a software that is loaded in a device

L-2 S 72. Local security policy is available in

A. Control Panel B. Desktop

C. Administrative Tool D. System Tray

L-2 S 73. "System Restore" properties can be accessed using

A. My Computer Icon B. Control Panel

C. Both of the above D. None of the above

L-2 S 74. List of available services along with their status can be acessed from

A. Control Panel B. Desktop

C. Administrative Tools D. System Tray

L-2 S 75. Grouping of computers meant to help users find shared resources within the group

A. Domain B. Group

C. Workgroup D. None of the above

L-2 S 76. If we have to set a program to be executed/started when windows loads, we have to put it in

A. Autorun folder B. Sysroot folder

C. Windows folder D. Startup folder

L-2 S 77. To obtain services from the operting system, a ———————— is made by a user program which traps into kernel and invoked the operating system

A. Requirement call B. System call

C. Interrupt D. Administration

L-1 T/F 78. You can convert the current drive from FAT to NTFS

A. TRUE B. FALSE

L-1 T/F 79. Multiple users cannot switch between accounts without having to restart the computer

A. TRUE B. FALSE

L-2 T/F 80. Restore points can not be created manually

A. TRUE B. FALSE

L-2 T/F 81. Restore points for system restore cannot be created by user

A. TRUE B. FALSE

L-2 T/F 82. In performing backup, system state data could also be backed up

A. TRUE B. FALSE

L-2 T/F 83. Work group in windows do provide centralized user accounts and authentication

A. TRUE B. FALSE

L-1 T/F 84. System files must never be deleted or moved.

A. TRUE B. FALSE

L-1 T/F 85. Fast user switching is available on stand-alone computers and on computers connected in a workgroup

A. TRUE B. FALSE

L-2 T/F 86. Power Users do not posses administrative powers at all

A. TRUE B. FALSE

L-2 T/F 87. "Guest: users have same access as "Users" except that the "Guest" account is further restricted

A. TRUE B. FALSE

L-2 T/F 88. Backup operator can override security restrictions for one and only purpose of backing up and restoring files

A. TRUE B. FALSE

L-3 T/F 89. ASR will not restore your data files

A. TRUE B. FALSE

Architecture

L-2 D 90. One and only software that executes at the most privileged level. It provides the mechanisms needed to implement an operating system, such as low-level address space management, thread management, and inter-process communication.

Ans Microkernel

L-2 S 91. The core of layered architecture of an Operating system.

A. Shell B. Core C. Brain D. Kernel

Drivers

L-1 D 92. Drivers are ———————— meaning that a running driver can be called a second time before the first call has completed

Ans Reenterant

Error Handling

L-2 S 93. A serious error which affects the operating system. It endangers the data and the process is stopped

A. Stop error B. Accidental error C. Fatal error D. System error

File Allocation

L-2 D 94. FAT

Ans File Allocation Table

L-2 D 95. A file system used by MS-DOS and some Windows-based operating systems to store and manage files.

Ans File Allocation Table (FAT)

L-2 D 96. FAT32 supports smaller cluster sizes and larger volumes than FAT, which results in more efficient space allocation on FAT32 volumes.

Ans FAT32

L-2 D 97. A randomly choosen text, data or stack segment will not fill an integral number of pages. On the average, half of the final page will be empty. The extra space in that page is wasted. This wastage is called

Ans Internal fragmentation

File Organization

L-2 D 98. Reference files contains keys of records in other files

File System

L-2 D 99. A file system that is more efficient, secure and reliable than earlier used FAT file system

Ans NTFS file system

L-2 D 100. In an operating system, the overall structure in which files are named, stored, and organized.

Ans file system

L-2 D 101. NTFS guarantees volume consistency by using standard transaction logging and recovery techniques

L-1 S 102. Windows 98 file system

A. NTFS B. NFS C. CD D. FAT

L-2 T/F 103.FAT file system is more secure than NTFS

A. TRUE B. FALSE

Functions

L-1 D 104. Basic functions that an OS performs - schedule jobs, manage hardware and software resources, maintain system security, enable multiple user resource sharing, handle interrupts, maintain usuage records

General

L-1 D 105. Upcall

Ans The term upcall is typically used in the context of using a framework, such as CORBA. When a request is sent from a client application to a server application, the framework is responsible for data marshaling, data transmission, and notification of the recipient that a request has been issued. An up call is the call into the user code from the framework. An upcall is also called a callback

L-1 D 106. Operating system acts as

Ans Extended machine or virtual machine

L-1 D 107. What is a distributed processing system?

Ans Computer systems that use more than one computer, or processor, to run an application. A single computer uses 2 or more CPUs to execute programs. A single program can run simultaneously at more than one location.

L-1 D 108. Operating system performs 2 basic functions

Ans Extending the machine and managing resources

L-1 D 109. PS/2 is the operating system for apple computers

L-1 D 110. The first block of the active partition is called

Ans Boot block

L-1 D 111. OSs function at 2 different levels, the hardware level and the user level

L-1 D 112. Multiprogramming is defined as execution of two or more programs that all reside in primary storage

L-1 D 113. The bootstrap loader is a program whose function is to start the computer software operating when power is turned on

L-1 D 114. A computer-based record about an authorized user that is created automatically on the computer the first time a user logs on to a workstation or server computer.

Ans Local user profile

L-1 D 115. The operating system does not care about the contents of a file. It looks at a file as a collection of bits. User level programs understand the contents of the file.

L-1 D 116. A folder name or file name longer than the 8.3 file name standard (up to eight characters followed by a period and an extension of up to three characters) of the FAT file system.

Ans Long name

L-1 D 117. Multiprocessing enables the computers to perform tasks simltaneously. This is done by either assigning different tasks to each processing unit or dividing a complex task among several processing units

L-1 D 118. With Windows XP Professional, a user can report system and program errors to Microsoft. Windows XP collects information about the problem and prepare a report which could be sent to Microsoft using an internet connection.

L-1 D 119. Linking is a technique that allows a file to appear in more than one directory. This system call specifies an existing file and a path name, and creates a link form the existing file to the name specified by the path. In this way, the same file may be accessed using more than one icon

L-2 D 120. MBR

Ans Master Boot Record

L-2 D 121. POSIX

Ans POSIX or "Portable Operating System Interface for Unix" is the name of a family of related standards specified by the IEEE to define the application programming interface (API), along with shell and utilities interfaces for software compatible with variants of the Unix operating system, although the standard can apply to any operating system.

L-2 D 122. Warm boot means

Ans The system is restarted using Ctrl+Alt+Del key combination

L-2 D 123. Linux was developed on

Ans MINIX

L-2 D 124. A keyboard shortcut for a command is called

Ans Accelerator key

L-2 D 125. A computer configuration that runs two or more operating systems

Ans Multiple boot

L-2 D 126. A computer configuration that can start two different operating systems

Ans Dual boot

L-2 D 127. A program which runs in kernel mode and does the allocation of resources

Ans ExoKernel

L-2 D 128. In the organization of computer 'Microarchitecture level is present between

Ans The physical devices and the machine language layer

L-2 D 129. Multitasking is the system's ability to execute two or more of a Single user's tasks concurrently

L-2 D 130. Saved copies of changed data that can be applied to an original volume to generate a volume shadow copy.

Ans Differential data

L-2 D 131. An operating system program which controls the operations and management of resources of a computer system. Examples of control program functions are job scheduling input output scheduling and program monitoring

Ans Control program

L-1 D 132. In the context of operating system process scheduling, LDT is

Ans Local Descriptor table

L-2 M 133. These are some of system state data

A. Registry B. Boot files including system files

C. Master Boot Record D. BIOS

L-2 M 134. These are some of system state data

A. Com+ class registration database B. Database metadata

C. Certificate services database D. All of the above

L-1 S 135. Programs desinged to control the operation of a computer system

A. Application programs B. System software

C. System utilities D. All of the above

L-1 S 136. Commands used to communicate with the operating system of the computer.

A. Low level commands B. System commands

C. Operating commands D. All of the above

L-1 S 137. The central module of an operating system is called ______________.

A. Shell B. Kernel C. Base D. Skeleton

L-2 S 138. A small program that is usually invoked to draw larger an more comprehensive program into a computer

A. Loader B. Bootstrap C. Linker D. Compiler

L 1 S 139. An operating system is a

A. System software B. Operating software

C. Application software D. Utility software

L-1 S 140. In Windows NT, NT stands for

A. New Technology B. New Terminal

C. New Technique D. None of the above

L-1 S 141. Which of the following is machine independent?

A. Machine Language B. Assembly Language

C. High Level Language D. None of these

L-1 S 142. Which of the following is not a multiuser operating system?

A. DOS B. MVS

C. UNIX D. All of the above

L-2 S 143. —————————— are strings that contain information such as drive, path or file name. They control the behaviour of various programs.

A. Environment variables B. Constants

C. Temporary files D. History

L-1 S 144. To achieve parallism, ————— are created

A. Processes B. Sub processes

C. Thread D. None of the above

L-1 S 145. Which of the following is more english like ?

A. Machine Language B. Assembly Language

C. High Level Language D. None of these

L-1 S 146. Which of the following is not an operating system ?

A. MVS B. DOS

C. UNIX D. DB2

L-1 S 147. For name of a file, ————— characters could be used

A. 11 characters B. Upto 128 characters

C. 8 characters D. Upton 255 characters

L-1 S 148. Which of the following is not a real time operating system ?

A. BLMX B. CCP

C. CTOS D. DOS

L-1 S 149. A disk that contains the MS-DOS system files necessary to start MS-DOS.

A. DOS disk B. Setup disk

C. System disk D. None of the above

L-1 S 150. The term which refers to the number of jobs per hour that the system completes

A. Resultant volume B. Work speed

C. Clock speed D. Throughput

L-2 S 151. Xenia is an ——————————

A. Compiler B. Super computer

C. Operating system D. Programming language

L-2 S 152. These are some of system state data

A. Active directory database B. Cluster service information

C. IIS Metadirector D. All of the above

L-2 S 153. Multitasking is also called ——————

A. Thread processing B. CPU sharing

C. Parallel proces D. Joint processing

L-2 S 154. A small program that runs when the computer is started is called the ————

A. Buffer B. Pointer C. Partition table D. Boot record

L-1 T/F 155.Commands in Unix as well as Ms-Dos are case sensitive

A. TRUE B. FALSE

L-1 T/F 156.Background printing uses additional system memory.

A. TRUE B. FALSE

Hardware

L-2 D 157. A conflict that occurs when the same system resources have been allocated to two or more devices.

A. Interrupt

L-1 D 158 The disk controller's cache is completely independent of the Operating system's cache

L-1 D 159. The disk controller's cache is divided into 2 sections, one for reads and another one for writes

L-2 D 160. —————— provides a way to set up and store different configuration

A. Hardware profile

L-2 D 161. Each device on a computer has a ——————, which may consist of IRQ lines, DMA, an I/O port, or memory address settings.

A. Hardware configuration

L-2 D 162. System resources in the context of conflict includes interrupt request (IRQ) lines, direct memory access (DMA) channels, input/output (I/O) ports, and memory addresses.

L-2 S 163. The partition table is located

A. At the end of the Master Boot Record B. At the beginning

C. In File allocation table D. None of the above

L-2 S 164. The part of the hard disk that contains the hardware specific files required to load windows

A. File system B. File allocation table

C. Partition table D. System volume

L-2 S 165. The partition of the hard disk drive which contains files required to load the operating system

A. Main partition B. Operating system C. System partition D. Hard partition

History

L-1 D 166. Third generation Operating systems

Ans 1965-80 (Cs and Multiprogramming)

L-1 D 167. Second generation Operating systems

Ans 1955-65 (Transistors and Batch Systems)

Input/Output

L-1 D 168. In —————————— CPU do all the work

Ans Programmed I/O

L-1 D 169. These devices can be added to the computer without the need to reboot

Ans USB

L-1 D 170. Memory mapped I/O makes the peripheral look like a block of RAM to the main processor

L-1 D 171. I/O bound Jobs Jobs that require more of Input/Output (I/O) operations as compared to computational operations

L-1 D 172. This file is used to track the operations performed. It contains messages generated by an application or service

Ans Log file

L-2 D 173. Full form of TLB is

Ans Translation Lookaside Buffer

L-2 D 174. Operating system runs in

Ans Kernel mode or supervisor mode

L-2 D 175. What is memory mapped I/O?

Ans Memory-mapped I/O is an I/O scheme where the device's own on-board memory is mapped into the processor's address space. Data to be written to the device is copied by the driver to the device memory, and data read in by the device is available in the shared memory for copying back into the system memory. "Memory-mapped I/O is frequently used by network and video devices. Many adapters offer a combination of programmed I/O and memory-mapped modes, where the data buffers are mapped into the processor's memory space and the internal device registers that provide status are accessed through the I/O space.

L-2 D 176. Layers of I/O software system

Ans Hardware → Interrupt handlers → Device drivers → Device independent operating system software → User level I/O software

L-2 D 177. System calls are processed in

Ans Kernel Mode

L-2 D 178. Compilers and editors runs in

Ans User mode

L-2 D 179. In I/O, function of device independent software are

Ans Naming & Protection

L-2 D 180 The code placed around the system call to do the checking is called a

Ans Jacket

L-2 D 181. For every I/O device, an associated ———————exists, which contains the address of the interrupt service procedure

Ans Interrupt Vector

L-2 D 182. The interrupt signal causes the CPU to stop what it is doing and start doing something else. The number on the address lines is used as an index into a table called the ————— to fetch a new program counter.

Ans Interrupt Vector

L-2 D 183. In Memory mapped I/O, each control register is assigned a unique memory address to which no memory is assigned.

A. TRUE

L-1 S 184. I/O devices can be roughly divided into 2 categories: block devices and

A. Stream devices B. Character devices

C. Bulk devices D. None of the above

L-2 S 185. Devices which stores information in fixed-size blocks, each block has its own address are called

A. Character devices B. Block devices

C. File devices D. Field devices

L-2 S 186. Generally Device Drivers run in

A. Kernel Mode B. User mode

C. Admin Mode D. All of the above

L-1 S 187. DMA means

A. Direct Memory Availability B. Disk Memory Access

C. Disk Memory Availability D. Direct Memory Access

L-1 S 188. Ways of I/O

A. Programmed B. Interrupt Driven

C. Using DMA D. All of the above

L-2 S 189. Full form of SPOOL is

A. Simultaneous Programmin Operation

B. System Peripheral Operation Online

C. Simultaneous Penpheral Operation Online

D. Simultaneous Peripheral Operator Online

L-2 S 190. Once the system call handler has completed its work, control may be returned to the user-space library procedure at the instruction following the ——— instruction

A. Loop B. Branch C. Call D. TRAP

L-1 S 191. I/O devices generally consists of two parts

Ans A controller and the device itself

L-2 T/F 192.No. of interrupts in DMA I/O is greater than in memory mapped I/O

A. TRUE B. FALSE

L-2 T/F 193.Drivers are not allowed to make system calls

A. TRUE B. FALSE

L-2 T/F 194. The DMA controller is much slower than the main CPU

A. TRUE B. FALSE

L-2 T/F 195 Error should be handled as close to the hardware as possible

A. TRUE B. FALSE

L-2 T/F 196. Each Device controller has control registers as well as data buffers

A. TRUE B. FALSE

L-2 T/F 197. The DMA controller has access to the system bus independent of the CPU

A. TRUE B. FALSE

Memory

L-1 D 198. Only data and programs currently needed by the processor reside in main memory

L-1 D 199. The content of each entry in the segment table or a segment register is called as Descriptor

L-1 D 200. Existence of two or more programs in different parts of the memory hierarchy at the same time

Ans Multiprogramming

L-1 D 201. The more page frames the memory has, the fewer page faults a program will get. But this is not always the case. This situation is called

Ans Belady's anomaly

L-2 D 202. Reason for locality of reference

Ans Loops, requirement of same data by the program over a period of time, subroutine calls etc

L-2 D 203. The working set is the set of pages used by k most recent memory references

L-2 D 204. A segment is a set of logically related instructions or data elements associated with a given name

L-2 M 205. The basic component of a memory management unit are

A. A facility for dynamic storage relocation

B. A provision for sharing common programs

C. Protection of information against unauthorized access

D. None of the above

L-1 S 206. ———————— compensates the difference between speed of main memory and processor

A. RAM B. Cache memory
C. Read only memory D. DMA

L-1 S 207. The ———————— is the address of the memory word where the instruction is stored

A. Point B. Structure
C. Location D. None of the above

L-2 S 208. A portion of memory that can be used by a process to pass information to another process

A. Buffer B. Log C. Named pipe D. Pager

L-1 D 209. Memory that cannot be paged to disk

Ans Non paged memory

L-1 D 210. Pages are loaded only on demand, not in advance

Ans Demand paging

L-2 M 211. Two ways the operating system use to keep track of memory usage

A. Bitmap B. Stack C. Linked list D. Free list

L-1 S 212. Transfers between RAM and disk are always in units of a

A. Block B. Character C. Byte D. Page

L-2 S 213 Most programs randomly access a small number of pages, and this set changes slowly with time

A. Random access B. Pattern based access
C. Locality of reference D. None of the above

L-1 S 214. When a page fault occurs in a virtual memory system, it signifies that the page referenced by the CPU is ————————

A. Not in memory B. Not in main memory
C. Not in CPU D. None of the above

Memory Allocation

L-2 D 215. The virtual memory comprises of the paging file on hard disk and the physical memory

L-2 D 216. Memory allocation procedures such as ———————— maintain crucial tables about memory usage

Ans Mallow

L-1 D 217. In the context of Os memory management, Full form of DMA is

Ans Direct Memory Access

L-1 D 218. Each storage location can hold one character

L-1 D 219. File mapping works best in a system that supports segmentation

L-1 D 220. If in second change page replacement algorithm, all the pages have been referenced, it degenerates into pure FIFO

L-1 D 221. The goal of the page replacement policy is to remove the page least likely to be referenced in the immediate future

L-1 D 222. The interrupt that occurs when software attempts to read from or write to a virtual memory location that is marked not present.

Ans Page fault

L-1 D 223. Virtual memory lets the programmer to write programs as though a large memory space is available, equal to the totality of axillary memory

L-1 D 224. If we increase memory size by one page frame and re-execute a process, at every point during the execution, all the pages that were present in the first run are also present in the second run, along with one additional page. Algorithms which possesses this property are known as

Ans Stack algorithms

L-2 D 225. Swapping

Ans To replace pages or segments of data in memory. Swapping is a useful technique that enables a computer to execute programs and manipulate data files larger than main memory. The operating system copies as much data as possible into main memory, and leaves the rest on the disk. When the operating system needs data from the disk, it exchanges a portion of data (called a page or segment) in main memory with a portion of data on the disk. DOS does not perform swapping, but most other operating systems, including OS/2, Windows, and UNIX, do. Swapping is often called paging or Virtual memory.

L-2 D 226. Overlaying

Ans In operating systems, an overlay is when a process replaces itself with the code of another program. On Unix-like systems, this is accomplished with the exec() system call.

L-2 D 227. Distributed Shared Memory

Ans Distributed Shared Memory (DSM), also known as a distributed global address space (DGAS), is a term in computer science that refers to a wide class of software and hardware implementations, in which each node of a cluster has access to a large shared memory in addition to each node's limited non-shared private memory.

L-2 D 228. Separate address spaces for data

Ans D-Space

L-2 D 229. Memory that cannot be paged to disk.

Ans Non paged memory

L-2 D 230. Separate address spaces for instructions

Ans I-Space

L-2 D 231. In Local page replacement algorithm, a fixed fraction of memory is allocated to every process

L-2 D 232. The system-allocated virtual memory that has been charged to a process and that can be paged.

Ans Page pool

L-2 D 233. A set associative cache of set size k will accommodate k words of main memory in each word of cache

L-2 D 234. Fragmentation is of two types: Internal fragmentation and External fragmentation.

L-2 D 235. A small block of memory temporarily assigned by operating system to hold information about an opened file

Ans File Control Block (FCB)

L-2 D 236. A page refers to the organization of address space, while a block refers to the organization of memory space

L-2 D 237. In Global page replacement algorithms, memory/page frames are dynamically allocated among runnable processes

L-2 D 238. Distance string could be used to predict the number of page faults that will occur with memories of different sizes

L-2 D 239. A page reference is denoted by the distance from the top of the stack where the referenced page was located. This is called

Ans Distance string

L-2 D 240. Best Fit allocation scheme tries to determine the best place to put the new data. (The smallest space which is big enough.)

L-2 D 241. In direct addressing, the value to be stored in memory is obtained by directly retrieving it from another memory location.

L-2 D 242. Paging systems that keep track of each process's working set and make sure that it is in memory before letting the process run

Ans Working set model.

L-2 D 243. The direct mapping cache organization uses the n-bit address to access the main memory and the k-bit index to access the cache

L-2 D 244. The Second chance page replacement algorithm is looking for an old page that has not Ben referenced in the previous clock interval

L-2 D 245. Memory protection is done by including protection information within the segment table or segment register of the memory management hardware

L-2 D 246. Page Fault Frequency algorithm tells when to increase or decrease a process's page allocation. It does not determine the page to be replace when a page fault occurs.

L-2 D 247. ________________ are completely independent address spaces, consisting of a linear sequence of addresses, from 0 to some maximum and of length from 0 to some maximum allowed

Ans Segments

L-2 D 248. The operating system protection condition is placed in the Descriptors of all operating system programs to prevent the occasional user from accessing operating system segments.

L-2 D 249. In general, a system with n pages and m blocks would require a memory-page table of n locations of which up to m blocks will be marked with block numbers and all others will be empty

L-2 D 250. Each page can be labeled with the number of instructions that will be executed before that page would be first referenced. The optimal page algorithm says that the page with the highest label should be removed

Ans Optimal page replacement algorithm

L-2 D 251. In NFU, software counter is associated with each page. These counters keep track of the number of times the pages have been referenced. When a page fault occurs, the page with the lowest counter is choosen for replacement

L-2 D 252. First Fit fits data into memory by scanning whole available memory from the beginning to the end, until the first free space which is at least big enough to hold the data is found. This space is then allocated to the data.

L-2 D 253. To ensure a plentiful supply of free page frames, many paging systems have a background process, called the ____________, that sleeps most of the time but is awakened periodically to inspect the state of the memory.

Ans Paging daemon

L-2 D 254. In the NOT RECENTLY USED page replacement algorithm, there are two status bits associated with each page. R is set whenever the page is referenced (either for read or write), M is set when the page is modified). These bits must be updated on every access

L-2 D 255. When a program require a page that is not in memory, it is called a page fault. The instruction causing the fault is stopped and a trap to the operating system occurs. After the operating system has fetched the page needed, the instruction causing the page fault is restarted.

L-2 D 256. A File Control Block contains - file's identification, its location on disk, and a pointer

L-2 D 257. If the virtual page number is not in the TLB (Transaction Lookaside Buffer), the MMU (Memory Management Unit) detects the miss and does an ordinary page table lookup.

L-2 D 258. ____________ technique is used to allow programs and data to be broken up into logically independent address spaces and to aid sharing and protection.

Ans Segmentation

L-2 D 259. If each procedure occupies a separate segment, with address 0 as its starting address, the linking up of procedures compiled separately is greatly simplified.

L-3 M 260. Memory management systems can be divided into 2 classes

A. Those that use Swapping and Paging
B. Those which do not use Swapping & Paging
C. Those which are operating system Dependent
D. Those which are kernel based

L-2 M 261. The address space contains

A. The executable Program
B. Linked Lists
C. Program's stack
D. Program's data
E. Data structures

L-2 M 262. Since segments varies in size, after the system has been running for a while, memory will be divided up into number of chunks, some containing segments and some containing holes. This phenomenon is called

A. Checkerboarding
B. Defragmentation
C. External fragmentation
D. All of the above

L-1 S 263. ———————— is the address of the instruction as written in the program

A. Physical address
B. Virtual address
C. Address
D. Temp Address

L-1 S 264. Locking a page in memory so that it will not be removed is called ———————— the page in memory

A. Thrashing
B. Pining
C. Fixing
D. Attaching

L-2 S 265. The amount of physical memory assigned to a process by the operating system

A. Memory allocation
B. Working set
C. File allocation
D. RAM

L-2 S 266. Temporary storage used by a computer to run programs that need more memory than it has.

A. Associative memory
B. Virtual Memory
C. Auxiliary memo
D. Primary memory

L-2 S 267 Memory access to and from a peripheral device that does not involve the microprocessor.

A. Paged access
B. Direct memory access
C. Interrupt
D. Memory mapping

L-2 S 268. In a technique called ————————, the operating system keeps part of the address space in main memory and part on disk and swaps pieces from and to as needed.

A. Associative memory
B. Virtual memory
C. Auxiliary memory
D. Primary memory

L-1 S 269. Which of the following among addresses is true ?

A. They have a unique identifier
B. Their contents will not change
C. Their identifiers
D. None of these

L-2 S 270. If the page is ———————— it must be written back to the disk

A. Dirty
B. Corrupt
C. Not found
D. Upto date

L-2 S 271. A file on the hard disk which is hidden and which is used by windows to hold parts of programs and data that do not fit in memory

A. Paging file
B. Boot.ini

C. Commandmen D. Autoexec.bat

E. Himem.sys

L-2 S 272. System state data

A. User Data B. Hardware data

C. Published data D. System files that are under Windows File Protection

L-2 S 273. The set of pages that a process is currently using is called its

A. Page fault B. Memory allocation

C. File allocation D. Working set

L-2 S 274. A portion of computer memory that can be allocated to a device or used by a program or the operating system

A. Interrupt B. Memory Addres

C. DMA D. None of the above

L-2 S 275. ———————— the moving of infrequently used parts of a program's working memory from RAM to another storage medium, usually the hard disk.

A. Thrashing B. Copying C. Swapping D. Paging

L-3 S 276. A code placed around the system call to do the various checking is also known as

A. Shell B. Jacket

C. Wrapper D. Windows file protection

L-1 T/F 277. In LRU page replacement algorithm, the associated linked list need not be updated on every memory reference

A. TRUE B. FALSE

L-2 T/F 278. Local page replacement algorithms work better than global page replacement algorithms

A. TRUE B. FALSE

L-2 T/F 279. Even if swapping is used, the system cannot handle more processes than its has room for in memory

A. TRUE B. FALSE

L-1 T/F 280. Memory references to data also tend to be localized

A. TRUE B. FALSE

L-2 T/F 281. Global Descriptor table is shared by all the programs on the computer

A. TRUE B. FALSE

L-2 T/F 282. The operating system can only use DMA if the hardware has a DMA controller

A. TRUE B. FALSE

L-2 T/F 283. In the inverted page table, there is one entry per page frame in real memory, rather than one entry per page of virtual address space

A. TRUE B. FALSE

L-2 T/F 284. When a page fault occurs, the operating system decides which page is to be removed from memory to make room for the page which is required

A. TRUE B. FALSE

L-1 T/F 285.The ———————— allows a program to be run even if only a part of it is in the main memory

A. Virtual Memory

L-2 T/F 286.The purpose of page table is to map virtual pages onto page frames

A. TRUE B. FLASE

L-1 D 287. Dynamic Memory Allocation - The means by which data objects can be created as they are needed during the program execution.

Memory Management

L-2 D 288. The significance of the Referenced bit is, it helps the operating system to choose a page to evict when a page fault occurs.

Memory organization

L-2 D 289. The current working set is the number of pages currently resident in memory.

L-2 D 290. In Task Manager, the peak amount of physical memory resident in a process since it started.

A. Peak memory usage

L-2 S 291. In segmentation there are ——— linear address spaces

A. 1 B. Many C. 2 D. 3

L-2 T/F 292.In Segmentation, sharing of procedures between users is done

A. TRUE B. FALSE

Ms-Dos 4

L-1 D 293. This command suspends processing of a batch file and displays a message.

Ans Stop

L-1 D 294. TIME/T displays the current system time and then the command prompt appears

L-1 D 295. Displays messages, or turns command echoing on or off.

Ans Comment

L-2 D 296. Part of the operating system which accepts commands given by the user and process them

Ans Kernel

L-1 D 297. DOS is

Ans Disk Operating System

L-1 D 298. PRINT command is used in dos to

Ans Print text file.

L-1 D 299. An Attribute is

Ans a special characterstics of a value or a command

L-1 D 300. In dos, this command is used to Sort input.

Ans SORT

L-1 D 301. Dos command - Show read only files

Ans Dir/ar

L-1 D 302. New long list format

Ans Dir/N

L-1 D 303. List in sorted order

Ans Dir/o

L-1 D 304. Creates a directory.

Ans MKDIR or MD

L-1 D 305. Removes a directory.

Ans RD

L-1 D 306. Displays system time

Ans TIME

L-1 D 307. Show directories only

Ans Dir/ad

L-1 D 308. Renames a file or files.

Ans Ren

L-1 D 309. Show directories pagewise

Ans Dir/p

L-1 D 310. List in sorted order by name

Ans Dir/oN

L-1 D 311. Shows directory and files list

Ans DIR

L-1 D 312. Searches for strings in files.

Ans FINDSTR

L-1 D 313. List the file only which is given

Ans Dir <File Name>

L-1 D 314. Displays or sets the system time.

Ans Time

L-1 D 315. MODE Configures a system device.

L-1 D 316. Shows directories and files in the current directory

Ans Dir *.*

L-1 D 317. Displays or sets a search path for executable files.

Ans Path

L-1 D 318. Show the directories and files present in the directory

Ans Dir *.*

L-1 D 319. Creates, changes, or deletes the volume label of a disk.

Ans LABEL

L-1 D 320. Records comments (remarks) in batch files or CONFIG.SYS.

Ans Rem

L-1 D 321. Show the directories and files present in the drive specified

Ans Dir <Drive Name>

L-1 D 322. Moves one or more files from one directory to another directory.

Ans Move

L-1 D 323. A series of instructions, or commands, that performs a repetitive task

Ans Command file

L-1 D 324. Compares two files or sets of files, and displays the differences between them

Ans FC

L-1 D 325. List directories and files present in the current directory and its subdirectories

Ans Dir/s

L-1 D 326. It is a part of the operating system, It accepts commands given by the user and acts on them

L-1 D 327. An operating system which contains the disk-oriented commands and uses disk devices pertaining to storage

Ans Disk Operating System

L-2 D 328. Attrib

Ans Displays or sets file attribute

L-2 D 329. In Ms-Dos, Attrib +R

Ans Set the read only file attribute

L-2 D 330. In Ms-Dos, Attrib -H

Ans Clear the hidden file attribute

L-2 D 331. In Ms-Dos, Attrib -S

Ans Clear the system file attribute

L-2 D 332 Compares the contents of two floppy disks.

Ans DISKCOMP

L-2 D 333. Directs the Windows command interpreter to a labeled line in a batch program

Ans GOTO

L-3 D 334. A command line utility for disk management which helps to partition the hard disk and make one active

L-1 D 335. In Ms-Dos, Deltree

Ans Deletes the directory with all its contents

L-1 F 336. MSDOS is

Ans Microsoft Disk Operating System

L-1 F 337. In Ms-Dos, creates a directory.

Ans MD

L-1 F 338. In Ms-Dos, displays output one screen at a time.

Ans MORE

L-1 F 339 This command is used to change the Windows command prompt.

Ans Prompt

L-2 F 340. The process which reads commands from a terminal is called

Ans Command Interpreter or Shell

L-2 F 341. In DOS, This command is used to recover readable information from a bad or defective disk.

Ans RECOVER

L-1 M 342. Deletes one or more files.

A. Erase B. Del C. Rd D. All of the above

L-1 S 343. Directory is also known as

A. File B. Folder C. Storage D. Drawer

L-1 S 344. It indicates one of the properties of a file

A. Fileq B. Attribute C. Chr D. Stamp

L-1 S 345. Performs conditional processing in batch programs.

A. Case B. If C. Condition D. All of the above

L-1 S 346. Starts a new instance of the Windows command interpreter.

A. Proc B. Cmd C. Dir D. Run

L-1 S 347. Date/T command outputs the current date and prompt to enter new date

A. TRUE B. FALSE

L-2 S 348. MS-DOS file system

A. FAT32 B. FAT16 C. NTFS D. CDFS

L-2 S 349. In Ms-Dos, Associates a path with a drive letter.

A. Prompt B. SUBST

C. Mount D. None of the above

L-1 S 350. DOS stands for

A. Disk Operating System B. Dynamic Operating System

C. Dirty Old System D. None of the above

L-2 S 351. Edits command lines, recalls Windows commands, and creates macros.

A. DOSKEY B. Home Key C. Prompt D. Batch file

L-1 S 352. XCOPY

A. Uploades files to a web server B. Moves files and directories

C. Copies files an directory trees. D. Execute Files

L-1 S 353. Displays a disk volume label and serial number.

A. Lab B. Ser

C. Vol D. None of the above

L-1 S 354. Remote desktop connection is located in ———— folder/program group.

A. Desktop B. Programs C. Communication D. System tools

L-1 S 355. Displays, sets, or removes Windows environment variables.

A. Clear B. Reset C. SET D. Load

L-1 S 356. A batch file which is automatically executed by the msdos operating system whenever the computer is started or restarted and it contains command that are intended to run when the computer is started

A. Config.sys B. Himem.sys C. Command.com D. Autoexec.bat

L-2 S 357. Copies the contents of one floppy disk to another.

A. Copy B. Xcopy

C. Diskcopy D. None of the above

L-1 S 358. Graphically displays the directory structure of a drive or path.

A. Tree

OS/2

L-2 D 359. A protected-mode, virtual memory, multitasking operating system for personal computers based on the Intel 80286, 80386, i486, and Pentium processors. OS/2 can run most MS-DOS-based programs and can read all MS-DOS disks.

Ans OS/2

Page Replacement

L-2 S 360. A program which is causing page faults every few instructions is said to be

A. Paging B. Caching C. Thrashing D. Deadlock

Processes

L-1 D 361. Generally Deadlocks involve

Ans Non preemptable resource

L-2 D 362. One of the prominent strategies used for dealing with deadlocks is to ——————

Ans Ignore them

L-1 D 363. What is spooling?

Ans To compensate the difference of speeds of different devices, spooling is used. It's a memory area in which a task is temporarily stored before it can be done

L-1 D 364. In ———— threads are very useful and often used

Ans Distributed Systems

L-1 D 365. What is the difference between a program and a process ?

Ans A process could be one of the parts of a program.

L-1 D 366. A list of memory locations which process can read and write

Ans Address space

L-1 D 367. Control unit and Arithmetic Logical Unit are part of CPU.

L-1 D 368. Processes which spend most of their time computing are called

Ans Compute-bound

L-1 D 369. If the ———————— is set, caching is disabled for the page

Ans Caching disabled

L-1 D 370. Processes which spend most of their time waiting for I/O are called

Ans I/O bound

L-1 D 371. The amount of CPU time a process has actually used since it started

Ans Current virtual time

L-1 D 372. A state where the system can guarantee that all processes will finish

Ans Safe state

L-1 D 373. A process and all of its children and further Dependents together form

Ans A process group

L-1 D 374. Processes which interacts with users and perform work for them are called

Ans Foreground Processes

L-1 D 375. The virtual address space and the control information necessary for the execution of a program

Ans Process

L-1 D 376. Proportionality is the time taken by the computer to finish a job in comparison to the time taken by the computer to finish some other job

Ans Proportionality

L-1 D 377. The structure and methods provided by an operating system to allow concurrent processes to communicate with each other

Ans Inter process communication

L-1 D 378. Threads are also called

Ans Lightweight Process

L-2 D 379. IPC

Ans Inter Process Communication

L-2 D 380. Clock software

Ans Handling the alarm system call made by user processes

L-2 D 381. Hold and wait condition

Ans Processes currently holding resource granted earlier can request new resources

L-2 D 382. Critical region is also called

Ans Critical section

L-2 D 383. What is a circular wait condition?

Ans There must be a circular chain of 2 or more processes, each of which is waiting for a resource held by the next member of chain

L-2 D 384. In two phase locking, in the first phase

Ans the process tries to lock all its records it needs, one at a time

L-2 D 385. The number of threads running in a process

Ans Thread Count

L-2 D 386. The main purpose of Working set model is to

Ans Reduce the page fault rate

L-2 D 387. Resource management means sharing (multiplexing) resources in 2 ways

Ans in time and in space

L-2 D 388. Threads in a process may not be ———— as different processes.

Ans Independent

L-2 D 389. Threads share same address space and all of its data among themselves

L-2 D 390. Multiprogramming by dividing memory into n possibly unequal partitions.

Ans Multiprogramming with fixed partitions

L-2 D 391. For deadlock prevention, attacking the hold and wait condition in the case where

Ans If we can prevent processes that hold resources from waiting for more resources

L-2 D 392. For deadlock prevention, attacking the mutual exclusion condition in the case where

Ans If no resource were ever assigned exclusively to a single process

L-2 D 393. Threads are part of the same job and are actively and closely cooperating with each other

Ans TRUE

L-2 D 394. Communication between procesees in a well structured way without the use of interrupts is called

Ans Inter process communication

L-2 D 395. Each process needs its own private ———— to keep track of the threads within it

Ans Thread table

L-2 D 396. Having multiple processes running at once means that when one process is blocked waiting for I/O to finish, another one can use the CPU. This concept is

Ans Multiprogramming

L-2 D 397. Foreground processing Automatic execution of high-priority (foreground) computer programs that have been designed to pre-empt the use of computer resources.

L-2 D 398. A data structure used for inter process communication, in which one processor writes into and the other reads from. Bytes are retrieved on a first in first out (FIFO) basis and random access is not possible

Ans Pipe

L-2 D 399. LFS has cleaner thread that spends its time scanning the log circularly to compact it

L-1 F 400. NFU

Ans Not frequently used algorithm

L-1 F 401. A Thread is

Ans One among many parts of a process

L-1 F 402. Processes that run in the background. These process usually handle activities such as email, printing etc.

Ans Daemons

L-2 F 403. An interrupt that leaves the machine in a well-defined state is called a

Ans Precise interrupt

L-2 F 404. The time the server waits when a command cannot be sucessfully completed. This time can also be configured

Ans Time-out interval

L-2 F 405. Most processes exhibit ———————— meaning that during any phase of execution, the process references only a relatively small fraction of pages.

Ans Locality of reference

L-3 F 406. A process that performs a specific system function to support other programs.

Ans Service

L-2 M 407. The three segments in which processes in UNIX are divided

A. Text Segment B. Linked Lists C. Stack Segment D. Data Segment

L-2 M 408. A process will terminate due to these conditions

A. Normal exit (voluntary)
B. Error exit (voluntary)
C. Both of the above
D. None of the above

L-2 M 409. A process will terminate due to these conditions

A. Fatal error (Involuntary)
B. Killed by another (Involuntary)
C. Both of the above
D. None of the above

L-2 M 410. A process's memory access can be characterized by an (ordered) list of page numbers. This list is called the

Ans Reference string

L-1 S 411. In OS concepts, a program in execution is called a

A. Thread B. Process C. Software D. All of the above

L-1 S 412. In ——— procedures and data could be separately protected and distinguished

A. Paging
B. Segmentation
C. In both paging
D. Not in both paging and segmentation

L-1 S 413. Execution of lower priority background programs when higher priority programs are not using the system resources

A. Multitasking
B. Background processing
C. Both of the above
D. Concurrent processing

L-1 S 414. A situation in which two or more processes cannot proceed because each needs access to data that is locked by the other

A. Contention
B. Deadlock
C. Collision
D. None of the above

L-2 S 415. ———————————— allows different parts of a single program to run concurrently

A. Multitasking
B. Multithreading
C. Concurrency
D. None of the above

L-2 S 416. Ranking of processes with respect to one another. This ranking determine how much and when a process is going to have access to resources

A. Process control B. Priority

C. Significance D. Labeling

L-1 S 417. Threads are useful on systems with ——— CPUs

A. Multiple B. Single

C. Doesn't matter D. None of the above

L-1 S 418. A program that runs while the user is working on another task.

A. Background program B. Foreground process

C. Module D. None of the above

L-1 S 419. In Round robin scheduling, each process is assigned a time interval called its

A. Quantum B. Time slice

C. Timestamp D. Time period

L-2 S 420. Among the methodologies used to recover from a deadlock situation

A. Through preemption B. Through restarting

C. Through killing D. Through rollback

L-2 S 421. This thread call allows a thread to voluntarily give up the CPU so that another thread can run

A. Thread_Yield B. Thread_Produce

C. Thread_Wait D. Thread_terminate

L-2 S 422. If n is the number of processes, p is the time a process spends waiting for I/O to complete, then the CPU utilization is

A. $1\text{-}p^n$ B. n C. n^p D. $2\text{-}p^n$

L-2 S 423. A special token known as ——— that is given to parent when a process is created. This token can be used to control the child

A. Handle B. Ticket C. Right D. Account

L-2 S 424. If n is the number of processes, p is the time a process spends waiting for I/O to complete, then the probability that all n processes are waiting for I/O (in which case CPU would be idle) is

A. $1\text{-}p^n$ B. n C. p^n D. $2\text{-}p^n$

L-1 S 425. In I/O, function of user processes are

A. Making I/O calls B. Format I/O

C. Spooling D. All of the above

L-1 S 426. Processes created by other prcoesses are called

A. Sub processes B. Branch process

C. Child Processes D. Peer processes

L-1 S 427. A program that remains in the memory while other programs are executing.

A. Memory programs B. Firmware

C. Software D. Resident programs

L-2 S 428. When a request of a process for a resource is denied, the process is put to

A. Kill the other process B. Run over

C. Wait D. Sleep

L-2 S 429. LIFO An acronym for Last In/First Out, a queueing technique in which the next item retrieved from a queue is the one that was most recently placed in the queue

A. TRUE

L-1 T/F 430. In ———— Operating System, all the processes are equal

A. UNIX B. Windows

L-1 T/F 431. Fewer resources are assigned to foreground processes then background processes by the operating system

A. TRUE B. FALSE

L-2 T/F 432. A unsafe state is a a deadlocked state

A. TRUE B. FALSE

L-2 T/F 433. Deadlocks cannot occur among different machines

A. TRUE B. FALSE

L-2 T/F 434 Each thread has its own stack

A. TRUE B. FALSE

L-2 T/F 435. Creation of a thread is faster than creation of a process

A. TRUE B. FALSE

L-2 T/F 436. Deadlocks can occur on hardware resources as well as software resources

A. TRUE B. FALSE

L-2 T/F 437. TLB helps mapping virtual addresses to physical addresses without accessing the page table

A. TRUE B. FALSE

L-2 T/F 438. The advantage of multiprogramming is that the CPU could be used by processes when it would be otherwise idle

A. TRUE B. FALSE

Programming

L-2 S 439. Executable routines which does a specific task are ———————— files. These routines are loaded only when needed by the program that calls them

A. Module B. dynamic-link libr C. Subroutine D. Function

L-2 T/F 440. Programmer must be aware that segmentation is being used

A. TRUE B. FALSE

Real Time Operating System

L-2 S 441. In this type of real time environment, missing a deadline once in a while is acceptable. This type of Operating system is called

A. False real time OS B. Simple real time

C. Hard real time D. Soft real-time OS

Resource

L-1 D 442. Mutual exclusion condition

Ans Each resource is either currently assigned to exactly one process or is available

L-1 D 443. Semaphore

Ans Is a protected variable or abstract data type which constitutes the classic method for restricting access to shared resources such as shared memory in a parallel programming environment. A counting semaphore is a counter for a set of available resources, rather than a locked/unlocked flag of a single resource.

L-2 D 444. One of the two volumes that make up a mirrored volume. Each mirror of a mirrored "volume resides on a different disk. If one mirror becomes unavailable due to disk, system or network failure Windows can use the remaining mirror to gain access to the volume

Ans Mirror

L-2 S 445. Resources previously granted cannot be forcibly taken away from a process, The must be explicitly released by the process holding them.

A. No preemption condition B. Preemption
C. Mutual sharing D. None of the above

L-2 T/F 446. Each mirror of a mirrored volume resides on same disk

A. TRUE B. FALSE

Scheduling

L-1 D 447. Concurrent access

Ans Programs in a multiprogrammed environment appear to run at the same time. Processes running in a multiprogrammed environment are called concurrent processes. In actuality, the CPU processes one instruction at a time, but can execute instructions from any active process

L-1 D 448. FIFO Page replacement algorithm

Ans The page which is in the memory for the longest time would be thrown out.

L-1 D 449. The WSClock page replacement algorithm

Ans Is based on working set

L-1 D 450. The Working set page replacement algorithm

Ans Keep track of working set of each process and ensure that it is there in the memory before the process is started to run

L-1 D 451. Another term for multi-user is time-sharing

L-1 D 452. Stick your head in the sand and pretend there is no problem at all

Ans Ostrich Algorithm

L-1 D 453. There are ——— conditions that must hold for a deadlock to occur

Ans 4

L-1 D 454. Banker's algorithm check to see if granting the request leads to a unsafe state.

L-2 D 455. Interrupt is

Ans A signal to a computer that stops the execution of a running program so that another action can be performed

L-2 D 456. Binary semaphore

Ans A binary semaphore takes only 0 and 1 as its values. They are used to implement mutual exclusion and synchronize concurrent process

L-2 D 457. Process bound jobs

Ans Those jobs which tend to occupy the CPU *i.e.,* they need access to the CPU for most of the part of their existence

L-2 D 458. Interrupt Vector is

Ans An interrupt vector is the memory address of an interrupt handler, or an index into an array called an interrupt vector table or dispatch table. Interrupt vector tables contain the memory addresses of interrupt handlers. When an interrupt is generated, the processor saves its execution state via a context switch, and begins execution of the interrupt handler at the interrupt vector.

L-2 D 459. Priority scheduling is for

Ans Interactive systems

L-2 D 460. What is priority inversion?

Ans In scheduling, priority inversion is the scenario where a low priority task holds a shared resource that is required by a high priority task. This causes the execution of the high priority task to be blocked until the low priority task has released the resource, effectively "inverting" the relative priorities of the two tasks. If some other medium priority task, one that does not depend on the shared resource, attempts to run in the interim, it will take precedence over both the low priority task and the high priority task.

L-2 D 461. Round robin scheduling is for

Ans Interactive systems

L-2 D 462. The Dining Philosophers Problem

Ans The dining philosophers problem is summarized as five philosophers sitting at a table doing one of two things: eating or thinking. While eating, they are not thinking, and while thinking, they are not eating. The five philosophers sit at a circular table with a large bowl of spaghetti in the center. A fork is placed in between each pair of adjacent philosophers, and as such, each philosopher has one fork to his left and one fork to his right. As spaghetti is difficult to serve and eat with a single fork, it is assumed that a philosopher must eat with two forks. Each philosopher can only use the forks on his immediate left and immediate right. "Illustration of the dining philosophers problem. The dining philosophers problem is sometimes explained using rice and chopsticks rather than spaghetti and forks, as it is more intuitively obvious that two chopsticks are required to begin eating. The philosophers never speak to each other, which creates a dangerous possibility of deadlock when every philosopher holds a left fork and waits perpetually for a right fork (or *vice versa.*)

L-2 D 463. Main disadvantage of Busy Waiting

Ans It wastes valuable CPU time and bandwidth

L-2 D 464. The Clock page replacement algorithm

Ans To keep all the page frames on a circular list in the form of a clock, as shown in Fig. 4-2. A hand points to the oldest page. When a page fault occurs, the page being pointed to by the hand is inspected. If its R bit is 0, the page is evicted, the new page is inserted into the clock in its place, and the hand is advanced one position. If R is 1, it is cleared and thc hand is advanced to the next page. This process is repeated until a page is found with R = 0. Not surprisingly, this algorithm is called clock. It differs from second chance only in the implementation.

L-2 D 465. Fair-share scheduling algorithm is for

Ans Interactive systems

L-2 D 466. Mulch queues are use for scheduling in

Ans Interactive systems

L-2 D 467. Guaranteed scheduling algorithm is for

Ans Interactive systems

L-2 D 468. Deadlock detection with one resource of each type

L-2 D 469. Shortest process next scheduling algorithm is for

Ans Interactive systems

L-2 D 470. Round robin scheduling assumes that all process are

Ans Equally important

L-2 D 471. Deadlock detection with multiple resource of each type

L-2 D 472. In the resource trajectories method of deadlock avoidance

Ans With a single processor, all paths must be horizontal or vertical but never diagonal

L-2 D 473. In the resource trajectories method of deadlock avoidance

Ans motion is always to the north or east, never to the south or west

L-2 D 474. A ——— is a variable that can be in one of two states, unlocked or locked

Ans Mute

L-2 D 475. Deadlock prevention could be done by attacking the four conditions of the deadlock

L-2 D 476. A ——————— resource is one that can be taken away from the process owning it with no ill effects

Ans Preemptable resource

L-2 D 477. Interrupt facility manages the data transfer for a program while another program is being executed by the CPU.

L-2 D 478. A——————— resource is one that cannot be taken away from its current owner without causing the computation to fail

Ans Non preemptable resource

L-2 D 479. The process of ———— means bringing each process to the memory in entirety, running it for a while, then putting it back on disk

Ans Swapping

L-2 D 480. Mono programming without swapping or paging means just one program runs at a time, sharing the memory between that program and the operating system.

L-2 D 481. A request for attention from the processor. When the processor receives an ——————, it suspends its current operations, saves the status of its work, and transfers control to a special routine known as an interrupt handler.

Ans Interrupt

L-2 D 482. With a local replacement strategy, the number of frames allocated to a process does not change. With global replacement, It may happen that a process select only frames allocated to other processes. In this way the number of frames allocated to a process is increased if that other processes do not choose its frames for replacement.

L-3 D 483. Degree of multiprogramming

Ans CPU utilization of a system can be improved by using multiprogramming. Let P be the fraction of time that a process spends away from the CPU. If there is one process in memory, the CPU utilization is (1-P). If there are N processes in memory, the probability of N processes waiting for an I/O is P*P...*P (N times). The CPU utilization is (1 - P^N) where N is called the multiprogramming level (MPL) or the degree of multiprogramming. As N increases, the CPU utilization increases. While this equation indicates that a CPU continues to work more efficiently as more and more processes are added, logically, this cannot be true. Once the system passes the point of optimal CPU utilization, it thrashes.

L-2 D 484. I/O bound jobs

Ans Those type of jobs in which most part of their existence is either input or output. They need access to CPU for a very short period of time and then get engaged in I/O

L-2 D 485. Starvation means a situation when a process does not get a resource even if there is no deadlock situation

L-2 F 486. Shortest job first is a —————— scheduling algorithm

Ans Non preemptive

L-2 F 487. A situation in which all the programs continue to run indefinitely but fail to make any progress is called

Ans Free run

L-2 F 488. Lottery scheduling algorithm is for

Ans Interactive systems

L-2 F 489. A lock which uses busy waiting is called

Ans Spin lock

L-2 F 490. A —————————— scheduling algorithm pics a process and lets it fun for a maximum of some fixed time

Ans Preemptive

L-2 F 491 After outputting a character, the CPU continuously polls the device to see if it is ready to accept another one.

Ans Busy waiting

L-2 F 492. —————————— or spinning is a technique in which a process repeatedly checks to see if a condition is true

Ans Busy waiting

L-2 F 493. A —————— is said to have occurred if each process in the set is waiting for an event that only another process in the set can cause

Ans Deadlock

L-2 F 494. A —————————— scheduling algorithm picks a process to run and then just lets it run until it blocks (either on I/O or waiting for another process) or until it voluntarily releases the CPU

Ans Non-Preemptive

L-2 S 495. Shortest remaining time next is a ——————————scheduling algorithm

A. Preemptive B. Batch Systems
C. Real time system D. None of the above

L-1 S 496. A technique used by the operating system to run process according to who come first and so on is called

A. LIFO B. FIFO
C. TIFO D. Shortest job first

L-2 S 497. Shortest job first is a scheduling algorithm for

A. Online systems B. Batch Systems
C. Real time syste D. None of the above

L-2 S 498. First-come First-Served is a —————— scheduling algorithm

A. Preemptive B. Non preemptive
C. Could be both D. None of the above

L-2 S 499. Continuously testing a variable until some value appears is called

A. Polling B. Busy waiting
C. Selecting D. Frequent view

L-2 S 500. —————————— operating systems enable several programs to run concurrently

A. Multiprocessor B. Multitasking
C. Multiuser D. None of the above

L-2 S 501. ———————— operating system allow two or more users to run program on the computer simultaneously

A. Multiprocessor
B. Multitasking
C. Multiuser
D. None of the above

L-2 S 502. The time duration in which a particular task is given control of the microprocessor in a multitasking environment

A. Timeliness
B. Time period
C. CPU Access
D. Time slice

L-2 S 503. In a deadlock situation, all the process ——— to wait forever

A. Continue
B. Don't have
C. Tend to
D. None of the above

L-2 S 504. Three level scheduling is for

A. Unequal transactions
B. Real time system
C. Online system
D. Batch systems

L-2 S 505. First-Come First-Served is a scheduling algorithm for

A. Multimedia systems
B. Online systems
C. Real time systems
D. Batch systems

L-2 S 506. Shortest remaining time next is a scheduling algorithm for

A. Real time systems
B. Preemptive system
C. Soft real time system
D. Batch system

L-2 S 507. ———————— maintains time of day and prevent one process from monopolizing the CPU

A. Online time
B. System time
C. Timers
D. None of the above

L-2 S 508. While one job was waiting for I/O to complete, another job could be using the CPU. This is called

A. Sharing
B. Multiplexing
C. Multitasking
D. Multiprogramming

L-2 S 509. If a process is running a user program in user mode and needs a system service, it has to execute a ——— instruction to transfer control to the operating system.

A. Send message to a web server
B. Restart the computer
C. Trap or System
D. Send a message to mobile phone

L-2 S 510. A ———— is a situation when two or more processes try to access the resource which is earlier locked by some other process and the other process is trying to access the resource locked by this process

A. Resource fight
B. Starvation
C. Deadlock
D. Segmentation

L-2 S 511. Time slice is also known as

Ans Time quantum or quantum

L-2 T/F 512. Starvation could be avoided by using a first-come, first-serve resource allocation policy

A. TRUE B. FALSE

L-2 T/F 513. Many processes can use a single resource at the same time

A. TRUE B. FALSE

L-2 T/F 514. Non resources deadlocks can also occur

A. TRUE B. FALSE

L-2 T/F 515. Most programs tend to make a large number of references to a small number of pages, and not the other way around

A. TRUE B. FALSE

L-2 T/F 516. If the processes which are in contention of occupying the cpu are both types, i.e., process bound and CPU bound types then it helps in optimizing the benefits of threads

A. TRUE

Security

L-1 D 517. It contains configuration information for a specific user.

Ans User profile

L-1 D 518. The execute-only condition protects programs from being copied

L-1 D 519. Created automatically the first time a user logs on to a computer. It contains settings such as desktop settings, permissions etc Each time the user logon to this computer, these settings are reloaded

Ans Local user profile

L-2 D 520. ———————— are tasks that a user is permitted to perform on a computer system or domain

Ans User rights

L-3 D 521. Pressing CTRL+ALT+Delete before logging on guarantees that the authentic windows logon prompt appears. Requiring the use of CTRL+ALT+Del increases security and helps to thwart certain trojan horses programs

L-1 D 522. Configuration information specific to each user includes desktop settings, application settings etc

Ans User profile

L-2 D 523. There are two types of user rights

Ans Privilleges and logon rights

L-1 M 524. Record of a user contains

A. User name B. Password C. Group to which

D. Rights and permissions the user have E. All of the above

L-1 S 525. An event log that contains information on security events as mentioned in the audit policy of a system

A. Event log B. Security log C. Antivirus log D. Audit log

L-2 S 526. Windows File Protection replaces the corrupted file from the backup stored in the

A. Driver B. DLL cache folde C. System files D. All of the above

L-1 S 527. The process of disguising a data in such a way as to hide its substance and it becomes useless for unauthorized person

A. Encryption B. Digital signature

C. Electronic data D. None of the above

L-2 S 528. Permissions on an object that are automatically assigned when the object is created

A. Explicit permissions B. Implicit permissions

C. Both of the above D. Inherent permissions

L-2 S 529. Windows File Protection detects attempts by other program to replace or move a protected system file. Windows check the file's ———————— to determine if the new file is the correct Microsoft version

A. Digital signature B. Checksum

C. Encryption D. Parity bit

L-1 S 530. UID

A. Useful Identity B. Use interval

C. User Identification D. None of the above

L-1 S 531. Converting data into a form so that it is prevented from being read by unauthorized persons

A. Text processing B. Password protecting

C. Encryption D. All of the above

L-2 S 532. Keeping data secure using various methods

A. Hiding B. Deleting C. Cryptography D. Encryption

L-1 T/F 533. A user can access files located on the network depending on account restrictions determined by the network administrator

A. TRUE B. FALSE

Software

L-1 D 534. A microprogam

Ans Controls the operation of the data path

L-2 D 535. A value rises above a configured threshold. This fact is communicated using a

Ans Performance alert

L-2 D 536. In Shadow copy backups, the fact that all files are backed up, regardless of their state.

Ans Crash consistency

L-2 D 537. With every device, the manufacture have to supply drivers for each Operating System that the device is supported on.

L-2 F 538. Programs can be run on a operating system for which they are not meant. They can be run in ———————— and may not provide full functionality

Ans Compatibility mode

L-1 S 539. To print a file, a process first generates the entire file to be printed and puts it in the

A. Temp directory B. Spooling directory

C. Print directory D. Windows directory

Type of Operating Systems

L-2 S 540. If the action absolutely must occur at a certain moment, the Operating System required is

A. Hard real time OS B. Real time OS

C. Soft real time D. None of the above

Types

L-1 D 541. Network Operating Systems

Ans The system software of a local-area network, which manages the network's resources, handling multiple inputs concurrently and providing necessary security. Abbreviated NOS.

L-1 D 542. Distributed Operating Systems

Ans Allows applications to be run on several processors

L-1 D 543. A scheduler real time system is

Ans Real time system but previously planned and have carefully set up steps

L-1 D 544. Real-time systems pertains to online computer processing systems which receive and process data quickly enough to produce output to control, direct, or affect the outcome of an ongoing activity or process

L-2 D 545. The two primary types of smart card operating systems are Fixed File Structure and __________

A. Dynamic Application System

L-2 D 546. A monolithic kernel is a kernel architecture where the entire operating system is run in kernel space as supervisor mode.

L-2 D 547. Time sharing is an operating system feature allowing several users to run several tasks concurrently on one processor, or in parallel on many processors.

L-2 M 548. Real time Operating Systems

A. VxWorks B. QNX C. Windows XP D. Linux

L-1 S 549. Dos, Windows and PS/2 are operating systems for the __________

A. Supercomputer B. Workstation

C. Both of the above D. Personal computers

Types

L-1 M 550. What are different types of operating system ?

A. Real time B. Distributed C. Multimedia D. Online

Types of Networks

L-1 D 551. The components of a distributed systems are connected by a multiplexer

Unix

L-1 D 552. A drive attached to an empty folder on an NTFS volume.

Ans Mounted Drive

L-2 D 553. Special files are kept in

Ans dev directory

L-1 D 554. In Unix, 'At' command

Ans Schedules commands and programs to run on a computer

L-1 D 555. TTY

Ans Displays the name of the currrent terminal

L-1 D 556. FORK creates an ———— duplicate of the original process

Ans Exact duplicate

L-1 D 557. Unix and OS/400 are examples of operating systems for minicomputers

L-1 D 558. UNIX . A popular operating system for 16-bit mini and, mIcro computers that was designed by Bell Telephone Laboratories, USA.

L-2 D 559. The original shell in UNIX is

Ans sh

L-2 D 560. A Daemon is a service running on a computer

L-2 D 561. A call which creates an exact clone of the calling process is known as

Ans Fork

L-2 D 562. In Unix operating system, special files are provided in order to make I/O devices look and behave like files

L-2 D 563. In Unix, a system call ———— forces all the modifed blocks out onto the disk immediately

Ans Sync

L-1 F 564. In Unix, system call to create a new process is

Ans Fork

L-1 F 565. A ——— sign is used after the command in UNIX so that the command is executed as a back ground job

Ans &

L-1 M 566. Server Operating Systems

A. Unix B. Windows 2000 C. Dos D. All of the above

L-1 S 567. UNIX command Interpreter is known as

A. Dos B. Shell C. Round D. Explorer

L-1 S 568. A non-proprietary graphical user interface developed by MIT is called

A. GUI B. X-Windows C. G-Windows D. Visual graphics

L-1 S 569. A system call which is executed by a child process to change its memory image and run a new program is

A. Fork B. Execve

C. Pid D. None of the above

L-1 S 570. Motif is a GUI for

A. Unix B. Windows

C. Dos D. None of the above

L-1 S 571. GUI in Unix is known as

A. X-Windows B. G-Window

C. GUI D. Window

L-1 S 572. Files in UNIX AR protected by assigning each one a —— bit binary protection code.

A. 9 B. 12 C. 15 D. 6

L-1 S 573. POSIX and MINIX are versions of

A. Windows B. Dos

C. Unix D. All of the above

L-1 S 574. In Unix, a special process, called —— is present in the boot image

A. Swap B. Loader C. Init D. Boot

L-2 S 575. A ———— call creates a child process identical to the parent

A. sidB. uid C. pid D. gid

L-1 S 576. In UNIX, all the processes in the whole system belong to a S tree with ——— at the root

A. init

Virtual Memory

L-1 D 577. The Leased recently used page replacement algorithm

Ans When a page fault occurs, throw out the page that has been unused for the longest time.

L-1 D 578. Loading the pages before letting processes run is called

Ans Prepaging

L-1 D 579. The virtual address space is divided up into units called

Ans Pages

L-1 D 580. Page A segment of data which can be moved into and out of storage in multiprogramming

L-1 D 581. In virtual memory, a virtual address in address space is mapped to a physical address in memory space

L-1 D 582. The virtual address space is divided up into units called Pages and the corresponding units int the physical memory are called

Ans Page frames

L-1 D 583. To translate one value into another usuable value. In virtual memory systems, a computer might map a virtual address into a physical address.

Ans Map

L-1 D 584. The state of a virtual memory system in which it is spending almost all its time swapping pages in and out of memory rather than executing applications.

Ans Thrashing

L-2 M 585. Among page replacement algorithms two better ones are

A. FIFO B. Aging C. LIFO D. WSClock

L-1 S 586. In a virtual memory system, data is brought from the disk to RAM in units called

A. Block B. Page C. Character D. Sector

L-2 S 587. The two best page replacement algorithms are

A. FIFO and LRU B. Ageing and WS

C. Ageing and FIFO D. Ageing and LRU

L-1 S 588. In paging there are ———— linear address spaces

A. Many B. 3 C. 1 D. 2

L-1 S 589. Programs written for a computer may be in one of the following categories

A. Binary code B. Octal or hexade C. Symbolic code

D. High level program E. All of the above

L-2 S 590. A ———————— bit keeps track of which pages are physically present in memory

A. Parity bit B. Most significant

C. Announcement D. Present/absent bit

L-1 T/F 591. Programs greater than the size of the RAM cannot be run

A. TRUE B. FALSE

Windows

L-2 D 592. Member in this group Supports file replication in a domain

Ans Replicators

L-2 D 593. Member in this group have full powers with respect to a system

Ans Administrators

L-1 D 594. GDT

Ans Global Descriptor Table

L-1 D 595. Sets the window title for a CMD.EXE session.

Ans Title

L-1 D 596. On command prompt, displays the version of the windows

Ans VER

L-1 D 597. A window display on the desktop used to interface with the Ms-Dos. Ms-Dos commands can be used here

Ans Command prompt window

L-1 D 598. A menu that contains commands you can use to manipulate a window or close a program. You click the program icon at the left of the title bar to open the System menu.

Ans System menu

L-2 D 599. System restore

Ans Restores system to a choose n restore point

L-2 D 600. User profile of a newly created user takes the settings of the default user.

L-2 D 601. An advanced file system that provides performance, security, reliabilit and guaranteed volume consistency

Ans NTFS file system

L-2 D 602. A section of the registry that appears as a file on hard disk. The registry subtree is divided into hives

Ans Hive

L-2 D 603. To specify which program windows automatically use for each internet services, we use ——— tab of the Internet properties

Ans Programs

L-2 D 604. A string consisting of environment information, such as a drive, path, or file name, associated with a symbolic name that can be used by Windows

Ans Environment variable

L-2 D 605. The first sector on a hard disk, which starts the process of booting the computer. It contains the partition table for the disk and a small amount of executable code called the master boot code.

Ans Master boot record

L-2 D 606. A utility that provides information about programs and processes running on the computer. Using Task Manager, you can end or run programs and end processes, and display a dynamic overview of the computer's performance.

Ans Task Manager

L-3 D 607. Restore points means

Ans A restore point for a computer hard drive is essentially a previous point in time that the user may reset the system to in the event of some severe problem. Sometimes referred to as a system restore, the restore point has been a common component in the overall restore utilities on hard drives that run Microsoft Windows as the base operation system

L-1 F 608. The horizontal bar at the top of a window that contains the name of the window.

Ans Title bar

L-1 M 609. Title bar contains

A. Maximize button B. Minimize button C. Send button D. Close button

L-2 M 610. At any instant, a process could be in either of the following

A. Running B. Ready C. Killed D. Blocked

L-1 S 611. Windows Movie Maker is located in ————.

A. Control panel B. Accessories

C. Startup folder D. Help

L-1 S 612. ———— is not available if a computer is part of a domain

A. Log off B. Fast user switch

C. Both of the above D. None of the above

L-2 S 613. The ———— is the first file on an NTFS volume.

A. Boot.ini file B. Master File Table

C. Partition table D. File allocation table

L-2 S 614. System restore monitors changes to a computer, and periodically makes easily identifiable

A. Checkpoints B. Restore points

C. Recovery point D. None of the above

L-2 S 615. ———— is a table in which operating system keeps information of each process

A. Process Table B. OS Table

C. Process log D. CPU register

L-3 S 616. ASR

A. Automated System Recovery B. Automatic Software Recovery

C. A System Recovery Line D. None of the above

L-1 S 617. System tools program group appears in

A. Help B. Setting C. Accessories D. Startup

L-2 S 618. ———— can be used to end programs and processes. It also display a dynamic overview of the computer's performance

A. Utility Manager B. Control Panel

C. Task Manager D. Security Center

L-2 S 619. In the event of a system problem, you can restore your computer to a previous state without losing your personal data files. This facility is provided by ————

A. Autorestore B. Backup C. System restore D. Re-installtion

L-2 S 620. ———— lets switching from one user to another without logging off and on.

Ans Fast user switching

L-2 T/F 621.NTFS file system does not provides guaranteed volume consistency

A. TRUE B. FALSE

Windows Xp

L-1 S 622. Win key + F is shortcut for

A. Search for computers B. Search for a file

C. Enable function D. Find text in a file

L-1 S 623. Win key + F1 is shortcut for

A. Display Windows Help B. Display Ms-Office

C. Display Display D. Display functions of computer

L-1 S 624. Win key + CTRL + F is shortcut for

A. Search for computers B. Search for webs

C. Find text in a file

L-1 S 625. Win key + U is a keyboard shortcut for

A. Opens Understanding windows B. Opens tutorials

C. Opens Utility Manager D. Display functions of computer

L-1 F 626. The right side of the taskbar is called

A. System Tray

L-1 S 627. The path and folder name where the Windows system files are usually located.

A. C:\i386 B.C:\Windows C. Temp folder D. History folder

L-1 S 628. The path and folder name where the Windows system files are located.

A. systemroot B. C:\i386 C. C:\Os D. Temp

L-2 S 629. These programs starts automatically when windows starts and they appear on

A. Desktop B. Control Panel C. Accessories D. System Tray

L-2 S 630. To know the folder in which windows system files are located, ———— command can be given on run dialog box

A. C:\i386 B. C:\Windows C. %systemroot% D. History folder

Windows, Unix

L-2 D 631. A process is said to be in safe state if it is not deadlocked and there is some schedule in which every process has to run to completion and even if these process could request their maximum number of resources immediately

A. Safe

L-2 F 632. Scheduler uses an ———— to decide which process to run next

A. Scheduler Algorithm

L-2 S 633. ———— decides which process is going to run next

A. Scheduler B. Batch command

C. Scheduled task D. Auto programming

Word

L-1 M 634. To get the command prompt in Windows XP the ———— command is used in the start-run

A. Command B. Prompt C. Cmd D. Run Dos

Programming

L-2 S 635. ISA is also known as

Ans Machine Language

Scheduling

L-2 D 636. In two phase locking, if the first phase succeeds, the second phase is restarted in which

Ans Updates are performed and locks are released.

Administration

L-2 D 637. A special group that contains all users who have user permissions on the server.

Ans Users

L-2 S 638. Group for the Help and Support Center

A. Users B. Help service group C. Administrators D. Guest

L-2 S 639. Processor and RAM information could be obtained from General tab of the

A. My computer properties B. System Properties

C. Network proper D. Windows explorer properties

L-2 S 640. The ———— have complete and unrestricted access to computer or domain

A. Users B. Administrators

C. Guests D. Everyone

L-2 S 641. ———— can track and reverse harmful changes to your computer

A. System restore B. Antivirus

C. Windows Firewall D. Dr. Watson

L-2 S 642. They can run certified applications, but not most legacy applications

A. Administrators B. Staff C. Users D. Power users

L-2 S 643. ———— are prevented from making accidental or intentional system-wide changes.

A. Administrators B. Staff C. Users D. Power users

Input/Output

L-2 S 644. ———— are used to allow the CPU to do something else while waiting for the printer to become ready

A. Interrupts B. Print Manager

C. Input Manager D. Output Manger

Windows

L-1 S 645. ———— helps to perform a tasks without using the menus

A. Function keys B. Shortcut keys

C. Mouse D. Monitor

Answers

Q. No.	Answer	Q. No.	Answer
46	A B	81	B
47	B	82	B
48	B	83	B
49	B	84	A
50	B	85	A
51	B	86	A
52	B	87	A
53	B	88	A
54	B D	89	A
55	B	91	D
56	B	93	C
57	B	102	D
58	B	103	B
59	B	133	A B
60	B	134	A C
61	A	135	B
62	A	136	B
63	A	137	B
64	A	138	B
65	A	139	A
66	A	140	A
67	A	141	A
68	C	142	A
69	D	143	A
70	C	144	C
71	C	145	C
72	C	146	D
73	C	147	D
74	C	148	D
75	C	149	C
76	D	150	D
77	C	151	C
78	B	152	D
79	B	153	C
80	B	154	D

Q. No.	Answer	Q. No.	Answer
155	B	269	A
156	A	270	A
163	A	271	A
164	C	272	D
165	C	273	D
184	B	274	B
185	B	275	D
186	A	276	C
187	D	277	B
188	D	278	B
189	C	279	B
190	D	280	A
191	A	281	A
192	B	282	A
193	A	283	A
194	A	284	A
195	A	285	A
196	A	286	A
197	A	291	B
205	A B C	292	A
206	B	342	A B
207	C	343	B
208	C	344	B
211	A D	345	B
212	D	346	B
213	C	347	B
214	B	348	B
260	A B	349	B
261	A C D	350	A
262	A C	351	A
263	B	352	C
264	B	353	C
265	B	354	C
266	B	355	C
267	B	356	D
268	B	357	C

Q. No.	Answer	Q. No.	Answer
358	A	445	A
360	C	446	B
407	A C D	495	A B
408	C	496	B
409	C	497	B
410	A	498	B
411	B	499	B
412	B	500	B
413	B	501	B
414	B	502	B D
415	B	503	A
416	B	504	D
417	A	505	D
418	A	506	D
419	A	507	C
420	A C D	508	C D
421	A	509	C
422	A	510	C
423	A	511	A
424	A C	512	A B
425	D	513	B
426	C	514	A
427	D	515	A
428	D	516	A
430	B	524	E
431	B	525	B
432	B	526	B
433	B	527	A
434	A	528	A
435	A	529	A
436	A	530	C
437	A	531	C
438	A	532	C
439	B	533	A
440	B	539	B
441	D	540	A

Q. No.	Answer	Q. No.	Answer
548	A B	615	A
549	D	616	A
550	A B C	617	C
566	A B	618	C
567	B	619	C
568	B	620	A
569	B	621	B
570	A	622	B
571	A	623	A
572	A	624	A
573	C	625	C
574	C	627	B
575	C	628	A
576	A	629	D
585	B D	630	C
586	B	633	A
587	B	634	A C
588	C	635	A
589	E	638	B
590	D	639	B
591	B	640	B
609	A B D	641	A
610	A B D	642	C
611	B	643	C
612	B	644	A
613	B	645	B
614	B		

6
SOFTWARE

Animation

L-1 D 1. 3-D models could be created using a wire frame view called modeling

Data Mining

L-2 D 2. Modern data mining systems self learn from the previous history of the investigated system, formulating and testing hypothesis about the rules, which this system obeys

Data Processing

L-1 S 3. The two types of data processing systems are

A. Distributed and centralized
B. Communication
C. Network
D. Switcher

Data Warehouse

L-2 D 4. One of the principal reasons for developing a Data warehouse is to integrate operational data from various sources into a single consistent architecture that supports analysis and decision making within the enterprise

Database

L-1 D 5. There are two types of file processing ―――――――― and ――――――――

Ans Sequential, Batch

L-1 D 6. There are two types of data processing systems ―――――――― and ――――――――

Ans File, database

L-1 D 7. QMF is a query language

L-1	D 8.	What is database design?
	Ans	To determine the grouping of various business entities and their characters so that using them is convenient
L-1	D 9.	OLAP (Online Analytical Processing) and Data warehouses are complementary
L-1	D 10.	What are the advantages of using a database?
	Ans	Better datamanagement, reduced redundancy, easy access, better data integrity etc
L-1	D 11.	Metadata is also called data warehouse architecture
L-1	D 12.	What were the deficiencies of pre-database information processing?
	Ans	Data redundancy, Lack of data integrity, difficult file access, difficult to apply business constraints, lesser data security
L-1	D 13.	A set of characters which are used to represent a specific data element
	Ans	Data field
L-1	D 14.	Data in a database can be shared among different users and applications
L-1	D 15.	Constraints describes the organization and relationships within the database
L-1	D 16.	A ———————————— is a self-describing collection of integrated records
	Ans	Database
L-1	D 17.	The software used for the management , maintenance and retrieval of the data stored in a database
	Ans	DATABASE Management System
L-1	D 18.	A system that receives requests from client applications over a network and and responds by returning requested data
	Ans	Database server
L-1	D 19.	The decentrailization of a computer system through the use of multiple computers interconnected by communications network.
	Ans	Distributed Database Processing - DDP
L-1	D 20.	The sequence of database operations that represents a logical unit of work and that accesses a database and transforms it from one state to another is called a ———
	Ans	Transaction
L-2	D 21.	Blank rows signal the end of a database. Don't leave a blank row between column headings and data records. Leave a blank row after all records and before totals, averages or other summary rows
L-1	F 22.	DBMS stands for————————
	Ans	Database Management Systems
L-1	F 23.	A collection of data related to a particular subject or purpose is called a ———
	Ans	Database
L-1	F 24.	A collection of data files integrated and organized into a single comprehensive file system

Ans Database

L-2 F 25. The system database that contains descriptions of the data in the database is known as ——————

Ans Data dictionary

L-2 F 26. —————— is a technique for inserting fault tolerance into computing systems. It basically consists on storing a snapshot of the current application state, and use it for restarting the execution in case of failure

Ans Checkpointing

L-3 F 27. In recovery procedure, it is updating a prior valid copy of the database with the necessary changes to produce a current version

Ans Rollback

L-2 S 28. Advantages of centralized processing

A. Changes to the software have to be done at central location only
B. Reports based on data from several sites are easy to prepare since data resides at only the central location.
C. Fast processing
D. Data redundancy

L-1 S 29. Two or more pieces of information in a file or a database are same

A. Similarity
B. Redundancy
C. Duplication
D. Replication

L-1 S 30. A statement that extracts information from the database based upon the input condition

A. Question
B. Query
C. Report
D. None of the above

L-2 S 31. In database design, a diagram that uses circles and arrows to represent the nature and direction of relationships between data items

A. Flowchart
B. Bubble chart
C. Data chart
D. Data flow chart

L-2 S 32. Interface for users for storing and retrieving data in a relational database

A. Structured Query Language
B. Filtering
C. Virtual Storage
D. None of the above

L-2 S 33. The process of keeping master files up-to-date by processing them with the latest transactions

A. Updating B. Processing C. Transacting D. Combining

L-1 S 34. Data about data

A. Database B. File C. Metadata D. Microdata

L-1 S 35. QMF and SQL are examples of ——————

A. Programming language
B. High level language
C. Query language
D. None of the above

L-1 S 36. Which of the following is a database management system ?

A. Ms-Word
B. Lotus 1-2-3
C. Oracle
D. None of the above

L-1 S 37. Which of the following is not true about distributed processing ?
A. They are modular B. They are more reliable
C. Maintenance costs are high D. Response is slow

L-1 S 38. A column in a table which contains specific information for each record
A. Group B. Key C. Field D. Set

L-1 S 39. A ———— key is a column in the table whose purpose is to uniquely identify records from the same table
A. Foreign key B. Singular key C. Null D. Primary key

L-2 S 40. DDE
A. Dynamic Data Export B. Dynamic Dot Exchange
C. Dynamic Data Exchange D. Data meta Data Exchange

L-2 S 41. ODBC
A. Open Database Concept B. Outgoing Database Connectivity
C. Open Database Connectivity D. None of the above

L-2 S 42. DDP stands for
A. Distributed Double Proces B. Double Decimal Processing
C. Distributed Data Programming D. Distributed Data Processing

L-2 S 43. Disadvantages of centralized processing
A. Hardware or software failure of central computer brings operations on all sites B. Full load on the centralized server
C. In case of physical damge to halt of the site, all data may get lost D. All of the above

L-2 S 44. Some of the advantages of distributed processing are
A. Better response time B. Modularity
C. Lower cost D. All of the above

L-2 S 45. The extent to which the data used for processing are reliable, accurate and free from error
A. Data Validity B. Data accuracy C. Correct data D. Data integrity

L-1 T/F 46. A collection of related information is called a file
A. TRUE B. FALSE

L-2 T/F 47. In a database system redundancy can be controlled
A. TRUE B. FALSE

L-2 T/F 48. ODBC is useful in accessing data from a variety of database management systems
A. TRUE B. FALSE

L-1 T/F 49. With distributed data processing the response times are better
A. TRUE B. FALSE

DBMS

L-1 D 50. In distributed processing several computers are used by processing and storage

L-1 D 51. The goal of a concurrency management mechanism is to allow concurrency while maintaining the consistency of the shared data

L-2 D 52. What is normalization ?

Ans Database normalization is a technique for designing relational database tables to minimize duplication of information and, in so doing, to safeguard the database against certain types of logical or structural problems, namely data anomalies

L-2 D 53. ________________ is data about data

Ans Metadata

L-2 D 54. A record consists of a group of data items related to an object of data processing

L-2 D 55. The different types of relationships are One to one, one to many and many to many

L-2 D 56. A schema separates physical aspects of data storage from the logical aspects of data representations

L-2 D 57. In ____________ data processing, data processing and storage can occur at ____________ locations

Ans Distributed, different

L-2 D 58. Schema The structures defined for a particular database system. Schemas are defined by using the DATA DEFINITION LANGUAGE of a DATA MODEL.

L-1 M 59. What are the characteristics of data in the DBMS?

A. Consistency B. Data independence

C. Security D. None of the above

L-1 M 60. What are the different types of Database Management Systems ?

A. Hierarchical B. Relational C. Equatorial D. Network

L-1 M 61. What are the services provided by a Database Management System ?

A. Storage management B. Security

C. Concurrency management D. Business process reengineering

L-2 M 62. What are the different normal forms ?

A. 1NF B. 2NF

C. 3NF D. BCNF E. 4NF

L-2 M 63. What are the advantages of distributed processing systems?

A. Faster processing B. Data security

C. Better availability D. none of the above

L-1 M 64. The information should be

A. Accurate and on correct time B. Accurate, on correct time & relevant

C. On time and relevant D. Relevant and accurate

L-2 M 65. The role of DBMS is to provide services such as

A. Transaction processing B. Concurrency management & security

C. Recovery and storage management D. All of these

L-1 S 66. The most popular database model is

A. Hierarchical B. Relational C. Object Oriented D. Deductive

L-1 S 67. In ________ database systems data are processed instantaneously

A. Distributed B. Real time C. Batch D. All of the above

L-2 S 68. Many-to-many relationships are usually expressed using ________ tables

A. Flat tables B. Intersection table

C. Union tables D. None of the above

L-1 S 69. The oldest database models are

A. Hierarchical and Network B. Relational and Object Oriented

C. Object Oriented & Deductive D. None of the above

L-1 S 70. OLTP stands for

A. On Linear Transaction Processing B. Online Transaction Parts

C. Online Transaction Processing D. Output Transaction Processing

L-1 S 71. The expansion of DBMS is ________

A. Database migration system B. Database management software

C. Database management system D. Data management system

L-1 S 72. It represents the correspondence between various data element

A. Keys B. Relationships C. Constraints D. Schema

L-1 S 73. Which of the following is a Relational Database Management System ?

A. DB2 B. Oracle C. Sybase D. All of these

L-1 S 74. A collection of data designed to be used by different people is called a ________

A. File B. Field C. Database D. Data structure

L-2 S 75. A structured repository of data about data.

A. Database B. Data field C. File allocation D. Data dictionary

L-2 S 76. What are the disadvantages of distributed processing systems?

A. Redundancy B. Lack of control C. Access problem D. All of the above

L-2 S 77. When all the columns in a table describe and depend upon the primary key, the table is said to satisfy

A. The first normal form B. The fifth normal form

C. The second normal form D. The third normal form

L-2 S 78. A ________ key is completely arbitrary, having no function or meaning other than identification of the row

A. Intelligent key B. Special key

C. Non-intelligent D. None of the above

L-1 S 79. What is a Database Management System ?

Ans Is a software which helps to manage data in a database. It maintains data integrity, reduces redundancy, ensures security etc.

L-1 T/F 80. Distributed processing systems are not modular

A. TRUE B. FALSE

Decision Support System

L-2 D 81. A decision support system helps the manager to extract information from the database analyze it, and then formulate a decision or a strategy for business planning

Drivers

L-1 D 82. The software that talks to a controller, giving it commands and accepting responses is called

Ans A Device Driver

General

L-1 D 83. In centralized data processing systems, processing and storage can take place at a central locations

L-1 D 84. Office automation systems help to keep track of the activities being performed in various departments in the company

L-2 D 85. A column in a data table is called a

Ans Field

L-2 D 86. Lotus Notes, Microsoft Exchange and Novell Groupwise are groupware products

L-2 D 87. OLAP (Online Analytical Processing) technology is being used in sales and marketing analysis, financial reporting and consolidation and budgeting and planning

L-2 D 88. OLAP ranges from basic navigation and browsing, to calculations, to more serious analysis such as time series and complex modeling

L-2 D 89. While OLAP systems have the ability to answer "who?" and "what?" questions, it is their ability to answer "what if?" and "why?" that sets them apart from data warehouses

L-2 F 90. Hardware or software that can compress and uncompress audio or video data compression/decompression

Ans Codec

L-1 M 91. Image processing softwares

A. Ms Paint B. Adobe Image ready C. Photography D. All of the above

L-2 S 92. OLAP stands for ——————

A. Online Analytical Production B. Online Analytical Processing
C. Online Artificial Processing D. None of the above

L-2 S 93. A voice recognition software works in 2 modes dictation mode and

A. Trial mode B. Command mode
C. Both of the above D. None of the above

L-1 S 94. Oracle is a

A. Programming language B. Front end
C. Database management system D. Accounting system

L-1 S 95. A fully compiled program which can be executed by the CPU

A. Source program B. Interpretor

C. Object program D. Program

L-2 S 96. Software components interact with each other in a network, regardless of the language which was used to create those components. This technology is known as

A. Embedding B. OLE

C. Com D. ActiveX

L-1 T/F 97. Oracle is a programming language

A. TRUE B. FALSE

Management Information System

L-1 D 98. Data warehousing make sure that the data is available for analysis and it doesn't affect the operational system.

Multimedia

L-1 D 99. MMX a set of instructions built in to the CPU specifically intended for improving the performance of multimedia or graphic applications — mainly games

Ans Multimedia extensions

L-1 F 100. MMX is ____________________

Ans Multimedia extensions

Programming

L-2 D 101. A function call that passes arguments to a function by passing the addresses of that arguments

Ans Call by address

L-2 D 102. A logically related set of data that can be decomposed into lower data elements. This set can be handled as a unit

Ans Database

L-1 D 103. Return Address

Ans is the address to which the operation is returned when execution of a subroutine or a function is finished

L-1 D 104. Turnkey systems

Ans A turnkey or a turnkey project is a type of project that is constructed by a developer and sold or turned over to a buyer in a ready-to-use condition.

L-1 D 105. Structured programming

A. Structured programming (sometimes known as modular programming) is a subset of procedural programming that enforces a logical structure on the program being written to make it more efficient and easier to understand and modify. Certain languages such as Ada, Pascal, and dBASE are designed with features that encourage or enforce a logical program structure.

L-1 D 106. LISP (List Processing) language is a natural language

L-1 D 107. What is a assembly language?

Ans Assembly language is a language is which programs are written for the system using symbols.

L-1 D 108. What is a programming language?

Ans A language which is used to write programs for the computer.

L-1 D109. COBOL is fifth generation language

L-1 D 110. A constant is a value that is not calculated.

L-1 D 111. What are HTML tags? And where are they used?

Ans HTML tags are used to define the output when the file is opened in a web browser. For example the title tag specifies what text would appear on the title bar of the window

L-1 D 112. Machine languages are also called First Generation languages

L-1 D 113. The main difference between a Compiler and a Interpreter is

Ans Compiler translates the whole program into machine language at once

L-1 D 114. A symbolic address in the label field is terminated by a comma

L-1 D 115. High level languages are also called Third Generation languages

L-1 D 116. The grammar and semantics governing the way a command is written is known as syntax

L-1 D 117. A program is a list of instructions telling the computer what to do

L-1 D 118. Many operating systems are designed as a collection of program modules

L-1 D 119. Full read and write privileges are given to a program when it is executing its own instructions

L-1 D 120. System software consists of low level programs that interact with the computer at a very basic level

L-1 D 121. Computer instructions written with the use of English words. Mathematical symbols could also be used.

Ans Symbolic code

L-1 D 122. The process of making sure that the software performs its intended task by trying it using sample data

Ans Testing

L-1 D 123. A program is a set of instructions or statements for directing the computer to perform a required task

L-1 D 124. Data Flow Chart — A flow chart showing the path of the data step by step in a problem solution or through a system

L-1 D 125. Programming language is a set of rules that provides a way of instructing the computer to perform certain operations

L-1 D 126. A symbolic address in Assembly language consists of one, two, or three but not more than three alphanumeric characters

L-1 D 127. A program is a set of instructions that specify the sequence of operations and sequence in which processing has to occur

L-1 D 128. A master file contains relatively permanent records for identification and some of the fields summarizes the transactions done

L-1 D 129. Each line of an assembly language program is arranged in three columns called fields. The fields are label, instruction and comment

L-1 D 130. The pointer points to the address of the current operand and the counter counts the number of times that the program loop is executed

L-1 D 131. —————————— is the formal process of developing data structures in a matter that eliminates redundancy and promotes integrity

Ans Normalization

L-1 D 132. HTML defines several aspects of a web page including heading levels, bold, italics, images, paragraph breaks and hypertext links to other resources

L-1 D 133. Because of one-to-one relationship between a symbolic instruction and its binary equivalent, an assembly language is considered to be a machine-level language

L-1 D 134. There are various types of programming languages that one may write for a computer, but the computer can execute programs only when they are represented internally in binary form.

L-1 D 135. A high level programming language suitable for handling logical operations and non numeric applications. Used mainly in areas of pattern recognition, artificial intelligence and games simulation

Ans LISP

L-1 D 136. Housekeeping In computer programming — The setup and initialization procedures (setting up con-straints, variables, and switches and clearing locations etc.) performed prior to the processing steps of the program.

L-2 D 137. A class from which other classes are derived.

Ans Base class

L-2 D 138. Stack

Ans Is an abstract data type and data structure based on the principle of Last In First Out (LIFO)

L-2 D 139. In the context of programming, a Pointer is an

Ans Address of a variable

L-2 D 140. Post script

Ans PostScript (PS) is a dynamically typed concatenative programming language created by John Warnock and Charles Geschke in 1982. PostScript is best known for its use as a page Dription language in the electronic and desktop publishing areas.

L-2 D 141. Main advantage of using JVM

Ans Java Virtual Machines operate on Java bytecode, which is normally (but not necessarily) generated from Java source code; a JVM can also be used to implement programming languages other than Java. Because JVMs are available for many hardware and software platforms, Java can be both middleware and a platform in its own right — hence the trademark write once, run anywhere. The use of the same bytecode for all platforms allows Java to be described as "compile once, run anywhere", as opposed to "write once, compile anywhere", which describes cross-platform compiled languages.

L-2 D 142. Extensible Markup Language (XML)

Ans A meta-markup language that provides a format for describing structured data.

L-2 D 143. A pseudofile that can be used to connect two processes is called a

Ans Pipe

L-2 D 144. A program statement which transfers program control to a subroutine

Ans Call statement

L-2 D 145. A stored set of "source" information used to connect to a database. "

Ans Data source

L-2 D 146. A study conducted to determine whether the proposed solution is feasible in all respect.

Ans Feasibility study

L-2 D 147. It should be possible to write programs that can access any I/O device without having to specify the type of device.

Ans Device independence

L-2 D 148. A pseudoinstruction is not a machine instruction but rather an instruction to the assembler giving information about some phase of translation

L-2 D 149. When the assembler translates the program from symbols to binary, the first scan is called the first pass, and the second scan is called the second pass

L-2 D 150. If you have a program that accesses data in a SQL database, data sources (ODBC) let the use of the same program to access data in a Visual foxpro database.

L-2 D 151. The internal data structure of an object is hidden from outside the object. The data can be accessed only by the functions declared within the class of that object

Ans Data hiding

L-2 D 152. A web archive that saves all the elements of a web site including any graphics, into one file. It helps to publish a whole website as a single MIME encapsulated aggregate HTML document

L-2 D 153. Description of a computer programming algorithm in english language with the use of structural conventions of a programming language. It is used for easy reading and understanding by humans.

Ans Pseudocode

L-2 D 154. A compiler translates full program into machine language program and then this machine language program is executed. An interpreter translates a line of a program and then it is executed before the next line is translated

L-2 D 155. When a subroutine is called, the calling program must transfer the data to the subroutine to work with. It is necessary for the subroutine to have access to data from the calling program and to return the results to that program

L-2 D 156. When translating from assembly language to binary form, after the first scan is completed, each label is associated with its location number and a table is formed. This table defines the hexa-decimal value of each symbolic address. This table is known as

Ans Address Symbol Table

L-2 D 157. In prototyping, a working model is first created based on what the user has asked for. On its completion, the prototype is again looked at by the user and other set of requirements and specification arises. This process is continued until a user and the developer think that the system is ready meets all the requirements of user and it can be implemented.

L-3 D 158. What is microcode?

Ans Microcode is a layer of lowest-level instructions involved in the implementation of machine code instructions in many computers and other processors; it resides in a special high-speed memory and translates machine instructions into sequences of detailed circuit-level operations.

L-3 D 159. Loops and subroutines tend to localize the references to memory for fetching instructions and data.

L-1 D 160. An error which occur during the execution of a program

Ans Execution error

L-1 F 161. Two values can be compared using ____________

Ans Comparison operators

L-1 F 162. Pre-defined symbols to describe the logic of a computer program

Ans Flowchart

L-1 F 163. The total time required to execute a program on a particular system is ____________ for that system

Ans Execution time

L-1 F 164. A program which translates a program written in a high level language to machine language is called a ____________

Ans Compiler

L-1 F 165. A procedure for evaluation and selection of hardware and or software in which lists are made of all the costs and benefits of each proposed data processing system

Ans Cost/benefit analysis

L-2 F 166. A function call that passes arguments to a function by passing the values of the arguments is known as ____________

Ans Call by value

L-2 F 167. ________________ keyword ensures that once a thread has started executing that method, no other thread can start executing any other synchronized method in that class

Ans Synchronized

L-3 F 168. API is ________________

Ans Application Programming Interface

L-1 M 169. 4GL examples -

A. Foxpro B. Clipper C. Powerbuilder D. Visual basic

L-1 M 170. Names of some high level languages

A. L-1 B. Visual basic C. Java D. Assembly

L-1 M 171. What are different of high level languages ?

A. Visual basic B. Java C. Foxpro D. Assembly

L-1 M 172. Four pseudoinstructions that are recognized by the assembler are

A. ORG B. END C. DEC D. OCT

E. Hex

L-1 M 173. Object Oriented Languages

A. C B. C++ C. C# D. Java

L-1 S 174. Pascal, Cobol, and Basic are ________________ languages

A. Compiler languages B. Programming language

C. Markup language D. None of the above

L-1 S 175. LISP and PROLOG are two popular ________________ languages

A. Natural B. Artificial intelligence

C. Algorithmic D. None of the above

L-1 S 176. A program written in a symbolic or high-level source language

A. Object code B. Source code

C. Binary code D. None of the above

L-1 S 177. A code which is used by a user to gain access to a computer system

A. Hexacode B. Password C. Code D. Watermark

L-1 S 178. A program that translates high level language to binary is called a

A. Interpretor B. Compiler

C. Linker D. Programming language

L-1 S 179. A set of computer instructions when executed, performs a specific tasks

A. Subroutine B. Program C. Function D. All of the above

L-1 S 180. ________________ are programs that translate assembly language into machine language

A. Compiler B. Assembler C. Interpretor D. Linker

L-1 S 181. An executing program, including the current values of the program counter, registers and variables

A. Thread B. Process

C. Command D. None of the above

L-1 S 182. A diagram that depicts the flow of data through a system and the processes that manipulate the data

A. Data dictionary B. Data Flow Diagram
C. Data direction D. None of the above

L-1 S 183. A high-level, mathematically oriented programming language used for scientific and engineering applications.

A. L-1 B. FORTRAN C. COBOL D. All of the above

L-2 S 184. The program submitted for compilation is called a

A. Object program B. Source program
C. Linker D. Binary program

L-2 S 185. When processor registers are used as pointers and counters they are called

A. Pointer registers B. Index registers C. Accumulator D. Counter

L-2 S 186. An entry in a computer program for the purpose of documentation or explanation.

A. Key point B. Comment C. Description D. Documentation

L-2 S 187. This program aid in detecting, locating and correcting errors in another program

A. Bugger B. Debugger C. Compiler D. Interpreter

L-2 S 188. Web browsers display ———— while pictures are loading or if they are missing

A. File name B. Alternative text
C. Website name D. Programmer name

L-2 S 189. Graphic representation of conditions and outcomes resembling the tree and its branches

A. Data flow diagram B. Decision Tree
C. Structured English D. Flowchart

-2 S 190. A branch instruction calls for a transferred a nonconsecutive instruction in the program

A. Jump B. Goto
C. Loop D. None of the above

L-2 S 191. The process of making sure that the forms and documents from a particular transaction are correct.

A. Verification B. Validation C. Checking D. Debugging

L-2 S 192. A point in a program at which the program can be halted and the values of variables and fields are analyzed to check and debug the program

A. Watch B. Break point C. Print D. Console

L-1 S 193. LISP

A. List Processing B. List Processor
C. List Pattern D. None of the above

L-1 S 194. JVM stands for

A. Java Virtual Machine B. Java Visual Machine

C. Java Visual Mechanics D. Java Virtual Mechanics

L-1 S 195. Examples of High Level Language

A. L-1 B. Assembly Language

C. Java D. C#

L-1 S 196. 3GL (Third generation languages)

A. C B. Visual Basic C. Pascal D. Cobol

L-1 S 197. COBOL stands for ——————

A. Common Business Oriented Language B. Computers Business Oriented Language

C. Common Business Official Language D. Common Business Oriented Literature

L-1 S 198. HTML stands for ——————

A. Hyper text markup language B. Hyper text marking language

C. Hyper text making language D. None of the above

L-1 S 199. Which of the following is represented as a series of 0s and 1s?

A. Machine Languages B. Assembly Language

C. High Level Languages D. None of these

L-1 S 200. Which of the following is the lowest level programming language?

A. Machine Languages B. Assembly Language

C. Natural Language D. None of these

L-1 S 201. The process of writing computer instructions in a programming language

A. Coding B. Writing C. Developing D. Setting

L-1 S 202. An instruction that transfers program control to one or more possible paths

A. Branch B. Loop C. Error path D. Exit

L-1 S 203. A programming language whose structure is application oriented and the language is independent of the architecture of the computer

A. High level language B. Low level language

C. Machine language D. None of the above

L-1 S 204. A language processor that translates a statement written in a high-level language and immediately executes it before translating the next statement.

A. Interpretor B. Compiler C. Translator D. Convertor

L-1 S 205. Various types of programming languages could be used to write a program for a computer. But the computer can execute programs only when they are represented internally in ——————

A. Binary form B. Symbolic form

C. English D. Assembly language

L-2 S 206. A memory in which information added last is on top and is retrieved first

A. Stack B. Pointer C. Linked list D. All of the above

L-2 S 207. A program file used to connect to a specific database. Different ———— are required for different DBMS systems

A. Data source driver B. Meta data

C. Data dictionary D. None of the above

L-1 S 208. An error in a computer program

A. Error B. Fault C. Blunder D. Bug

L-1 S 209. Execution error is also known as

A. Dry error B. Processing fault C. Bug D. Run time error

L-1 S 210. Calls one batch program from another.

A. Execute B. Command C. Run D. Call

L-1 S 211. Fifth-generation languages are called

A. Machine Languages B. Assembly Languages

C. Natural Languages D. None of these

L-1 S 212. FORTRAN is the abbreviation of ————

A. For translation B. Formula translation C. For transmission

D. Formula Termination

L-1 S 213. Which of the following is an interpretor language?

A. COBOL B. C C. C++ D. L-1

L-1 S 214. An algebraic, high level language similar to FORTRAN

A. Pascal B. Cobol C. Algol D. L-1

L-1 S 215. Main use of COBOL language is to develop softwares for

A. Developing operating system B. Writing Drivers

C. Develop business data processing application

D. To develop antivirus solutions for businesses

L-1 S 216. Its easy to understand a program written in High Level language than

A. Machine Level Language B. Assembly Language

C. Low level D. All of the above

L-1 S 217. A type of computer code that can be used to make a Web page dynamic.

A. Program B. Snippets C. Web scripts D. Module

L-1 S 218. A named storage location capable of containing a specific type of data

A. Constant B. List C. Variable D. Reference

L-1 S 219. The time required by an object program to complete its single, continuous execution

A. Dry run time B. Execution time C. CPU time D. Run time

L-1 S 220. The set of rules of a programming language like rules of grammar for languages like English

A. Semantics B. Version C. Syntax D. Structure

L-1 S 221. A sequence of precise and unambiguous instructions for solving a problem in a finite number of operations

A. Flowchart B. Structured engling C. Formula D. Algorithm

L-1 S 222. ―――――――― become part of source file and once inserted, are no longer part of the source file

A. Linked object B. Connection

C. Shortcut D. Embedded Object

L-1 S 223. A program written by a user may be either dependent or independent of the physical computer that runs his program

A. Compatible B. Master C. Universal D. Portable

L-1 S 224. A ―――――――― is a single instruction that performs several different commands in a sequence determined by the user, and is triggered when you run it

A. Command B. Database C. Macro D. Function

L-2 S 225. XML is

A. Xtra Machine Language B. Extensible Markup Language

C. Extensible Method Limit D. None of the above

L-2 S 226. A stack is ――――――――

A. FIFO B. FILO C. LIFO D. LILO

L-2 S 227. DSS stands for ――――――――

A. Dictation support system B. Decision scanning system

C. Decision support system D. Dictation scanning system

L-2 S 228. A small application unable to run by itself.

A. Subroutine B. Function C. Applet D. Snippet

L-2 S 229. A system of record is the source of the data that feed the data warehouse

A. Object code B. Linker C. Interpretor D. compiler

L-2 S 230. Representation of the essential features of something without including much detail

A. Encapsulation B. Hiding C. Abstraction D. Protection

L-2 S 231. A set of common instructions that can be used in a program many times is called a ――――――――

A. Script B. Snippet C. Subroutine D. Procedure

L-2 S 232. A test that verifies that the software Operate to system specifications and data integrity is maintained.

A. Validation testing B. Debugging

C. Verification D. User acceptance test

L-2 S 233. A ―――――――― is a set of instructions that performs a specific task and may be called from many places within a software or from many softwares

A. Snippet B. Command

C. Subroutine D. None of the above

L-2 S 234. A "What if" approach that uses an information system to assist management in formulating policies and projecting the likely results of following a decision

A. Excel B. Software

C. Management In D. Decision support system

L-2 S 235. Prior to starting the assembly process, the symbolic program must be stored in memory. A ———— program is used to input the characters of the symbolic program into memory

A. Swapping B. Linker

C. Loader D. None of the above

L-1 S 236. Writing a program for a computer consists of specifying, directly or indirectly, a sequence of machine instructions

A. TRUE

L-1 S 237. Which of the following is not a procedural language ?

A. COBOL B. LISP C. FORTRAN D. Pascal

L-1 T/F238. Passwords are not case sensitive

A. TRUE B. FALSE

L-1 T/F239. Fortran is not a high level language

A. TRUE B. FALSE

L-1 T/F240. Assembly languages are machine independent

A. TRUE B. FALSE

L-1 T/F241. A function does not return a value but a subroutine does

A. TRUE B. FALSE

L-2 T/F242. A assembler is more complicated program than an compiler

A. TRUE B. FALSE

L-2 T/F243. It is not required to store the return address for the subroutine to know where to return

A. TRUE B. FALSE

L-1 T/F244. Assembler languages are also called Second Generation languages

A. TRUE B. FALSE

L-1 T/F245. Functions are structured programs that calculate a specific result

A. TRUE B. FALSE

L-1 T/F246. Its easy to write a program in Assembly language then in Machine language

A. TRUE B. FALSE

L-1 T/F247. Assembly Level Language is distinct for computers with different architectures

A. TRUE B. FALSE

L-1 T/F248. Programs written in any other language must be translated to the binary form before they can be executed by the computer.

A. TRUE B. FALSE

L-2 T/F249. Almost every commercial computer has its own particular assembly language

A. TRUE B. FALSE

L-2 T/F250. A program written by a user may be either dependent or independent of the physical computer that runs his program

A. TRUE B. FALSE

Speech Recognition

L-1 D 251. Speech recognition converts voice to machine readable input

L-1 D 252. Speech recognition is not designed for completely hands-free operation in order to get best results one has to use mouse and keyboard along with the voice

L-2 D 253. Speech recognition systems use powerful and complicated statistical modeling systems

L-2 D 254. Accuracy may be measured in terms of performance accuracy which is usually rated with word error rate (WER), whereas speed is measured with the real time factor. Other measures of accuracy include Single Word Error Rate (SWER) and Command Success Rate (CSR)

L-3 D 255. To validate a user's identity using various characteristics of their voice is also done using speech recognition techniques.

System Software

L-1 S 256. Write protection is useful for sharing system programs such as utility programs and other library routines

Ans TRUE

Types

L-1 D 257. Application software

Ans Application software is any tool that functions and is operated by means of a computer, with the purpose of supporting or improving the software user's work

L-1 D 258. Utility programs or service programs

Ans Utility software (also known as service program, service routine, tool, or utility routine) is computer software designed to help manage and tune the computer hardware, operating system or application software by performing a single task or a small range of tasks. Some utility software has been integrated into most major operating systems.

L-1 D 259. Groupware includes Email, Electronic Meeting Systems, Desktop Video Conferencing as well as systems for workflow and business process reengineering

L-1 M 260. There are basically 3 types of software → System software, application software, general purpose utility software

A. System software B. Compiler software

C. Application software D. General purpose software

L-1 S 261. Which among the following is an application program?

A. COBOL B. L-1
C. Powerpoint D. None of these

L-1 S 262. A software that interprets HTML files and display them

A. Frontpage B. Word C. Browser D. All of the above

Types of Softwares

L-1 D 263. What is a word processor?

Ans Any application software designed to type, format, edit and print text content. It may contain some graphics according to the capability of the word processor

L-1 D 264. What is systems software?

Ans System software is closely related to, but distinct from operating system software. It is any computer software that provides the infrastructure over which programs can operate, i.e., it manages and controls computer hardware so that application software can perform. Operating systems, such as Microsoft Windows, Mac OS X or Linux, are prominent examples of system software.

L-1 M 265. What are the different types of computer software?

A. System software B. Operating system
C. Application software D. Utility software

L-1 S 266. Programming languages are

A. Firmware B. System software C. Application software
D. Utility software

L-1 S 267. Which of the following is a word processor?

A. Ms-Word B. Wordstar C. WordPerfect D. All of the above

Voice Recognition

L-1 D 268. Naturalness describes how closely the output sounds like human speech, while intelligibility is the ease with which the output is understood

L-1 D 269. Voice recognition systems are used in mobile phones now-a-days.

L-2 D 270. Formant synthesis does not use human speech samples at runtime. Instead, the synthesized speech output is created using an acoustic model.

L-2 D 271. In order to reproduce the natural sound of each language, a narrator records a series of texts, (poetry, political news, sports results, stock exchange updates, etc.) which contain every possible sound in the chosen language.

L-2 D 272. Domain-specific synthesis concatenates prerecorded words and phrases to create complete utterances

L-2 D 273. Concatenative synthesis is based on the concatenation (or stringing together) of segments of recorded speech

L-2 D 274. Language is comprised of sound elements called phonemes. These phonemes are combined to create words and language

L-2 D 275. Diphone synthesis uses a minimal speech database containing all the diphones (sound-to-sound transitions) occurring in a language

L-2 D 276. ______________________ is a technique for synthesizing speech by replacing the formats (main bands of energy) with pure tone whistles

Ans Sinewave synthesis

L-2 D 277. One can use speech recognition by clicking or saying the name of buttons on the Language bar. A user can also switch between two modes — Dictation mode and Voice Command mode by saying the mode she want.

L-2 D 278. Articulatory synthesis refers to mathematical computational techniques used for synthesizing speech. These computation are based on models of the human vocal tract and the articulation processes occurring there.

L-2 D 279. Unit selection synthesis uses large databases of recorded speech. During database creation, each recorded utterance is segmented into some or all of the following: individual phones, diphones, half-phones, syllables, morphemes, words etc.

L-2 S 280. Switches between command mode and dictation mode.

A. Alt B. Ctrl C. Esc D. F1

L-2 T/F 281.Speech recognition can be use only in Ms Word and not in Ms Excel

A. TRUE B. FALSE

Answers

Q. No.	Answer	Q. No.	Answer
3	A	44	D
28	A B	45	D
29	B	46	A
30	B	47	A
31	B	48	A
32	A	49	A
33	A	59	A B C
34	C	60	A B D
35	C	61	A B C
36	C	62	A B C D E
37	D	63	A B C
38	C	64	B
39	D	65	D
40	C	66	B
41	C	67	B
42	D	68	B
43	D	69	A

Q. No.	Answer	Q. No.	Answer
70	C	188	B
71	C	189	B
72	D	190	B
73	D	191	B
74	C	192	B
75	D	193	A
76	D	194	A
77	D	195	A C D
78	C	196	A C D
80	B	197	A
91	A B	198	A
92	B	199	A
93	B	200	A
94	C	201	A
95	C	202	A
96	D	203	A
97	B	204	A
169	B C D	205	A
170	B,C	206	A
171	A B	207	A
172	A B C E	208	D
173	B C D	209	D
174	B	210	D
175	B	211	C
176	B	212	B
177	B	213	D
178	B	214	C
179	B	215	C
180	B	216	D
181	B D	217	C
182	B	218	C
183	B	219	D
184	B	220	C
185	B	221	D
186	B	222	D
187	B	223	D

Q. No.	Answer	Q. No.	Answer
224	C	242	B
225	B	243	B
226	C	244	A
227	C	245	A
228	C	246	A
229	D	247	A
230	C	248	A
231	C	249	A
232	D	250	A
233	C	256	A
234	C	260	A C D
235	C	261	C
236	A	262	C
237	B	265	A C D
238	B	266	B
239	B	267	D
240	B	280	B
241	B	281	B

7

NETWORKING

Address Resolution Protocol

L-2 M 1. Address resolution algorithm can be of ———— type.

A. Table lookup B. Closed form computation

C. Operating system D. Message exchange

Addressing

L-2 S 2. A 32 bit value that is used to distinguish network ID and host ID portions from an IP address is

A. IP mask B. Subnet mask

C. Class mask D. Network Identifier

L-1 S 3. This is a subdivision of an IP network

A. Subnet B. Small network

C. 'A' level network D. None of the above

L-2 T/F 4. Subnet masks use the format 255.x.x.x.

A. TRUE B. FALSE

Administration

L-1 D 5. He/she is responsible for planning, configuring and managing the day-to-day operations of the network

Ans Network Administrator

Communication

L-1 D 6. Point to point protocol

Ans A data link protocol commonly used to establish a direct connection between two networking nodes. It can provide connection authentication, transmission encryption privacy, and compression. PPP is used over many types of physical networks including serial cable, phone line.

L-1 D 7. The condition of modem in which it is in listen mode and waiting for incoming calls

Ans Waiting for Call

L-2 D 8. A tunnel that is initiated by the client. It tunnels PPP over IP from the client to the tunnel server, then the data is forwarded to the target host by the tunnel server.

Ans Voluntary level

L-2 D 9. This service maps IP addresses to computer netbios names. This is done dynamically. It helps users to access resources by name instead of IP address. IP addresses are difficult to remember.

Ans Windows Internet Name Service (WINS)

L-1 D 10. Full form of MPI is

Ans Message Passing Interface

L-1 D 11. Modem means

Ans Modulation Demodulation

L-1 D 12. In the context of communication, ECC is Error Correcting Code.

L-1 D 13. What are microwave systems?

Ans Microwave system is a system of equipment used for microwave data transmission. The typical microwave system includes radios located high atop microwave towers, which are used for the transmission of microwave communications using line of sight microwave radio technology.

L-1 D 14. A computer system which is not connected to the internet/network is said to be

Ans Offline

L-1 D 15. What is a modem and how does it work?

Ans Is a modulator-demodulator. It converts signals from digital to analog and send them over a analog media. At the receiving end it converts them back to digital

L-1 D 16. What is communication media?

Ans Medium used to transfer data from one host to another. Data travel through it from source to destination. E.g. Coaxial cable, optical Fiber etc.

L-1 D 17. Why does an organization needs an intranet?

Ans So that people using computers within the company can communicate and work together

L-1 D 18. A node which is not connected to the internet

Ans Offline

L-1 D 19. Short waves have a frequency range of 150-285 KHz

L-1 D 20. A path for carrying signals between a source and a destination

Ans Channel

L-1 D 21. For transmitting audio waves, long antennas are required.

L-1 D 22. In the case of TV, ——————— waves carry picture information

Ans AM (Amplitude modulation)

L-1 D 23. A processing unit that coordinates networks and data communications,

Ans Communication processor

L-1 D 24. A high-speed digital telephone service with speeds of 128Kbps or more

Ans ISDN (Integrated Services Digital Network)

L-1 D 25. The type of wiring and lower level protocols used for data transmission

Ans Network media

L-1 D 26. The communication satellites are placed in orbits called ———————

Ans Equatorial Geosynchronous

L-1 D 27. Communication between a computer and another computer or device without wires.

Ans Wireless communication

L-1 D 28. An end point of a branch in a network or a common Junction of two or more network

Ans Node

L-1 D 29. Modems, multiplexes and frontend processors are examples of communications channels

L-1 D 30. Communication satellites are placed in the orbits which is 42282 miles above sea level

L-1 D 31. The precise meaning of well-connected is determined by the particular needs of the client

Ans Well-connected

L-1 D 32. The connection to your network if you are using a device that uses the telephone network.

Ans Dial-up connection

L-1 D 33. Terminals linked to the computer system by a direct cable are known as hard wired terminals

Ans Hard wired terminals

L-1 D 34. Integrated Services Digital Network (ISDN) — A phone line that is configured to supports modem

L-1 D 35. One or more of the nodes in a cluster cannot communicate with the other cluster nodes. Such a state is

Ans Network partition

L-1 D 36. A state in which one or more of the nodes in a cluster cannot communicate with the "other cluster nodes.

Ans Network partition

L-1 D 37. The word modem is a combined abbreviation of the two words ——————— —— and ———————

Ans Modulator and demodulator

L-1 D 38. A CRC error indicates that one or more characters in the data packet received were found incorrect on arrival

Ans CRC errors

L-1 D 39. A network is a group of computers and other devices such as printers and scanners connected by a communication link.

Ans Network

L-1 D 40. A form of data transmission in which information is sent and received at irregular intervals, one character at a time.

Ans Asynchronous Communication

L-1 D 41. A state that refers to a resource in a cluster when the resource is in the process of being brought online or taken offline.

Ans Pending

L-1 D 42. The number of bits transmitted every second, used as a measure of the speed at which a device such as modem can transfer data

Ans Bits per second (bps)

L-1 D 43. ______________________ consists of high frequency radio waves that travel in straight lines through the air rather than through wires

Ans Radiowaves

L-1 D 44. For sending a print to a printer connected to another computer on LAN, that printer should be installed as ______________________ on this computer

Ans Network Printer

L-1 D 45. An analog or analogue signal is any continuous signal for which the time varying feature (variable) of the signal is a representation of some other time varying quantity, i.e., analogous to another time varying signal.

L-2 D 46. Interleaving

Ans Interleaving is used in digital data transmission technology to protect the transmission against burst errors. These errors overwrite a lot of bits in a row. Interleaving is used to help stop this from happening. To reduce the effect of such burst errors, the bits of a number of codewords are interleaved before being transmitted. This way, a burst error affects only a correctable number of bits in each codeword, and the decoder can decode the codewords correctly.

L-2 D 47. Full form of UART is

Ans Universal Asynchronous Receiver Transmitters

L-2 D 48. What is modulation?

Ans Modulation is the process of varying some characteristic of a periodic wave with an external signals. Modulation is utilized to send an information bearing signal over long distances. Radio communication superimposes this information bearing signal onto a carrier signal. These high frequency carrier signals can be transmitted over the air easily and are capable of traveling long distances. The characteristics (amplitude, frequency, or phase) of the carrier signal are varied in accordance with the information bearing signal. In the field of communication engineering, the information bearing signal is also known as the modulating signal. The modulating signal is a slowly varying signal — as opposed to the rapidly varying carrier frequency.

L-2 D 49. What are different types of modulation?

Ans Amplitude, phase, frequency modulation

L-2 D 50. A concentrator is essentially a smart multiplexer

L-2 D 51. What is uplink, downlink, and cross link?

Ans An uplink (UL or U/L) is the portion of a communications link used for the transmission of signals from an Earth terminal to a satellite or to an airborne platform. An uplink is the inverse of a downlink. An uplink or downlink is distinguished from reverse link or forward link

L-2 D 52. The passage of a data packet between two network nodes

Ans Hop

L-2 D 53. Phase modulation is in reality a second form of frequency modulation

L-2 D 54. A set of rules and procedures pre established to interconnect different computers

A. Communication protocol

L-2 D 55. A parity bit is an extra bit included with a binary message to make the total number of 1's either odd or even

L-2 D 56. A type of ATM service which supports constant bandwidth allocation and is used for audio and video transmissions

Ans Constant Bit Rate (CBR)

L-2 D 57. A communications system that handles moderate volumes of data, typically from 300 to 9600 bauds. E.g., Phone lines.

Ans Voiceband Data

L-2 D 58. Modems come in several forms including small stand-alone units, plug in circuit boards and microelectronic modem chips

L-2 D 59. A link between the I/O ports of two computers. This link is created with a Single cable connecting the computers directly

Ans Direct cable connection

L-2 D 60. The parity method detects the presence of one, three, or any odd number of errors. An even number of errors is not detected

L-2 D 61. A —————————— is a communication device that multiplexes several signals for transmission over a single medium

Ans Multiplexer

L-2 D 62. Modulation permits the transmission to occur at high frequencies while simultaneously allows the carrying of the audio signal

L-2 D 63. For Network Load Balancing, a set of configuration parameters that determine the filtering mode to be applied to a range of ports.

Ans Port rule

L-2 D 64. A frontend processor is responsible for handling communications to and from all the remote terminals connected to the computer system

L-2 D 65. Distributed applications running at different times communicate across heterogeneous networks and with computers that may be offline

Ans Message Queuing

L-2 D 66. The address of the local computer used for routing outgoing packets back to the source computer. This address is used primarily for testing.

Ans Loop back address

L-2 D 67. The process of changing some characteristics of a carrier wave in accordance with the intensity of the signal is known as ——————————

Ans Modulation

L-2 D 68. When the amplitude of the high frequency carrier wave is changed in accordance with the intensity of the signal is known as ——————————

Ans Modulation

L-2 D 69. A device responsible for monitoring a token ring. The active monitor ensures that tokens are not lost and that frames do not circulate indefinitely

Ans Active monitor

L-2 D 70. A technique used to reduce the number of characters without losing the data. The data which is shorter in size is transmitted and at the receiver end, the reverse process is done to obtain the full content

Ans Modem compression

L-2 D 71. Wins proxy is a computer that listens to name query broadcasts and responds for those names not on the local subnet. The proxy communicates with a WINS server to resolve names. These names are also cached for a specific time period.

Ans WINS proxy

L-2 D 72. A client on a network connects to the proxy server for the network and request a service such as a file, connection, web page, or other resource, residing on a server on a different network. Proxy server take the request and forwards to the server. When the reply comes, the proxy server send the reply to the client who requested that service or resource.

L-3 D 73. Tunneling

Ans Computer networks use a tunneling protocol when one network protocol (the delivery protocol) encapsulates a different payload protocol. By using tunneling one can (for example) carry a payload over an incompatible delivery-network, or provide a secure path through an untrusted network.

L-3 D 74. By immediately hanging up when called and then dialing the caller back, the server ensures that the calling system is a trusted one.

Ans Callback

L-1 D 75. Wi-Fi means

Ans Wireless Fidelity

L-2 D 76. It is necessary for the modems to operate at the same baud rate in order to communicate with each other

L-2 F 77. A number used to indicate the cost of a route in the IP routing table is known as

Ans Metric

L-2 F 78. In the context of active directory replication, ———————— to the set of connections that domain controllers use to replicate information among themselves

Ans Topology

L-1 M 79. Which of the following is a function of the telecommunication software ?

A. Modulation B. Demodulation
C. Access control D. None of the above

L-1 S 80 CRC is

A. Cyclic Reduction Check B. Cyclic Redundancy Check
C. Circular Redundancy Check D. Circular Redemption Check

L-1 S 81. Signal booster in a network

A. Amplifier B. Repeater C. Bridge D. Hub

L-1 S 82. The frequency range of medium waves is

A. 150-285KHz B. Upto 1605KHz
C. Up to 100MHz D. None of the above

L-1 S 83. Ability to send data in only one direction at a time but at a other time, data could be send in other direction as well.

A. Duplex B. Half duplex C. Full duplex D. Simplex

L-1 S 84. Medium waves have frequencies up to ———————— KHz

A. 1200 B. 1605 C. 1350 D. 650

L-1 S 85. Which of the following gives high fidelity reception ?

A. Amplitude modulation B. Frequency modulation
C. Phase modulation D. Digital modulation

L-1 S 86. The clarke orbit is ———————— mile above sea level

A. 36000 B. 22282 C. 12000 D. 25000

L-1 S 87. Wireless communication between computers use ———————— to transmit files

A. Violet light B. Infrared light C. Ultraviolet light D. Laser beam

L-1 S 88. Using any host computer on the Internet as if a user is directly connected is called

A. FTP B. Telnet C. E-mail D. PPP

L-1 S 89. It consist of a node address and a port number. It identifies a particular service on a particular node

A. Port identifier B. Socket C. Service D. All of the above

L-1 S 90. When you connect to your ISP using a telephone line and modem, that type of connection is called the ————————

A. Broadband B. Dial up connection
C. ISDN D. Telnet

L-1 S 91. Determination of the next router where a packet has to be sent en route to its destination and then sending the packet there

A. Trafficking B. Forwarding C. Communication D. Sending

L-1 S 92. Transmission of pictures, texts, maps, graphs, etc., via phone lines, and other carriers between geographically separated locations. An image is scanned at a transmitting point and duplicated at a receiving point

A. Email B. Facsimile C. Snail mail D. Tele-message

L-2 S 93. A device that can both transmit and receive signals

A. Duplex transmitter B. Transceiver
C. Receiver D. None of the above

L-2 S 94. A technique for detecting when data is lost during transmission

A. Error correction B. Error detection C. Line testing D. Parity bit

L-2 S 95. A condition whereby network traffic has reached or is approaching network capacity

A. Jam B. Congestion
C. Stagnation D. None of the above

L-2 S 96. Rate of information arriving at, and possibly passing through, a particular point in a network system.

A. Throughput B. Throughout
C. Bandwidth D. None of the above

L-2 S 97. An extra bit added to a string of bits meant for transmission that enables the computer to detect internal errors in the transmission of binary data

A. Check digit B. Parity bit
C. Altra bit D. None of the above

L-2 S 98. A process that resides in a device which is to be managed remotely. This process record the values of various variables and report these to the specified management stations

A. Logger B. Agent C. Router D. Gateway

L-1 S 99. FM stand for

A. Frequency Modulation B. Frequent Modulation
C. Frequency Modification D. Functional Module

L-1 S 100. Data that is not encrypted. Sometimes also called

A. Plaintext B. Text
C. Cleartext D. Simple text

L-1 S 101. Communication satellites are placed in the orbits called

A. Clarke orbit B. Asynchronous orbit
C. Newton orbit D. None of the above

L-1 S 102. Networks can be broadly classified as ________ or ________

A. Peer to peer B. Star C. Client server D. All of the above

L-1 S 103. It forwards packet to specific ports for which the packet is meant rather than to all ports

A. Switching hub
B. Hub
C. Transmitter
D. None of the above

L-1 S 104. Process of breaking a packet into smaller units when it is to be transmitted over a network medium that cannot support the original size of the packet.

A. Fragmentation
B. Frame division
C. Segregation
D. None of the above

L-2 S 105. Can link lans with different topologies. Connects lans and wans.

A. Router
B. Hub
C. Switch
D. All of the above

L-2 S 106. Is an API that are used by hosts on a LAN to communicate with each other

A. Network basic input/output
B. NLM protocol
C. DHCP
D. None of the above

L-2 S 107. The difference between the highest and lowest frequencies in a given range

A. Bandwidth
B. Band interval
C. Frequency interval
D. Frequency band

L-2 S 108. Separating of multiple input streams that were multiplexed into a common physical signal back into multiple output streams.

A. Demultiplexing
B. Segregation
C. Both of the above
D. None of the above

L-3 S 109. A message queuing and routing system for Windows that enables distributed applications running at different times to communicate across heterogeneous networks and with computers that may be offline

A. Message Queuing
B. Message buffering
C. Message storage
D. Information buffering

L-1 S 110. ISDN stands for ____________

A. International services digital network
B. Integrated services departmental network
C. Integrated services digital network
D. None of the above

L-1 S 111. A TV uses two kinds of waves ____________ and ____________

A. AM and SW
B. SW and FM
C. AM and FM
D. AM and MW

L-1 S 112. A mark that denotes the time of creation or transmission of a document.

A. Bookmark
B. Bookstamp
C. Timestamp
D. Timeliness

L-1 S 113. What is the amount of data that can be transmitted in a fixed amount of time called?

A. Refresh rate
B. Resolution
C. Pixel density
D. Bandwidth

L-1 S 114. Logical grouping of information sent as a network layer unit over a transmission medium without prior establishment of a virtual circuit

A. Data piece
B. Data packet
C. Datagram
D. Fragments

L-2 S 115. Radar stand for

A. Radio detection and reflection
B. Radio deflection and reflection
C. Radio detection and ranging
D. None of the above

L-2 S 116. A method for sending voice over a LAN

A. Voice over Lan
B. Voice over network
C. Virtual packet
D. Voice over Internet Protocol

L-2 S 117. Components of a communication satellite

A. Transponder
B. Antenna system
C. Rocket thruster
D. All of the above

L-2 S 118. Which of the following is a modulation technique?

A. Amplitude modulation
B. Phase modulation
C. Frequency modulation
D. All of the above

L-2 S 119. Third party certifies that a particular message existed at a specific time and date.

A. Checkpointing
B. Time certification
C. Time stamp
D. None of the above

L-2 S 120. The process of sending a message simultaneously to more than one destination on a network.

A. Calling
B. Broadcast
C. Multicasting
D. None of the above

L-2 S 121. This command is used to disable all new traffic handling. It is used for network load balancing

A. Netbalance
B. Net traffic
C. Drainstop
D. None of these

L-2 S 122. The technique by which a digital signal is converted to analog and transmitted over an analog medium

A. Modulation
B. Keying
C. Multiplexing
D. Compression

L-2 S 123. An application programming interface (API) standard for software that provides a TCP/IP interface under Windows.

A. Port
B. Servlet
C. Winapi
D. Winsock

L-2 S 124. Routing metric used to measure the distance between a source and a destination in number of routers between two hosts

A. Light years
B. Router count
C. Host count
D. Hop count

L-2 S 125. A dedicated physical path is established between the two communicating parties for the duration of information exchange

A. Packet switching
B. Datagram switching
C. Session switching
D. Circuit switching

L-2 S 126. When two or more computers wish to use a channel, they use ———— method to determine whether access is available

A. Collision
B. Context
C. Contention
D. None of the above

L-1 S 127. Microwaves cannot bend with the curvature of the earth, they are relayed by antennas

Ans TRUE

L-1 T/F 128. In a peer to peer network, one system controls all the others.

A. TRUE B. FALSE

L-2 T/F 129. In Full duplex file transfer, data can be transmitted in both the directions but only in one direction at a time

A. TRUE B. FALSE

L-1 T/F 130. ISDN is high speed fully digital service

A. TRUE B. FALSE

L-1 T/F 131. Reception quality is better in Frequency Modulation

A. TRUE B. FALSE

L-1 T/F 132. A microwave system consists of towers located 100 miles apart

A. TRUE B. FALSE

Communication Devices

L-2 S 133. A device that supports lan to lan communication

A. Switch B. Hub C. Bridge D. Port

Email

L-2 S 134. A protocol used for receiving email messages

A. Yahoo B. POP3 (Post Office Protocol)
C. IMAP D. SMTP

FDDI

L-2 S 135. Frame from a token ring or FDDI device indicating a serious problem with the ring.

A. Destination host unreachable B. Time out
C. ACK D. Beacon

File Access

L-1 D 136. To make resources, such as folders and printers, available to others

Ans Share

L-1 D 137. Permissions that restrict a shared resource's availability over the network to only certain users.

Ans Shared folder permissions

L-1 S 138. A folder on another computer that has been made available for other people to use on the network.

A. Shared folder B. Network folder
C. Web server D. Multiple use folder

FTP

L-2 D139. Although data connection appear and disappear frequently, the control connection persists the entire session

General

L-1 D140. LAN stands for

Ans Local Area Network (LAN)

L-1 D141. Copying of data to multiple computers

Ans Replication

L-1 D142. Add, remove and configure local and network printers and fax printers.

Ans Network connections

L-1 D143. This computer ensures that all the nodes in the network have synchronized time

Ans Time server

L-1 D144. A ———————————— is a group of two or more computes systems linked together

Ans Network

L-1 D145. Synchronized time ensures that the time used by the network computers, services and functions remain accurate

Ans Time server

L-1 M146. A computer on a network is called

A. Host B. Node C. Both of the above D. Terminal

L-1 S 147. The different locations is a network are called

A. Points B. Nodes

C. Module D. None of the above

L-1 S 148. Intranet is also called a ——————

A. Intranet B. Extranet

C. Internet D. None of the above

L-1 S 149. ———— utility is used to verify connections to remote hosts

A. Ping B. ARP C. Zip D. Con-tester

L-1 S 150. The components of a network are

A. Terminals, computers, and Software B. Tele-communication Processors

C. Tele-communication media D. All of the above

L-1 S 151. The identifier of your computer on the network.

A. Network name B. File name C. Operating system D. Name

L-1 S 152. Logical arrangement of network "nodes within a network

A. Internet B. Design

C. Topology D. None of the above

L-1 S 153. A network within an organization which is not accessible from outside the organization

A. Internet B. Extranet

C. Intranet D. None of the above

L-1 S 154. A network that connects many networks and acts as the primary path for traffic between those networks

A. Bridge B. Backbone C. LAN D. Gateway

L-2 S 155. A system that has two or more network interfaces each of which is connected to a different network

A. Hub B. Switch

C. Dual connection D. Dual homed system

L-1 T/F 156. Failure of a single system hampers all the systems from performing in a peer to peer network

A. TRUE B. FALSE

Hardware

L-1 D 157. A common connection point for computers in a LAN.

Ans hub

L-1 D 158. A device that connects the computer to a network.

Ans Network adapter

L-2 D 159. Switch

Ans A networking device used to connect devices in the internal network together and to connect to an external network

L-1 S 160. A server or router that terminates tunnels and forwards traffic to the hosts on the target network.

A. Router B. Tunnel server

C. Server D. Traffic controller

L-1 S 161. A device that is used to interface two otherwise incompatible networks

A. Hub B. Switch C. Gateway D. All of the above

L-2 S 162. A router that is directly reachable by this computer

A. Default subnet B. DNS

C. Default gateway D. None of the above

L-2 S 163. It interconnects 2 or more physically and logically separate network segments

A. Hub B. Switch C. Gateway D. Bridge

L-1 S 164. A device connected to multiple physical TCP/IP networks capable of routing or "delivering IP packets between them

Ans Gateway

L-1 T/F 165. Network hardware understand protocol address

A. TRUE B. FALSE

L-1 T/F 166. A hub transmits the incoming data to all the outgoing ports, whereas a switch transmits the data only to the port for which it is meant

A. TRUE B. FALSE

Internet

L-2 D 167. Software services that support Web site creation, configuration, and management, along with other Internet functions. Internet Information Services

Ans Internet Information Services

L-2 D 168. If the system is using a proxy server for internet, the proxy server's address can be mentioned in ———————— of the connection tab of Internet explorer dialog box

Ans LAN settings

Media

L-1 D 169. The wider the bandwidth of a communication system, the lesser time it will take to transmit the data

L-1 D 170. What are the advantages of Fiber optic cables?

Ans Cheap over a period of time, easy to handle, high speed

L-1 D 171. The term uses for the range of frequencies available for data transmission

Ans Bandwidth

L-1 D 172. What is the importance of Fiber optics in communications systems?

Ans Lightweight, fast, easy to install, durable

L-1 D 173. Any device that is used to transmit data from one location to another

Ans Carrier

L-1 D 174. A path or link through which noncontrol information passes between two devices

Ans Channel

L-1 D 175. A modem that operates over the coaxial cable that is used by cable tv providers.

Ans Cable modem

L-1 D 176. The 'core' of Fiber optic cable is very thin strand of highly refined cylindrical glass

L-1 D 177. The type of physical wiring and lower-layer protocols used for transmitting and "receiving packets; for example, Ethernet, FDDI, and Token Ring.

Ans Network media

L-2 D 178. A digital phone line used to provide higher bandwidth

Ans Integrated Services Digital Network

L-2 D 179. The fastest carriers which have data transfer rates of 1 million baud (bits/second) or more

Ans Broadband channel

L-2 D 180. A T-1 line can handle 1280 Kilobytes per second and a T-3 Line can handle ten times that speed.

Ans Address Resolution Protocol

L-2 D 181. Speed of download traffic is more than upload traffic. It's a high bandwidth digital transmission

A. Asymmetric Digital Subscriber Line (ADSL)

L-2 D 182. Capacity - the data carrying capability of a circuit or network, measured in bits per second (bps)

L-2 D 183. A device that enables a broadband connection to the Internet by using "cable television infrastructure.

A. Cable modem

L-2 D 184. Twisted pair wire is the oldest and still most common transmission line and consists of copper wires twisted into pairs

L-2 D 185. Access speeds in networks using cable modems vary greatly, with a maximum throughput of 10 megabits per second (Mbps).

L-1 M 186. What are different types of communication media?

A. Coaxial cable B. Twisted pair cable

C. Optical Fibre D. Air E. Electric cable

L-1 S 187. Any device that is used to transmit data "from one location to another

A. Wire B. Carrier C. Media D. Link

L-1 S 188. The core in a Fiber optic cable is surrounded by a second layer of glass called

A. Yoke B. Clad C. Cap D. Pipe

L-2 S 189. A system capable of transmitting information in both directions over a communications channel.

A. Simplex B. Duplex C. Full duplex

D. None of the above

L-1 S 190. Which is the oldest and most common transmission line?

A. Coaxial cable B. Fiber optic cable

C. Twisted pair wire D. None of the above

L-1 S 191. How many channels can a half inch diameter Fiber optic cable carry?

A. 5000 B. 5500

C. 50000 D. None of the above

L-1 S 192. A unit of information transmitted as a whole from one device to another on a network.

A. Megabyte B. Kilobtye C. Data packet D. Box

L-2 S 193. A communication system in which information can be transmitted in both the directions simultaneously

A. Simplex B. Multiplex

C. Full duplex D. None of the above

L-2 S 194. A system capable of transmitting information in only one direction at a time over a communications channel. It may reverse the direction some other time

A. Duplex B. Simplex C. Half duplex D. Multiplex

L-2 T/F 195. A router operates at network layer

A. TRUE B. FALSE

Protocols

L-1 D 196. A host can forward packet using the protocol address

L-2 D 197. The type of address resolution technique in which bindings or mappings are stored in a table in memory, which the software searches when it needs to resolve and address, is called

Ans Message exchange

L-2 D 198. Address resolution can be made trivial in certain circumstances

L-2 D 199. The type of address resolution technique in which computers exchange messages across a network to resolve an address.

Ans Message exchange

L-2 D 200. If a network uses configurable addressing, the network administrator must choose a hardware address as well as IP address. These two values can be choosen to make address resolution trivial

L-2 D 201. The type of address resolution technique in which the protocol address assigned to a computer is choosen carefully so the computer's hardware address can be computed from the protocol address using basic boolean and arithmetic operations

A. Hardware mapping

L-1 D 202. In DNS, the use of wildcard characters is supported which are used to resolve multiple names.

Ans Wildcarding

L-1 D 203. cd command in FTP

Ans to change directory on the remote machine

L-1 D 204. Full form of IP is

Ans Internet Protocol

L-1 D 205. Get command in FTP

Ans To copy one file from the remote machine to the local machine

L-1 D 206. Full form of TCP is

Ans Transmission Control Protocol

L-1 D 207. In FTP, File name translation

Ans In ftp if the machines between which file transfer is taking place uses different file naming system, file name translation allows to change the file name accordingly on the target computer

L-1 D 208. What are network protocols ?

Ans A protocol is a set of rules governing communication between two hosts on a network. These rules specify the formats of messages, the rules for creation and termination of connections, the way of sending messages etc.

L-1 D 209. To control the mode verbose command is used

L-1 D 210. TCP/IP stands for ——————————

Ans Transmission control protocol/Internet protocol

L-1 D 211. The identifier of your computer on the network.

Ans Name

L-1 D 212. Direct connection between two devices is either by way of SLIP or PPP

L-1 D 213. Binary transfer could be used for all non-text files

L-1 D 214. FTP was originally defined a a part of ARPANET protocols

L-1 D 215. FTP can accommodate multiple representations of text files

L-1 D 216. Dialing to establish a connection to a remote by using a modem

Ans Dial up networking

L-1 D 217. IP addresses are virtual because they are maintained by software

L-1 D 218. The ARP defines two basic message types: a request and a response

L-1 D 219. Output from FTP begin with a 3 digit no. that identifies the message

L-1 D 220. A 3 digit no. is used for identification of messages in an FTP session

L-1 D 221. One of the most popular protocols for LANs is called ——————

Ans Ethernet

L-1 D 222. Once connected via Telnet, the user's computer emulates the remote computer

L-1 D 223. A —————— domain is any tree or subtree with the DNS namespace.

Ans DNS domain

L-1 D 224. HTTP does not provide access to other Internet protocols like FTP, SMTP, NNTP, WAIS etc.

L-1 D 225. Translation from a computer's protocol address to an equivalent hardware address is known as

Ans Address resolution

L-1 D 226. The DNS name of a device on a network. These names are used to locate computers on the network

Ans Host name

L-1 D 227. The method used to resolve an address depends upon the protocol and hardware addressing schemes

L-1 D 228. In an ARP message an address length field is present for both hardware address as well as protocol address

L-1 D 229. To accommodate applications that only need to read or write part of a file, TCP/IP includes a file access service

L-1 D 230. A user can choose whether FTP should issue informational messages (verbose mode) or omit such messages (Quiet mode)

L-1 D 231. End-of-file to indicate that a transfer has completed is important because it permits a file to be created dynamically

L-1 D 232. HTTP Hypertext transport protocol, the Internet protocol that defines how a Web server responds to requests for files.

L-1 D 233. Sent through a packet switching network, one unit of information which contains destination address and other information

Ans Datagram

L-1 D 234. TFTP is especially useful for bootstrapping a hardware device that does not have a disk on which to store system software

L-1 D 235. A low-level protocol that routes packets of data across separate networks connected together by routers to form a network.

Ans Internet Protocol (IP)

L-1 D 236. Sending a ARP request every time data has to be sent is inefficient, so the host stores recently known address and their resolution

L-1 D 237. If an FTP user supplies login name Nm, the user will have same file access permissions as someone who logs in as Nm on the remote machine

L-1 D 238. FTP characteristics — Authentication and ownership, Interactive access, arbitrary file contents, format specification, accommodates heterogeneity, client server paradigm

L-1 D 239. The most popular file transfer service in the internet uses FTP. The FTP is general purpose protocol that can be used to copy an arbitrary file from one computer to another

L-1 D 240. Before protocol software can send a packet across a physical network, the software must translate the IP address of the destination computer into an equivalent hardware address

L-1 D 241. Although the ARP message format is sufficiently general to allow arbitrary protocol and hardware address, ARP is almost always used to bind a 32 bit IP address to a 48 bit ethernet address

L-1 D 242. An ARP message receiver extracts the sender's address binding and checks to see if the sender's address is present in the cache. If so, the receiver uses the binding in the incoming ARP message to replace the previously stored bindings

L-2 D 243. What is FTP?

Ans File transfer protocol is used to transfer files between two systems, usually remote to each other.

L-2 D 244. Subnet address

Ans A subnet (short for "subnetwork") is an identifiably separate part of an organization's network. Typically, a subnet may represent all the machines at one geographic location, in one building, or on the same local area network (LAN).

L-2 D 245. Features of TFTP

Ans Useful in booting systems which do not have storage device, It uses UDP, no authentication mechanism

L-2 D 246. What is Telnet?

Ans Telnet is a remote login method in which keystrokes are sent to the server as if they are typed on the remote machine. Output appears as if it would appear on the remote machine.

L-2 D 247. TFTP, UDP protocols are stored in ROM of a computer so full booting up of a computer is not required.

L-2 D 248. What is anonymous FTP?

Ans Logging of a user who do not have permission on an FTP server. This user provides "Anonymous" as its user name and its email address as a password. The FTP server gives limited access as per its policies and configuration

L-2 D 249. Advantages of using two connections in FTP

Ans Dynamic file size, no intersection of data and control, no data connection when no file transfer is occurring, file transfer can be aborted any time etc

L-2 D 250. ARP message is encapsulated in a hardware frame

L-2 D 251. An FTP server requires a username and a password to login.

L-2 D 252. What is a domain name and how it is different from an IP address?

Ans IP address is name of a computer in a network or internet which identifies it. Domain name have to be translated to IP address before a data packed could be forwarded towards its destination

L-2 D 253. An IP address that is shared among the hosts of a Network Load Balancing cluster.

Ans Virtual IP address

L-2 D 254. ARP maintains a small table of bindings in memory. This table is maintained as cache

L-2 D 255. FTP delivers two basic types of transfer that accommodates most files — textual and binary

L-2 D 256. The type field in a hardware frame header specifies that the frame contains an ARP message

L-2 D 257. File transfer is complicated because an Internet can connect to heterogeneous computer systems

L-2 D 258. A protocol of netware family that controls addressing within and between Local area networks.

Ans Internet Packet Exchange (IPX)

L-2 D 259. In an ARP message, the operation field specifies whether the message is a request or a response

L-2 D 260. Acknowledgement from a computer that a packet of data has been received and verified to be correct

Ans ACK

L-2 D 261. Application as well as higher layers of protocol software are built to use protocol addresses only

L-2 D 262. A file used by the Domain Name System (DNS) server to preload its names cache when service is started.

Ans Cache file

L-2 D 263. A range of IP addresses that are available to be leased or assigned to DHCP clients by the DHCP service.

Ans Scope

L-2 D 264. A network configuration, usually on a separate Internet Protocol (IP) subnet, that gives data a direct path to system hardware

Ans System Area Network

L-2 D 265. A computer that has multiple network adapters or that has been configured with multiple IP addresses for a Single network adapter

Ans Multihomed computer

L-2 D 266. This protocol complements TCP and offers a connectionless datagram service which does not guarantee delivery and sequencing of delivery

Ans User Datagram Protocol (UDP)

L-2 D 267. In message exchange address resolution method, Message exchange can be either done with a centralized server or with the target computer

Ans TRUE

L-2 D 268. In ARP message, a fixed size field is included at the beginning of an ARP message to specify the size of the hardware addresses being used

L-2 D 269. After a computer replies to an ARP request, the computer extracts the sender's address binding from the request and adds the binding to its cache for latter use

L-2 D 270. In Simple Network Management Protocol (SNMP), a message sent by an agent to a management system indicating that an event has occurred on the host running the agent.

L-2 D 271. Issues related to file transfer with respect to heterogeneous nature of internet - file name, file extension, login accounts, file representations, file protection mechanisms

L-2 D 272. To handle incompatibilities among computer systems, many FTP clients permits a user to define rules that specify how to translate a file name when moving to a new computer system.

L-2 D 273. TFTP vs FTP only file transfer in FTP, UDP used in TFTP, No interaction in TFTP, Dir and listing cannot be seen/used in TFTP, no authorization in TFTP, code for TFTP require less memory than FTP

L-2 D 274. The ARP specifies that an ARP request message should be placed in the hardware frame and broadcast to all computers on the network. Each computer receives the request and examines the IP address.

L-2 D 275. Table lookup is usually employed to resolve IP addresses across a WAN, closed-form computation is used with configurable networks, and message exchange is used on LAN hardware that has static addressing

L-2 D 276. The most common use of FTP the internet file transfer protocol that allows anonymous FTP do not require a password or access to that FTP site. One only has to log in as anonymous and enter one's email address as a password

Ans Anonymous FTP

L-2 D 277. In message exchange address resolution method, when a computer needs to resolve an address it sends a message across a network and receives a reply. The message carries a request that specifies the protocol address, and the reply carries the corresponding hardware address

L-2 D 278. Mapping between a protocol address and a hardware address is called address resolution, A host or router uses address resolution when it needs to send a packed to another computer on the same physical network. A computer never resolves the address of a computer on a remote network

L-3 D 279. A challenge/response authentication protocol. The NTLM authentication protocol is used for network authentication in windows NT and 2000

Ans NTLM authentication protocol

L-1 D 280. ls command in FTP

Ans to list the names of the files in the current remote directory

L-1 D 281. cdup command in FTP

Ans Makes the parent of the current directory be the current directory

L-1 D 282. Data travels in packets called IP datagrams

L-2 D 283. FTP does not interpret the contents of a file transferred in binary mode, and does not translate from one representation to another. Instead, it merely produces a copy

L-2 D 284. Each computer that handles a packet resolves a next-hop address before sending. It does not resolve the address of the target computer if the target computer is not on the same network as this computer

Ans TRUE

L-2 M 285. FTP disadvantages over NFS

A. Whole file to be download in FTP to work

B. Cannot append file before downloading

C. No abstraction

D. None of the above

L-2 M 286. The password for anonymous account for FTP access could be

A. Blank B. Guest

C. 123456 D. abcdef E. Email address

L-2 M 287. Two types of connections in FTP

A. Bits connection B. Data connection

C. Stream connection D. Control connection

L-1 S 288. FTP

A.File Transfer Process B. File Transfer Protocol

C. Fragment Transfer Protocol D. None of the above

L-1 S 289. TFTP

A. Testing FTP B. Trival FTP

C. Trial FTP D. None of the above

L-1 S 290. ARP is

A. Address Resolver Protocol B. Address Resolution Protocol

C. Address Resolution Program D. None of the above

L-1 S 291. HTTP is short for

A. Hyper Text Transmission Protocol B. Hyper Text Transfer Protocol

C. High Level Text Transfer Protocol D. None of the above

L-1 S 292. It matches domain names to IP Address

A. HTTP B. DNS C. HTML D. URL

L-1 S 293. ________________ is a remote login protocol

A. FTP B. Telnet C. SMTP D. All of the above

L-1 S 294. Actual Internet addresses are numerical and are called

A. Domain Name Systems B. IP addresses

C. DNS D. Domain Addresses

L-1 S 295. A logical connection created between two hosts to exchange data

A. Contact B. Session C. Handshake D. Contract

L-1 S 296. The address of the local computer used usually for testing purposes

A. Test address B. Loop back address

C. Duplicate address D. Default address

L-1 S 297. The ________________ completes the task of matching domain names to IP addresses

A. DHCP B. DNS

C. Web server D. Internet provider

L-1 S 298. It is the ratio of received bits that contain errors to the total number of received bits

A. Bit Enhancement Rate B. Bit Error Rate

C. Bit Entry Rate D. None of the above

L-2 S 299. In FTP direction of data connection is

A. From client to server B. From server to client

C. From webserver to server D. From client to webserver

L-2 S 300. Placing a message inside a frame for transport is called

A. Hiding B. Encapsulation C. Tunneling D. Abstraction

L-2 S 301. If an expected packet is not received in time, this condition is called

A. Hop B. Time-out error

C. Time to Live (T) D. Timestamp

L-1 S 302. The name given by a network administrator to a group of networked computers that share a common directory

A. Domain name B. Host name C. Computer name D. Network name

L-2 S 303. The process of translation of host names to numerical IP addresses is called

A. Name resolution B. Lease grant

C. Domain name translation D. Hop count

L-2 S 304. A command-line tool used to diagnose Domain Name System (DNS) infrastructure.

A. NsLookup B. ARP

C. PING D. None of the above

L-2 S 305. A protocol which is a member of the TCP/IP suite of protocols and it governs email transfers

A. Simple Mail Transfer Protocol B. Outlook Express

C. Telnet D. HTTP E. OSI

L-2 S 306. For a DNS, a store of resource records, locally stored for recently resolved names of remote hosts

A. Cache B. Temp store C. ARP D. Buffer

L-2 S 307. The process of having the software translate between names that are easy for users to work with and numerical IP addresses, which are difficult for users but necessary for TCP/IP communications

A. Name resolution B. Address resolution C. Telnet D. SMTP

L-1 S 308. Ways to run FTP

A. Command prompt B. In the browser window

C. Through IIIrd party PTP Client D. All of the above

L-1 S 309. Which of the following is a network protocol ?

A. Ethernet B. Xmodem C. HTTP D. All of the above

L-1 S 310. FTP is a protocol from ———— protocol stack

A. ISO B. OSI C. TCP/IP D. All of the above

L-1 S 311. A set of rules and conventions for sending information over a network.

A. Interpreter B. Convention C. Theory D. Protocol

L-1 S 312. A TCP/IP protocol that specifies how electronic mails are exchanged by computers

A. SNMP B. POP C. FTP D. SMTP

L-1 S 313. When a user requests a file download, ———— protocol is invoked by the browser

A. Telnet B. HTTP C. SMTP D. FTP

L-1 S 314. A software system that sends a file from one computer to a file on another is known as

A. Telnet B. HTTP C. FTP D. TCP/IP

L-1 S 315. After ———— expires, the client must either renew or obtain a new lease for its IP address from DHCP

A. Contract B. Grant period C. Lease time D. Renewal time

L-1 S 316. ———— is actually a collection of protocols or rules, that governs the way data travels from one machine to another across networks

A. FTP B. Telnet C. ARP D. TCP/IP

L-2 S 317. TFTP uses this protocol to transfer files

A. TCP B. FTP C. UDP D. HTTP

L-2 S 318. Control connection uses ———— and is used to send commands

A. UDP B. Telnet C. TCP D. SMTP

L-2 S 319. How long to hold or use the packed before expiring and discarding it

A. Hop B. Time out

C. Time to Live (TTL) D. Timestamp

L-2 S 320. Protocols that enable the transmission of voice calls over IP networks

A. Telnet B. FTP C. VOIP D. Yahoo

L-2 S 321. Used in the internet for translating names of network nodes into addresses

A. File name system B. Host name system

C. Network system D. Domain name system

L-2 S 322. In login to an FTP site as anonymous user password is ________

A. 123 B. abc

C. email address D. Website address

L-2 S 323. The length of time for which a DHCP client can use a dynamically assigned IP address

A. Assigned name period B. DHCP period

C. Both of the above D. Lease

L-2 S 324. ________ Permits files to be transferred from one computer to another using a TCP connection.

A. TCP B. HTTP

C. File Transfer Protocol D. UDP

L-2 S 325. To avoid conflict between the control and data connections, FTP uses a different protocol ________for each connection

A. Network address B. Session number

C. Port number D. Connection number

L-2 S 326. A local text file that maps NetBIOS names (commonly used for computer names) to IP addresses for hosts that are not located on the local subnet

A. Host file B. Network.ini file

C. Lmhosts file D. None of the above

L-2 S 327. When two computers or a computer and a terminal device are interconnected in such a way that they can exchange information. These two do a ________ and agree to communicate in a certain way until the connection exits

A. Declaration B. Agreement C. Protocol D. Handshake

L-1 S 328. The process of sending a message simultaneously to more than one destination on a network. The receivers may belong to different networks and all hosts in a network may not be the recipients

Ans Multicasting

L-2 S 329. FTP has two transfer modes - for text file and for all non-text files. Although binary transfer produces an exact copy of the bits, the resulting copy may be meaningless. This is because FTP does not convert values to the local representations.

L-1 T/F 330. Hardware understands IP Address

A. TRUE B. FALSE

L-1 T/F 331. Hardware does not understand IP address

A. TRUE B. FALSE

L-1 T/F 332. FTP allows file transfer only from client to the server

A. TRUE B. FALSE

L-1 T/F 333. The direction of control connection in FTP is from server to the client

A. TRUE B. FALSE

L-1 T/F 334. The TCP/IP suite does not contain a standard address resolution protocol

A. TRUE B. FALSE

L-2 T/F 335. ARP response is a broadcast

A. TRUE B. FALSE

L-2 T/F 336. An ARP request is a multicast

A. TRUE B. FALSE

L-2 T/F 337. IPX guarantee that a data packets would not be lost during transit

A. TRUE B. FALSE

L-2 T/F 338. FTP translates the downloaded file to the respective representation

A. TRUE B. FALSE

L-2 T/F 339. Direction of control connection in ftp is from the server to the client

A. TRUE B. FALSE

L-2 T/F 340. Even if a computer is attached to more than one network, it would need only one address translation module

A. TRUE B. FALSE

L-2 T/F 341. The control connection remains in place during the data transfer and it diminishes as soon as the data transfer completes

A. TRUE B. FALSE

L-2 T/F 342. Domain names are unique

A. TRUE B. FALSE

L-2 T/F 343. An ARP request is a broadcast

A. TRUE B. FALSE

L-2 T/F 344. ARP response is not a broadcast

A. TRUE B. FALSE

L-2 T/F 345. Address resolution is local to a network

A. TRUE B. FALSE

L-2 T/F 346. Two machines can have the same IP address

A. TRUE B. FALSE

L-2 T/F 347. In FTP, Control connection is used to send commands

A. TRUE B. FALSE

L-2 T/F 348. Direction of datal connection in ftp is from the server to the client

A. TRUE B. FALSE

L-2 T/F 349. A computer that is connected to more than one network may need more than one address translation module

A. TRUE B. FALSE

L-2 T/F 350. Hardware frame use special bits to denote that whether the encapsulated arp message is a request or response

A. TRUE B. FALSE

L-2 T/F 351. Separate address binding table is used for each physical network in table lookup method of address resolution

A. TRUE B. FALSE

L-2 T/F 352. A hardware frame has nothing to do with an arp message. An arp message is just like a data for a hardware frame

A. TRUE B. FALSE

L-2 T/F 353. In closed form method of address resolution, a resolver uses a mathematical function to map IP address to a hardware address

A. TRUE B. FALSE

L-2 T/F 354. If protocol addresses are assigned from a compact range then only direct indexing technique of searching in table lookup address resolution method can be used

A. TRUE B. FALSE

L-2 T/F 355. One computer can resolve the address of another computer only if both computers attach to the same physical netowrk - a computer never resolves the address of a computer on a remote network

A. TRUE B. FALSE

Remote Communication

L-2 S 356. ——————— allows user to connect remotely to a computer

A. Remote Desktop Connection B. Win connection

C. Com connection D. Remote link

Resource

L-1 D 357. Moving of resources back to the original preferred node after the node has failed and then has come back online

A. failback

L-2 D 358. Working of NFS

Ans Network file system, A network file system is any computer file system that supports sharing of files, printers and other resources as persistent storage over a computer network. The file has not to be downloaded for changes unlike ftp.

L-2 D 359. A resource type that provides Windows Internet Name Service (WINS) from a cluster.

Ans WINS resource

L-2 S 360. ——————— is a network service that stores information about resources, such as computers and printers. If not used the Find Printer button is not available.

A. Resource sharing B. Active resource
C. Active directory D. None of the above

Routing

L-1 D 361. A number used to indicate the cost of a route in the IP routing table that enables the selection of the best route among possible multiple routes to the same destination.

A. Metric

L-2 D 362. In a routing table, routes that are permanent. They are manually configured by a network administrator

A. Static routes

L-1 S 363. A routable protocol in the TCP/IP protocol suite that is responsible for IP addressing, routing, and the fragmentation and reassembly of IP packets.

A. TCP B. IP C. FTP D. Telnet

L-2 S 364. The process of forwarding a packet through an internetwork

A. Forwarding B. Routing C. Packet sending D. Trafficking

L-2 S 365. Routes in a routing table that are permanent

A. Dynamic routes B. Manual routes C. Configured routes D. Network routes

L-2 S 366. These routes are manually configured by the network administrator

A. Configured routes B. Manual routes C. Dynamic route D. Static routes

Security

L-2 D 367. ——————— is used when a message sender needs to encrypt large amounts of data

Ans Asymmetric encryption

L-2 D 368. The nonsecret half of a cryptographic key pair that is used with a public key algorithm

Ans Public key

L-1 D 369. At the top of a certification authority CA is Root certification authority

L-1 D 370. An error detection code is a binary code that detects digital errors during transmission

L-1 D 371. An intelligent key is based upon data values such as date, a last name of a combination of values

L-2 D 372. A Worm is

Ans A computer worm is a self-replicating computer program. It uses a network to send copies of itself to other nodes (computers on the network) and it may do so without any user intervention

L-2 D 373. Technique used for authentication and secure exchange of information on internet.

Ans Certificate

L-2 D 374. Identification data for security. It is issued for the purpose of user authentication.

Ans Ticket

L-2 D 375. Rules for packet filters/firewalls that define which packets to pass and which to block

Ans Access control list

L-2 D 376. A logical relationship which is established between domains to allow pass through authentication.

Ans Trust relationship

L-2 D 377. Operating system and its software should be regularly updated with ——— so that vulnerablities in them could be taken care of

Ans Security Patches.

L-2 D 378. Firewall Router or remote-access server (or several routers or access servers) designated as a buffer between connected networks. A firewall uses access lists and other methods to ensure the security of a network.

L-2 D 379. Operates at the application layer. It uses various proxy servers to proxy the traffic. So it does not route the traffic. At the application layer blocking of various traffic which is thought of as inappropriate could be done.

L-3 D 380. A Virus is

Ans A computer virus attaches itself to a program or file enabling it to spread from one computer to another, leaving infections as it travels

L-2 D 381. Two forms of tickets in Windows are ticket-granting tickets (TGTs) and service tickets.

L-2 F 382. One party asks a question and another party have to provide a correct answer to get authenticated. E.g.: Password authentication

Ans Challenge response

L-2 F 383. For security reasons, ——————— is used. In this the originators of a message, file, or other digitally encoded information, binds its identity to the information.

Ans Digital signature

L-2 S 384. Settings of automatic updates can be accessed from automatic updates tab of

A. Internet explorer B. System Properties C. Start menu D. Accessories

L-2 S 385. A program that behaves like a system logon to retrieve user names and password is a

Ans Virus B. Trojan horse C. Worm D. Script

L-2 S 386. A program that masquerades as another common program in an attempt to receive information.

A. Virus B. Trojan horse C. Worm D. Daemon

L-2 S 387. Use ——————————— for viewing the security status of a PC and access important settings

A. Security Pol B. Security Center C. Antivirus D. Firewall

L-2 S 388. The process of determining what types of activities are permitted on an object by a specific user

A. Authentication B. Authorization C. Security D. Check

L-2 S 389. This part of a cryptographic key pair is secret. It is used with a public key algorithm for decrypting a symmetric session key, digital signature and decryption

A. Public key B. Private key
C. Could be both of the above D. None of the above

L-2 S 390. An attack in which an attacker exploits a weakness or a design limitation of a network service to overload or halt the service, so that the service is not available for use

A. Dictionary attack B. Denial-of-service
C. Wiretapping D. Spoofing

L-2 S 391. A program that masquerades as another common program in an attempt to receive information.

A. Trojan horse B. Virus C. Script D. Worm

L-2 S 392. The process of determining the identity of a user that is trying to access an object for eg. A computer

A. Authentication B. Authorization
C. Security D. Check

L-2 S 393. Same secret key is used for both encryption and decryption

A. Asymmetric encryption B. RSA algorithm
C. Digital signature D. Symmetric encryption

L-2 S 394. A system which detect break-ins or attempts to break-in using logs and expert softwares

A. Break detection system B. Intrusion detection system
C. Anti hacking system D. None of the above

L-2 S 395. A hash algorithm that creates a 128-bit hash value and was developed by RSA Data Security, Inc.

A.Triple hash B. RSA Hash C. MD4 D. DES

L-2 S 396. On a network, protection of a computer so that only authorized users can gain access to respective files

A.Antivirus B. Authority C. Check posting D. Security

L-2 S 397. Assuming DNS name of another system by either corrupting the name service cache of a victim system or by compromising a domain name server for a valid domain

A. Phishing B. DOS C. DNS spoofing D. Eavesdropping

L-3 S 398. A system that has been hardened to resist attack, and which is installed on a network in such as way that it is expected to potentially come under attack.

A. Web server B. Trial host C. Proxy D. Bastion host

L-3 S 399. Authentication vs Authorization

Ans Authentication is a test to determine what or who the user is. And authorization tests what a user has, i.e., what rights a user have for a particular object

L-2 T/F 400. It is not possible to interrupt the email on its way

A. TRUE B. FALSE

L-2 T/F 401. Public keys are used to encrypt a session key

A. TRUE B. FALSE

Sharing

L-1 D 402. NFS is integrated into a computer's file system

L-1 D 403. NFS advantages

Ans Abstraction from user, File transfer not required

L-1 D 404. Sharable devices

Ans Devices that can be used by many users at the same time

L-1 D 405. A computer that runs a service to be used by network and remote clients

Ans Host

L-1 D 406. Entering Username and password and ———— to begin using a network

Ans Log on

L-1 D 407. Each shared folder on a server has a name (share name) used by computers in the network

Ans Share name

L-1 D 408. A computer in a LAN that uses shared network resources provided by another computer which is called a server

Ans Client

L-1 D 409. A folder on a Web server. You can view files and folders on Web servers just as you would view files and folders on network servers

Ans Network place

L-2 D 410. A file access service also permits file sharing in which multiple clients can access a file that resides on a server

L-1 S 411. To access another computer on LAN ———— icon is used

A. My Computer B. My Network Place

C. Control panel D. My documents

L-1 S 412. A computer or program that request the services of another computer or program

A. Requester B. Client

C. Customer D. None of the above

L-2 S 413. The process of attaching a laptop computer to a docking station while the computer is running

A. Quick attach B. Hot docking

C. Plug and play D. None of the above

L-2 S 414. A set of information that includes identification and proof that is used to gain access to resources, local and network

A. Rights B. Credentials

C. Permission D. None of the above

L-2 S 415. A group of computers that are part of a network and share a common directory database

A. Workgroup B. Network C. Domain D. LAN

L-2 S 416. A computer that is dedicated to managing the printers on a network. The print server can be any computer on the network.

A. File server B. Server C. Network server D. Print server

Topology

L-2 D 417. In VLAN, hosts from one or more LANs are logically grouped for communication as if they were on the same physical LAN

Ans Virtual local area network (VLAN)

L-1 D 418. What is a network topology?

Ans How the various components of a network are connected together. The structure of the network

L-1 D 419. What is a centralized processing system?

Ans A central computer or group of computers gives the services especially data, to all the other hosts which may be situated locally or remotely. The central computer is called the server and all the systems which uses the services of the server are called clients

L-1 S 420. A physical communications network that spans large geographical distances.

A. LAN B. WAN

C. Both of the above D. None of the above

L-1 S 421. In which network the ends are not connected

A. BUS B. Ring C. Star D. All of the above

L-1 S 422. A network topology in which a S connecting line is shared by a number of nodes

A. BUS B. STAR C. RING D. MESH

L-1 S 423. Which of the following is a network topology?

A. BUS B. STAR C. RING D. All of the above

L-1 S 424. A network connecting geographically separated computers

A. Local Area Network (LAN) B. System area network

C. Wide area network D. Metropolitan area network (MAN)

L-1 S 425. ______________________ is the geometric arrangement of the computers in a network

A. Design B. Alignment C. Configuration D. Topology

L-1 S 426. A communications network connecting a group of computers, printers, and other devices located within a relatively limited area

A. Geographical Area Network B. Metropolitan Area Network

C. Wide Area Net D. Local Area Network (LAN)

L-1 T/F 427. WANs usually operate at higher speeds than LANS.

A. TRUE B. FALSE

L-1 T/F 428. A LAN consists of essentially group of computers only

A. TRUE B. FALSE

Types

L-2 D 429. Neural networks

Ans A real or virtual device, modeled after the human brain, in which several interconnected elements process information simultaneously, adapting and learning from past patterns

L-2 D 430. WAIS stands for ———————

Ans Wide area information server

L-1 D 431. An extranet is the part of a corporate intranet that allows companies to communicate with the intranets of their customers and suppliers, facilitating electronic transactions

Ans Extranet

Types of Networks

L-1 D 432. What is Intranet?

Ans An intranet is a private network that is contained within an enterprise. It may consist of many interlinked local area networks and also use leased lines in the wide area network

L-1 D 433. Ethernet is a LAN technology invented by Xerox and later on developed jointly by Xerox, Intel, and Digital Equipment Corporation. These networks use CSMA/CD.

L-1 D 434. A configuration of computers on a network that is similar to a client/server architecture, except that the server is mostly a repository of a data on which it cannot itself perform queries or processing.

Ans File Server architecture

L-2 D 435. Tunneling offers private and secure link between a remote user or host and a private network

Ans Tunneling

L-2 F 436. A logical connection over which data is encapsulated

Ans Tunnel

L-1 M 437. What are different types of network topologies?

A. Bus B. Ring C. Ball D. Star

L-1 M 438. What are different types of computer networks?

A. VAN B. WAN C. LAN D. FAN

L-2 M 439. In tunneling, these are performed

A. Modulation B. Encapsulation C. Encryption D. All of the above

L-1 S 440. WAN stands for

A. Wire and Network B. Wire Accessible Network

C. Widely Accessible Network D. Wide Area Network

VPN

L-2 F 441. ―――――――― provide remote access and routed connections to private networks over the Internet (Shared public network)

Ans Virtual Private Network (VPN)

Communication

L-1 D 442. Pull

Ans Pull technology or client pull is a style of network communication where the initial request for data originates from the client, and then is responded to by the server.

L-1 D 443. Push In client/server information-dissemination applications

Ans Sending data to a client without the client requesting it

L-1 D 444. Rs-232 terminals are hardware devices containing both a keyboard and a display and which communicate using a serial interface, one bit at a time. These terminals are character oriented

L-2 D 445. Delay between the time a device requests access to a network and the time it is granted permission to transmit

Ans Latency

L-2 D 446. SSL is a open standard for establishing secure communications channels to prevent the interception of vital information

L-2 D 447. A bi-directional pipe for incoming and outgoing data that enables an application program to access the TCP IP protocols.

Ans Socket

L-2 D 448. Since both computers and terminal work internally with whole characters but must communicate over a serial line a bit at a time, chips have been developed to do the character-to-serial and serial to character conversions. They are called

Ans Universal Asynchronous Receiver Transmitters

L-3 D 449. Load balancing In routing, the capability of a router to distribute traffic over all its network ports that are the same distance from the destination address. Sometimes called load sharing to indicate that most routing protocols do not evenly balance traffic

Ans Load balancing

L-2 F 450. Delay between the time a device receives a frame and the time that frame is forwarded out the destination port.

Ans Latency

L-1 S 451. INTELSAT stands for ――――――――――

Ans A. International Telecommunication Satellite Organisation

B. Intelligent Satellite

C. International Telephonic System

D. None of the above

L-1 S 452. A communication path between two nodes or channel

A. Link B. Connection

C. Session D. None of the above

L-1 S 453. NFS

A. New file system B. New technology

C. Network file system D. None of the above

L-1 S 454. SSL is

A. Secure Software Layer B. Security Service

C. Secure Socket D. Secure Server Layer

L-1 S 455. Communication line distortion caused by the variation of a signal from its reference timing positions

A. Disturbance B. Signal lag

C. Jitter D. None of the above

L-2 S 456. A command line tool useful in diagnosing DNS

A. Traceroute B. Ping C. NsLuokpup D. ARP

L-2 S 457. ICMP echo message and its reply to test the reachability of a network place

A. Arp B. Net view C. Workgroup explorer D. Ping

L-2 S 458. Traffic-passing technique used by network connecting devices such as switches and bridges, in which traffic received on an interface is sent out through all interfaces except the interface on which the information was received.

A. DOS B. Spoofing C. Flooding D. Eavesdropping

General

L-2 D 459. Ability to handle growing amount of work "Capability of a system to increase total throughput under an increased load when resources are added.

A. A Scalable system

Media

L-1 S 460. A type of high-speed Internet connection using standard telephone wires.

A. Digital Subscriber Line (DSL) B. Broadband Connection

C. Both of the above D. None of the above

Protocols

L-1 D 461. put command in FTP

Ans To copy one file from the local machine to the remote machine

L-1 D 462. pwd command in FTP

Ans To find out the pathname of the current directory on the remote machine

L-1 D 463. mput command in FTP

Ans To copy multiple files from the local machine to the remote machine

L-1 D 464. To copy multiple files from the remote machine to the local machine;

L-1 D 465. A 32-bit number in dotted decimal format that represents an Internet Protocol (IP)

Ans IP Address resource

L-1 S 466. Software must translate the protocol address to an equivalent hardware address before sending a packet

A. Name resolution B. Target determining

C. Address resolution D. Destination mapping

L-1 S 467. A 32-bit address used to identify a computer (node) on an IP internetwork. It's a unique address and it consists of network ID, plus a unique host ID.

A. ARP address B. IP addresses

C. Ethernet address D. Web address

Security

L-1 D 468. The technique of securing an individual system from attack

L-3 F 469. The act of manipulating people into performing actions or divulging confidential information.

Ans Social engineering

L-3 S 470. Passively eavesdropping on network traffic in order to capture valuable or secret data

A. Phishing B. Snooping C. Spamming D. Dos

L-2 S 471. A system in which hardware and software work collectively to secure an internal network or intranet from unauthorized access from outside

A. Antivirus B. Password C. Stoppage D. Firewall

Sharing

L-1 D 472. An account that uniquely identifies a computer on a domain

Ans Computer account

L-2 D 473. A group of computers on a windows network which share a directory database and security policies

Ans Active directory domain

Transmission

L-1 S 474. AM stands for

A. Amplitude modulation B. Altitude modulation

C. Angle modulation D. None of the above

Answers

Q. No.	Answer	Q. No.	Answer
1	A B D	110	C
2	B	111	C
3	A	112	C
4	A	113	D
79	A B	114	C
80	B	115	C
81	B	116	D
82	B	117	D
83	B	118	D
84	B	119	C
85	B	120	C
86	B	121	C
87	B	122	A
88	B	123	D
89	B	124	D
90	B	125	D
91	B	126	C
92	B	127	A
93	B	128	B
94	B	129	B
95	B	130	A
96	B	131	A
97	B	132	A
98	B	133	C
99	A	134	B
100	A C	135	D
101	A	138	A
102	A C	146	A B D
103	A	147	B
104	A	148	A
105	A	149	A
106	A	150	D
107	A	151	D
108	A	152	C
109	A	153	C

Q.No.	Answer	Q.No.	Answer
154		301	B
155	D	302	A
156	B	303	A
160	B	304	A
161	C	305	A
162	C	306	A
163	D	307	A
164	A	308	D
165	B	309	C
166	A	310	C
186	A B C D	311	D
187	B	312	D
188	B	313	D
189	B C	314	C
190	A	315	C
191	C	316	D
192	C D	317	C
193	C	318	C
194	C	319	C
195	A	320	C
285	A B C	321	D
286	E	322	C
287	B D	323	D
288	B	324	C D
289	B	325	C
290	B	326	C
291	B	327	D
292	B	330	B
293	B	331	A
294	B	332	B
295	B	333	B
296	B	334	B
297	B	335	B
298	B	336	B
299	B	337	B
300	B	338	B

Q No.	Answer	Q No.	Answer
339	B	398	D
340	B	399	A
341	B	400	B
342	A	401	A
343	A	411	B
344	A	412	B
345	A	413	B
346	B	414	B
347	A	415	C
348	A	416	D
349	A	420	B
350	A	421	A
351	A	422	A
352	A	423	D
353	A	424	C
354	A	425	D
355	A	426	D
356	A	427	B
360	C	428	B
363	B	437	A B D
364	B	438	B C
365	C	439	B C
366	D	440	D
384	B	451	A
385	B	452	A
386	B	453	C
387	B	454	C
388	B	455	C
389	B	456	C
390	B	457	D
391	A	458	C
392	A	460	C
393	D	466	C
394	B	467	B
395	C	470	B
396	D	471	D
397	C	474	A